The International Journal on Media Management

A Publication of the Institute for Media and Communications Management
University of St. Gallen, Switzerland

Subscriber Information

Contributor Information

Editorial Scope: *The International Journal on Media Management (IJMM)* provides a global view in the fields of media management, communications, and media economics. The goal of the journal is to offer a close analysis of new industry structures, organizational forms, and critical competencies developing as a result of reconfigurations in the media value chain. The journal serves as a forum for discussion, bringing together academics and industry figures to explore the transition from "classic" to "new" media and to identify the factors that will determine organizational success and economic efforts in a fast-changing and converging environment.

The journal embraces a wide and rich array of media related issues and focuses on the changes in this field evoked by rapid technical developments and the convergence in the media industry and communications.

Audience: Academics, researchers, and managers with an interest in aspects of media management; policymakers in all sectors of the media industry.

Contributer Information: *IJMM* publishes original research and scholarship on changes in the media and communications industries. The content is both interdisciplinary, combining a number of different academic disciplines (strategy, media technology, marketing, finance, media studies, etc.) and multisectoral, exploring the interrelationship between developments in related industries. The journal is open to all theoretical and methodological approaches.

Submission: Submitted papers should be no longer than 5,000 words excluding tables and figures. Submit the manuscript to the Editors via e-mail: media.editors@netacademy.org

Manuscript Preparation: Manuscripts should be prepared according to the guidelines of the *Publication Manual of the American Psychological Association* (5th ed.). Double space all material in the following order: title page, abstract, text and quotations, acknowledgments, references, appendixes, tables, figure captions, and footnotes. Footnotes should be kept to a minimum. The title page should include the title of the manuscript; names and affiliations of all authors; address, phone, and fax numbers; the e-mail address of the corresponding author; and a running head of not more than 48 letters and spaces. Only the title page should contain identifying information. The second page should include the manuscript title, and an abstract of 150 to 200 words. All pages must be numbered. All figures must be camera ready.

Double Blind Peer Review: Every submitted article will be subject to peer review. The normal review period is three months. Authors should take care that the manuscript contains no clues as to identity.

Permissions and Copyright Statement: Authors are responsible for the content of their work and for obtaining permission from copyright owners to use a lengthy quotation (500 words or more) or one or more lines of poetry or song lyrics or to reprint or adapt a table or figure published elsewhere. Authors should write to the original author(s) and publisher of such material to request nonexclusive world rights in all languages for use in the article and in future print and nonprint editions. Provide copies of all permissions and credit lines obtained.

Production Notes: After a manuscript is accepted for publication, the author is asked to provide a computer disk containing the word processing file. Files are copyedited and typeset into page proofs. Authors read proofs to correct errors and answer editor's queries. Reprints may be ordered when proofs are returned.

Book Reviews: *IJMM* regularly publishes reviews of books pertaining to media management, communications management, and media economics. The reviews reflect a modest attempt to locate contours of the emerging and interdisciplinary field of media management. If you are interested in reviewing books for IJMM, contact the editors at media.editors@netacademy.org

Contents

Volume 6 Numbers 3 & 4 2004

Editors' Note **149**
Beat F. Schmid, Peter Glotz, Joachim Haes,
Bozena I. Mierzejewska, Yingzi Xu

Introduction: The Impact of Regulatory Change on **150**
Media Market Competition and Media Management
Philip M. Napoli

Focus Theme Articles

Digitalizing Diversity: Public Service Strategies and **152**
Television Program Supply in Finland in 2002
Minna Aslama, Heikki Hellman, and Tuomo Sauri

Bundling in Cable Television: A Pedagogical Note **162**
With a Policy Option
Keith Brown and Peter J. Alexander

Managing Competition Through Barriers to Entry **168**
and Channel Availability in the Changing
Regulatory Environment
Robert G. Picard and Bum Soo Chon

Diversity in Broadcast Television: An Empirical Study **176**
of Local News
Peter J. Alexander and Brendan M. Cunningham

Pie Sharing or Food Fight? The Impact of Regulatory **184**
Changes on Media Market Competition in Singapore
Marc Edge

General Research Articles

The Dual Structure of Global Networks **194**
in the Entertainment Industry: Interorganizational
Linkage and Geographical Dispersion
Bum Soo Chon

Market Competition and Cultural Tensions Between **207**
Hollywood and the Korean Film Industry
Eun-mee Kim

Selling the Niche: A Qualitative Content Analysis of **217**
Cable Network Business-to-Business Advertising
Walter S. McDowell

Radio Station Innovation and Risk Taking: A Survey of **226**
Programmers and General Managers
John W. Owens and Francesca Dillman Carpentier

Optimizing Radio Advertising in North Queensland, **235**
Australia: A Mathematical Programming Approach
Adee Athiyaman

Book Reviews

The Wired Homestead, An MIT Press Sourcebook on **247**
the Internet and the Family
reviewed by Navneet Anand

Media and Economics, **251**
Volume 1/1: Foundations of Media Economics:
Communication and Media Science, Economics;
Volume 1/2: Foundations of Media Economics:
Sociology, Culture, Politics, Philosophy, International,
History, Technology, Journalism
reviewed by Gürhan Kurucu

A Handbook of Cultural Economics **255**
reviewed by Josh Heuman

Calendar of Events **257**

Associated Reviewers

JMM – The International Journal on Media Management

■

Editors' Note

Dear Readers,

Welcome to the second double-issue of JMM in 2004! You had to wait a long time, but here it comes: the focus topic, "The Impact of Regulatory Changes on Media Market Competition and Media Management," guest edited by Philip M. Napoli, Director of the Donald McGannon Communication Research Center at Fordham University. We express our gratitude for Phil's cooperation and involvement throughout the editorial process.

In the general research section of this issue, we have gathered research that we found inspiring but that does not lay within the scope of this issue's focus topic. As it is our aim to publish a broad array of articles on all aspects of media management, five articles cover a broad subject matter, and their research methodologies vary considerably. There is one thing, however, that they have all in common: They constitute significant contributions to our field.

The first article included in the general section is by Bum Soo Chon: "The Dual Structure of Global Networks in the Entertainment Industry: Interorganizational Linkage and Geographical Dispersion." In this article, Chon analyzes the structure of organizational networks and the geographical dispersion of global media conglomerates. Using multidimensional scaling and quadratic assignment procedure correlation analysis, Chon finds significant similarities between the geographical and organizational structures as well as surprising properties regarding the nature of these networks. Chon's conclusions contribute to the understanding of global media networks and factors affecting their creation.

In the last decade, global media networks have benefited greatly from the expansion to Asian markets that challenge new entrants with their distinct cultural setting. In Eun-mee Kim's article, "Market Competition and Cultural Tensions Between Hollywood and the Korean Film Industry," he analyzes the Korean motion picture market and examines how Hollywood productions compete for attention and market share in the dynamically growing local market. The analysis shows that American and Korean movies depend on different success factors and that direct competition is rather the exception than the rule.

Walter S. McDowell's "Selling the Niche: A Qualitative Content Analysis of Cable Network Business-to-Business Advertising" focuses on problems associated with branding strategies of cable networks. Using content analysis of business-to-business advertising, McDowell identifies strategies networks use to sell their programming to specific market niches and reveals marketing shortfalls.

We close this issue with two articles devoted to managing radio stations. In John W. Owens and Francesca Dillman Carpentier's article, "Radio Station Innovation and Risk Taking: A Survey of Programmers and General Managers," they find out that radio executives often overstate the innovativeness of their own station and see competitors as conservative and lacking innovation in their playlists. This research also indicates that both station managers and owners support more innovation in their stations and are willing to take the risks. In Adee Athiyaman's "Optimizing Radio Advertising in North Queensland, Australia: A Mathematical Programming Approach," he deals with profiling radio audiences and identifies "triggers" for product purchases and an "optimal" mix of commercial and public radio stations to reach a given audience. Albeit developed on the example of Australia, it provides interesting facts for those dealing with radio management in practice or in teaching and research.

In this issue, you will also find our book review section and a conference calendar. To find out about upcoming issues, calls for papers, and books available for review, please check our Web site at http://www.mediajournal.org To send us your comments or works for publication, please e-mail us at media.editors@netacademy.org

With the publication of this issue, the transition to our publishing partner, Lawrence Erlbaum Associates, is complete. We thank you, our readers, for your patience and support and wish you an inspiring reading on media market regulation and beyond.

Sincerely,
Beat F. Schmid
Peter Glotz
Joachim Haes
Bozena I. Mierzejewska
Yingzi Xu

Introduction: The Impact of Regulatory Change on Media Market Competition and Media Management

Philip M. Napoli

The regulation of media industries is undergoing a period of intense change. New technologies such as direct broadcast satellite, digital television, satellite radio, and the Internet are dramatically changing the competitive landscape and placing strains on traditional regulatory models. In many nations, the transition from a government-controlled to a commercial, privatized media system is ongoing. Regulatory philosophies, as well as the processes by which regulatory decisions are made are, in many nations, in a state of flux as well. All of these regulatory changes have significant implications for media market competition and for media management.

Perhaps what is most interesting about this period of transition is that—based on casual observation—research appears to be playing a more prominent role in the decision-making processes than it has in the past. In the United States, for example, the Federal Communications Commission's (2003) decision to relax a number of different media ownership regulations was preceded by the commissioning of a dozen studies addressing a broad range of topics relevant to the ownership proceeding. Moreover, research questions and controversies (addressing issues such as consumers' media usage behaviors and the minimum number of firms required for a competitive market) were at the core of the recent decision by the U.S. Court of Appeals for the Third Circuit to remand the bulk of these rules back to the Commission (see United States Court of Appeals for the Third Circuit, 2004) for further consideration and, most likely, further research.

From a managerial standpoint, media organizations seeking to respond to the opportunities offered to them by a changing regulatory environment find themselves (often very publicly) struggling to integrate units (and corporate cultures) previously separated by regulatory structures that were once less permissive of interindustry and intraindustry mergers and acquisitions (the travails of AOL-Time Warner—now once again simply Time Warner—provide a useful case in point). Or, as is the case in many nations, media organizations find themselves struggling to respond effectively to a more procompetitive media regulatory environment (see, e.g., Edge's, 2004, article on the situation in Singapore in this issue).

Given this management and policy environment, the topic of this focus theme issue seems particularly timely—and we were particularly fortunate to have authors submit manuscripts addressing a wide range of very timely issues from a wide range of national contexts.

The submissions included in the focus theme section of this issue address not only the impact of regulatory change on media market competition from an economic standpoint but also the impact of regulatory change on competition in the "marketplace of ideas." Although it is tempting to approach regulation and policy questions pertaining to media industries through the somewhat narrow lens of economics (given that these are the analytical tools that are, perhaps, the most highly developed and the most widely accepted in the policy-making arena), policymakers, policy analysts, and scholars are all increasingly realizing that this is not a viable approach to promoting and sustaining a media system that effectively performs the full range of functions required of them in democratic societies. This collection of articles reflects this perspective through its attention to both economic competition and competition in the marketplace of ideas.

For instance, the lead article by Aslama, Hellman, and Sauri (2004) examines the transition to digital television in Finland and the role and function of the concept of diversity (a key element of a competitive marketplace of ideas) as a policy objective, a public service imperative, and a programming strategy in this transition. Too often, research addressing the diversity principle has focused primarily on diversity exclusively as a policy objective to the neglect of its role as both an ethical imperative for media organizations (within public service and commercial media organizations alike) and as a potential strategy for content providers. Aslama et al.'s article is a rare instance of a unified treatment of these various functions of the diversity principle. Moreover, Aslama et al. provide what is, to my knowledge, one of the first empirical explorations of how the digital transition might impact the television programming landscape.

Address correspondence to Philip M. Napoli, Graduate School of Business, Fordham University, 113 W. 60th St. New York, NY 10023. E-mail: pnapoli@fordham.edu

The second focus theme article by Brown and Alexander (2004; both of the U.S. Federal Communications Commission) addresses the subject of channel bundling in cable television—an issue that has grown quite prominent as of late in the United States as the result of proposed legislation that would require cable systems to offer channels on an a la carte basis. Brown and Alexander's article explores the strategic rationales behind bundling as well as the public welfare pros and cons of bundling. Brown and Alexander then develop a potential alternative (which they label "quasi-bundling") in which cable operators sell packages of channel space, which subscribers could then fill in with their own channel choices. Brown and Alexander then consider the welfare implications of such an approach under different competitive conditions. It is particularly exciting to have the work of policy professionals who are addressing a current policy concern included in this focus theme issue—and to be able to make this work available to the broader public while the issue is still under consideration (for this I have the *International Journal on Media Management* [JMM] staff and their lightning-fast production schedule to thank).

Picard and Chon's (2004) article explores the issues and challenges facing policymakers in their efforts to manage barriers to entry in television broadcasting and to maintain a competitive environment that effectively serves both economic and social policy objectives. Picard and Chon's article examines not only the full range of barriers to entry present in the broadcasting industry but also the effects (both positive and negative) of new entrants. Picard and Chon's article provides a useful overview of the challenges facing policymakers in their efforts to craft regulatory structures that are sensitive to new technological developments as well as to consumer and producer welfare.

The issue returns to the subject of diversity with Alexander and Cunningham's (2004) analysis of diversity in local broadcast television news. This study not only takes a unique and creative approach to the measurement of content diversity and its relation to market structure but also provides indications of how regulatory changes (specifically, changes in ownership regulations) might impact the diversity of news content offered by local television stations. In recent years, great strides have been made in the realm of diversity analysis, and Alexander and Cunningham's article is a prime indicator of the increased theoretical and methodological rigor being brought to bear on media diversity research.

The focus theme section concludes with Edge's (2004) overview and analysis of the move toward "controlled competition" in the Singaporean media industry and its impact on the management and economics of Singaporean media firms. In this article, Edge addresses the fascinating question of the extent to which competitive national media markets can operate effectively in small nations. Can a nation be too small to effectively sustain a competitive media system? What regulatory or stra-

tegic initiatives can be employed to help sustain competition? Edge's chronicle of the situation in Singapore raises these and other interesting questions.

I would like to extend my thanks to all of the authors who submitted their work for consideration for inclusion in this focus theme issue and to the reviewers from across the globe who evaluated the submissions under very tight deadlines. Thanks are due as well to the members of the *JMM* team (particularly Joachim Haes, Bozena Mierzejewska, and Yingzi Xu) who walked me through this process of serving as guest editor—and bore most of the burden of putting this focus theme issue together. The end result is, I believe, a valuable collection of work that sheds new light on the subject of the impact of regulatory change on media market competition and media management that hopefully will inspire further work in this area.

Philip M. Napoli
pnapoli@fordham.edu

is an Associate Professor in the Schools of Business at Fordham University and is the Director of the Donald McGannon Communication Research Center. He is the author of Audience Economics: Media Institutions and the Audience Marketplace *(Columbia, 2003) and* Foundations of Communications Policy: Principles and Process in the Regulation of Electronic Media *(Hampton, 2001).*

References

Alexander, P. J., & Cunningham, B. M. (2004/this issue). Diversity in broadcast television: An empirical study of local news. *International Journal on Media Management, 6,* 176–183.

Aslama, M., Hellman, H., & Sauri, T. (2004/this issue). Digitalizing diversity: Public service strategies and television program supply in Finland in 2002. *International Journal on Media Management, 6,* 152–161.

Brown, K., & Alexander, P. J. (2004/this issue). Building cable television: A pedagogical note with a policy option. *International Journal on Media Management, 6,* 162–167.

Edge, M. (2004/this issue). Pie sharing or food fight?: The impact of regulatory changes on media market competition in Singapore. *International Journal on Media Management, 6,* 184–193.

Federal Communications Commission. (2003). *2002 biennial regulatory review, report and order and notice of proposed rulemaking.* Retrieved July 7, 2004, from http://hraunfoss.fcc.gov/edocs_public/attachmatch/FCC-03-127A1.pdf

Picard, R. G., & Chon, B. S. (2004/this issue). Managing competition through barriers to entry and channels availability in the changing regulatory environment. *International Journal on Media Management, 6,* 168–175.

United States Court of Appeals for the Third Circuit. (2004). *Prometheus Radio Project v. Federal Communications Commission.* Retrieved July 12, 2004, from http://www.ca3.uscourts.gov/opinarch/033388p.pdf

FOCUS THEME ARTICLES

Digitalizing Diversity: Public Service Strategies and Television Program Supply in Finland in 2002

■

Minna Aslama
University of Helsinki, Finland

Heikki Hellman
Helsingin Sanomat, Helsinki, Finland

Tuomo Sauri
Statistics Finland, Helsinki, Finland

In this article, we examine content supply as a public service strategy in Finland, one of the forerunner countries of digital terrestrial television in Europe. Regarding digitalization, European broadcasters face several options from full service to a specialized mission. The case at hand is the first full digital year of 2002 in Finland. The focus is on one of the traditional principles of public service broadcasting, the diversity of programming, as it is realized in the new, digital, multichannel environment. We examine content diversity by comparing channel profiles as well by analyzing indexes of the horizontal and vertical breadth and dissimilarity of programming. In a market of two public service and two commercial analogue generalist TV channels, the five new thematic digital channels have radically altered the amount of system-wide supply, but the diversity of programming has not suffered. This is due to the specializing strategy of the public service broadcaster. Its approach to focus on factual programming is clear in its digital output but can be detected in moderation also in its analogue supply. However, with the expected increase on commercial digital supply also in terrestrial networks, there is the possibility of the generalist public service broadcaster to turn into a fragmented one.

Digitalization of television and of public service television is underway in most European countries. According to the European Commission (2003), the penetration of digital television (DTV) in the European Union (EU) area in 2002 was 21%, equaling some 32 million households. Of that figure, satellite networks comprised some 14%, cable some 5%, and terrestrial networks close to 2%.

In Europe, developing terrestrial networks has been the most popular strategy for public service to take charge of digitalization (Hujanen, 2004; Syvertsen & Aslama, in press). By opting for terrestrial infrastructure for digital transmissions, public service broadcasters have aimed at gaining control and countering the digital satellite and/or cable transmissions run by commercial companies. As of 2003, digital terrestrial television networks exist and function in six European countries. The United Kingdom (UK) was the first to launch full-scale digital terrestrial broadcasting in 1998 and despite the initial difficulties has managed to reestablish its operations full scale. Sweden followed with digital terrestrial starting in 1999 and Finland as well as Spain in the first years of the new Millennium. The most recent terrestrial DTV operations have been launched in Germany and the Netherlands, in both countries full scale in 2003 (Ministry of Transport and Communications of Finland [MINTC], 2003). In addition to the ones that have already begun with digital terrestrial

Address correspondence to Minna Aslama, Department of Communication, Swedish School of Social Science, PO Box 16, 00014 University of Helsinki, Finland. E-mail: minna.aslama@helsinki.fi

television, at least 10 other European countries are planning to launch it full scale in 2004 to 2005.

In this article, we examine content supply as a public service strategy in Finland as one of the forerunner countries of digital terrestrial television. As universality of contents has conventionally been one of the main ideologies of public service, the focus here is on one of its aspects: on the diversity of programming as realized in the new, digital, multichannel environment.

Context: European Dilemmas

Digitalization of television broadcasting in any single European country is a European-wide issue that interests international device manufacturers as well as the EU. The EU stand on digitalization of broadcasting is that the process must be market driven, and the development must abide by EU-level telecom directives regarding technology neutrality, minimum regulation, and transparency (European Commission, 2003). However, one could say paradoxically, as the EU relies on market forces and consumer demand to foster the development, the pan-European strategies and policies for redefining the remit of public service television are nonexistent. Thus, stages and directions of developments vary greatly by country. The future estimate for Europe is that DTV will reach 80 million European households by the end of 2007. Satellite will remain the prominent digital platform, accounting for some 40% of European DTV, but there are high hopes for both cable and terrestrial DTV. The rapid growth of DTV will be experienced especially in the small, multiplatform markets such as Portugal and the Nordic countries. Conversely, the market development will be slower in advanced pay-TV markets such as France, Italy, Spain, and the UK (MINTC, 2003).

Despite the technical and funding dilemmas, the most crucial question for public service television is that of its new mission. Traditionally, for European public broadcasters, diversity is the main defining notion of their remit. It is a principled concept, a normative criterion of quality, and a deliberately sought policy goal aiming at pluralism at various levels: in reflecting the various sectors of society, serving the multiplicity of audiences, and supplying a wide range of choice in program content (Blumler, 1991; Hellman, 2001; McQuail, 1992). In this article, we make a distinction between the broad ideal that is often referred to as the universality principle, with all its dimensions (equal access, minority services, etc.), and one of the more specific performance goals, the diversity of program content or supply. Prior to the multichannel environment, diversity has been viewed as the task of generalist, full-service channels.

Now, in debates of the new era remit, the various aspects of universality are revisited, but the question of the new role of public service goes even beyond them: Digital Strategy Group of the European Broadcasting Union (EBU; 2002) identified as the two main challenges not only defining the kinds of activities that would be identified as the public service remit but also deciding on the kind of institutional framework that should be used for performing the public service role. Both of these questions challenge the ideal of universality in access (broadcasting free of charge and available to all) as well as in content (from a variety of program types to a diversity of "voices" seen and heard in public service channels).

One of the new stances in the matter, much advocated by the commercial competitors, is the call for diversity without public service. Indeed, as Harrison and Woods (2001) pointed out, European public service seems to be in the cross fire of competing concerns: Competition and state aid policies have much higher value than other social and cultural policy concerns, as the former provide legal basis for action. As long as the public service remit is uncertain at the EU level, national public service broadcasters face uncertainty, and the commercial competitors will take advantage of the EU competition policies against them. The liberalist argument claims that the shift to multichannel, on-demand broadcasting offered by digitalization will enable the market to fulfil its public service task with no special broadcasters needed. Two variants of this line of discourse are, in Jakubowicz's (2003) terms, the "attrition model," according to which digital development should be left entirely to the commercial sector, and the "distributed public service model" that refers to a situation in which public service programming would be commissioned by regulators from any broadcaster.

Another idea is to provide diversity with a division of labor, something that Hujanen (2004) called "fragmented public service" and Jakubowicz (2003) called the "monastery model." Here, the logic is that public service broadcasters would fill gaps or concentrate on kinds of programs and services that are not offered by their commercial counterparts. Surely, public service television has already done so to a minor extent in situations in which both public and commercial analogue channels have in principle provided full service with a broad range of genres: The former channels have perhaps chosen more information-oriented profiles and supported some cultural or experimental programming. Today, with the expanding channel capacity, the issue pertains very much to thematic channels.

Despite the just described scenarios for the conventional public service ideal, the approach taken in the forerunner countries of digital terrestrial television is to follow the "full portfolio model" (Jakubowicz, 2003) that in terms of television contents means including both generalist as well as specialized channels in the public service channel palette. When going digital, the British Broadcasting Corporation (BBC), the German ARD, the Swedish SVT, and the Finnish Broadcasting Company (YLE) have combined the broad mixed-genre channels with thematic or niche channels (Hujanen, 2004).

Case Study: the Diversity of Finnish Television Supply 2002

The year 2002 in Finnish television provides an interesting case study on one kind of programming strategy public service broadcasting can follow in the digitalization process. It also addresses the crucial question of whether a digital, multichannel environment supports or challenges content diversity.

Public Service Broadcasting and the Finnish Television Landscape

The decade leading Finland to the digital era has witnessed major changes in the television market. Whereas most European countries in the beginning of the 2000s employed by dual systems of public service and commercial broadcasting, in Finland, this has been the case almost from the beginning of television broadcasting. Since 1957, there existed a "comfortable duopoly" (Hellman & Sauri, 1994), as the Mainostelevisio (MTV) sent its own programs as well as advertisements in the two channels of the public service YLE, thus amongst YLE's programming. Finally, in 1993, MTV became MTV3, an independent channel operator, and in 1997, the second nationwide commercial channel Nelonen ("Channel Four") entered the market. Two public channels competing with two commercial ones equals very moderate competition in an affluent country with 5.2 million inhabitants, especially when compared to the neighboring Sweden with two public and five commercial channels or the Netherlands with three public and no less than eight private channels (Brants & De Bens, 2000). Audience shares show that the public service YLE with its two analogue channels, TV1 and TV2, is still the market leader, reaching a share of 44% on its two channels in 2003. The commercial MTV3 accounts for 38% and the commercial Nelonen 11% (Finnpanel Oy, 2004b).

A new kind of competition, however, has begun digitally. After some postponements, Finland was the sixth country in the world to begin with terrestrial DTV broadcasting in August 2001. The Finnish policies on public service and digital broadcasting can be summarized as on one hand entailing an unambiguous stand on going for terrestrial platform led by the public service YLE. The government's motives, in short, were to save money in the future with digital broadcasting technology and to compete against foreign digital satellite supply. On the other hand, although developing the platform was a clear-cut decision, the development of demand and content was in practice to be taken care of by market forces (Brown, 2002, 2003). Digitalization was framed as a business activity: For example, there was a definite decision not to subsidize the prices of new transmission devices for the viewers. Instead, it was believed that the increasing choice and "quality of content" would create consumer demand in spite of the extra cost from DTV set-top boxes and rising license fees (e.g., Aslama, 2003). In 2002, the MINTC released its new DTV strategy that reemphasizes the approach taken from the start: The state is to create good operating prerequisites for DTV, but the state is not to bear economic responsibility (Österlund-Karinkanta, 2003).[1]

As of 2002, the first full year of DTV, a total of nine digital TV channels operated in Finland.

As Table 1 depicts, the digital licenses are divided into two multiplexes, and one separate multiplex is entirely reserved for the public service YLE. Of the five new digital terrestrial TV channels introduced in August 2001, three are operated by YLE; one by Alma Media (Sub-TV), the owner of MTV Finland; and another (Urheilukanava) by Urheilutelevisio Oy. All of them are free of charge, but extra pay-TV services (MTV3+, Nelonen+) as well as entire channels will eventually be part of commercial digital broadcasting.

Table 1. Finnish Digital Channels, 2002

Multiplex	A	B	C
Administrator	YLE	MTV3	Nelonen (Channel Four)
Channels	TV1–D: Simulcast of analogue full service	MTV–D: Simulcast of analogue full service with extra programming	Nelonen: Simulcast of analogue full service with extra programming
	TV2–D: Simulcast of analogue full service	Sub-TV: Entertainment-oriented channel for young adults—also on cable	
	YLE24: News and current affairs channel	Urheilukanava: Sports channel—also on cable	
	YLE Teema: Culture, science, and education-oriented channel		
	FST–D: Swedish-language, full service channel		

Note. YLE = Finnish Broadcasting Company; MTV = Mainostelevisio; FST = Finlands Svenska Television.

The digital take-up was marked with economic, financial, and technical difficulties, one of them the nonavailability of multimedia home platform (MHP)-standard digital receivers. As a result, four commercial subscription channels decided not to commence their services, and their licenses, granted in 1999, were eventually withdrawn (Brown, 2003). Nevertheless, the second round of licence applications was completed, and due to new commercial newcomers, the extension of the DTV network concerning the Multiplexes B and C was started in 2004.[2] Also, a fourth multiplex is envisioned, but it will be reserved for data transfer (Österlund-Karinkanta, 2003).

Finnish Diversity Policies

The kind of expansion of channel capacity and content supply described previoulsy could be expected to prompt media policymakers to impose some content performance goals, especially for public service. Traditionally, given the fundamental role of the notion of diversity for public service, some European countries have included specific content requirements, even quotas, in the public service remit. Yet, in Finland, diversity as a performance goal has not been expressed in too much detail either in the Act on YLE of 1993,[3] or the Act on Television and Radio Broadcasting of 1998, which regulates the commercial sector. The 10-year-old law on public service broadcasting simply stipulates YLE to provide a variety of information, opinions, and debates on social issues for the general public as well as for minorities and special groups. As for commercial broadcasters, the law states that when granting licenses, the government should aim at promoting freedom of speech and increasing the diversity of programming.

The preceding depicts that the Finnish policy approach has been to address content diversity implicitly, and the digital era has not brought about any changes. Instead of detailed stipulations of programming, the focus is on the structural approach, that is, on the regulation of the broadcasting market. Diversity is best promoted, the rationale goes, by granting broadcasting licenses to "appropriate" firms only. In other words, if industry structure is kept viable and competition moderate, program diversity follows as a by-product. In the digitalization process, the policy-making has focused on developing the technological infrastructure for terrestrial television, led by the public broadcasting company YLE, and the diversity considerations remained indistinct, being dealt with at the level of market-entry regulation (Aslama, Hellman, & Sauri, 2004; Brown, 2002).

Still, the pressures for public service to justify its existence remain. In 2002, the new Communication Markets Act (MINTC, 2004) was ratified and parallel to that process, stricter demands than before for monitoring the performance of public service were introduced. The require-

ment is that YLE must produce two annual reports for appraising the universal service duties: one to the Parliament and one to the Finnish Communications Regulatory Authority (which in turn would issue its own statement to the Finnish government). It could be expected that diversity will be one of the core issues to be addressed in those reports, as well as in the assessments of the parliamentary and Ministry working groups that have been set up to redefine the role of YLE in the digital era.

Digitalizing Diversity: Supply of the First Digital Year 2002

One indication of the importance of content diversity to the new era of television is that the MINTC of Finland has since 2001 commissioned studies depicting Finnish television supply. Thus far, the research has covered the years 1997 through 2001 with a specific diversity analysis included. This empirical look at the first digital year of 2002 is based on one of the studies (Aslama & Wallenius, 2003). The data covers altogether 7 sample weeks in 2002, amounting to a total of over 10,500 programs in the four analogue and five digital channels. The data was coded by using a 13-category classification that closely follows the standard typology used by Finnish broadcasters.[4]

An overall look at the programming profiles of the four analogue channels (TV1 and TV2 of YLE and the commercial MTV3 and Nelonen) and the five brand new digital channels (YLE24, YLE Teema and Finlands Svenska Television (FST)–D of YLE, the commercial Sub-TV, and Urheilukanava) reveals a curious result. The five digital channels, of which four are thematically highly specialized, together provide a very similar output to the four analogue full-service channels. Looking at individual channels, they form an interesting continuum in the scale of information and entertainment orientation.

At the outset, the channel profiles featured in Figure 1 seem self-evident. The analogue channels that find their places quite near the center of the information-entertainment axis reflect the generalist tradition. The digital channels, then, exemplify the thematic, fragmented approach that positions public service and commercial channels further apart in the scale. Admittedly, the analogue Nelonen is more entertainment oriented than the digital Sub-TV. This is due to the fact that the former targets a broader audience mainly with Anglo-American fiction, whereas the latter caters to trendy youth and young adults, including a significant proportion of infotainment and factual programs on popular culture. However, three interesting issues emerge from Figure 1. One is the obvious division of labor between all the channels. The analogue channels engage in the division of labor and have increasingly done so since the birth of Nelonen in 1997 (Aslama et al., 2004). The distinction

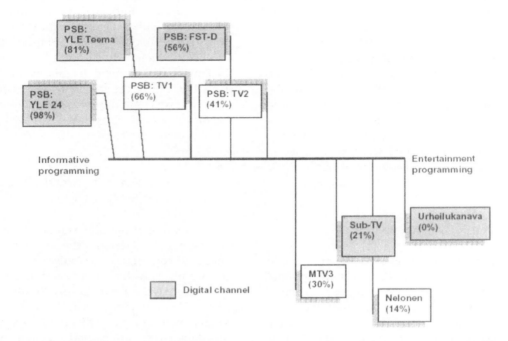

Figure I. Profiles of Finnish analogue and digital TV channels (share of informative programming, %), 2002.

Based on the program typology used in this study, *informative programming* is here defined to include the following categories: news, current affairs, features and documentaries, cultural programs, hobby and 30 personal interest programs, and educational programs. *Entertainment programming* refers to domestic and foreign fiction, sports, feature films, and entertainment programs. Children's programs and miscellaneous other programs are not included in these compilation categories. PSB = public service broadcasting; YLE = Finnish Broadcasting Company; FST = Finlands Svenska Television; MTV = Mainostelevisio.

between analogue and digital channels will eventually vanish when the national switch off of analogue television broadcasting takes place in 2007. Yet, already in 2002, the profiles of the analogue channels catering to the majority of the Finnish viewers have fit nicely together with the profiles of the new digital channels. Another issue is the clear position of public service YLE as the information provider. In fact, since the start of Nelonen, both TV1 and TV2 have reduced the entertainment orientation of their programming. The third point is the question of the digital channel FST–D, which offers all 13 program types and features the most "even" program profile regarding the shares of information and entertainment. In its generalist approach, it is still a specialized channel that serves to justify YLE's public service operations. A special case in the European context, FST–D provides full-service programming to the Swedish-language minority that forms some 6% of the Finnish population.

The program profiles positioned in the scale of information–entertainment give an overview of the Finnish television system as of 2002 but reveal little of how balanced different channels are, that is, how evenly different program categories are featured in their program profiles. To specifically examine diversity of the first digital year in Finland, two different indexes of program-type diversity are used, one measuring the breadth of programming and the other indicating the difference between the channels. According

to Hellman (2001), these measures, called here *diversity* and *dissimilarity*, respectively, represent different dimensions of program-type variety.

Breadth is measured by the Relative Entropy Index (H; e.g., Hellman, 2001), which expresses how varied and balanced the program output is on a channel, that is, vertically (channel diversity). When calculated as a summary measure of the overall program output across channels, it serves as a horizontal measure (system diversity). The index varies between 0 (all programming in one category) to 1 (all program types have an equal share in the supply).[5] Difference between the channels, then, is measured by the Dissimilarity Index (D), which indicates how much the content of one network in terms of program types represented in its schedule deviates from the content of another (channel dissimilarity). By calculating the average dissimilarity per year, the index serves as a horizontal measure of difference across channels (system dissimilarity). The minimum value for this index is 0 (channels have exactly same kinds of programming profiles), whereas the maximum is 2 (channels utilize completely different program types).[6]

The channel and system-wide breadth of programming of 2002, featured in Figure 2, prove that diversity as performed by the channel system in the first digital year could be assessed to be beneficial to the viewer. The analogue channel system scores very high for diversity (0.90), but the new digital channels together reach almost the

M. Aslama, H. Hellman, and T. Sauri

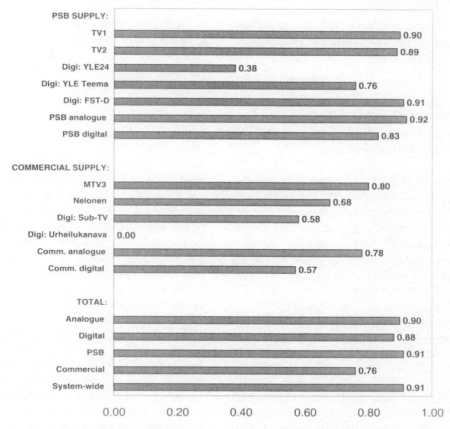

Figure 2. Diversity of Finnish television supply, 2002.

same level (0.88). Through counterprogramming, the digital channels even manage to make an increase—although a marginal one—in the total system-wide diversity (0.91).

As further illustrated by Figure 2, the difference between the diversity provided by commercial and public service is apparent—in total, in analogue, as well as in digital supply.

Admittedly, both YLE as well as its commercial counterparts demonstrate a degree of diversity that is well above average in comparison with the situation in many other countries (e.g., Ishikawa et al., 1996; van der Wurff & van Cuilenburg, 2001). Yet YLE's strategy to emphasize information-oriented programming, manifested in moderation by the analogue TV1 and emphasized with the digital YLE24 and YLE Teema, seems to be successful in two ways. First, it remains "inclusive" enough to maintain very high levels of diversity both in analogue and digital supply. Only the news and current affairs channel YLE24 remains below the threshold of high diversity. Also, YLE Teema, thematically focused in education, culture, and science, manages to offer a more balanced mix of program types than the full-service commercial analogue channel Nelonen. Second, as of 2002, YLE's full-service analogue and thematic digital channels are information oriented enough to act as counterforces to the entertainment-led commercial channels so that system-wide diversity remains very high.

The chosen public service strategy is also illustrated by the analysis of the differences between the channels. Although the digital channels together offer a very diverse array of programs, they also manage to make a positive effect on system dissimilarity due to their specialized and differing profiles: In 2002, the system-wide dissimilarity was notably higher when digital channels were included (1.21) than when measured only with the analogue supply (0.75). The dissimilarity scores also reveal that the five analogue and digital public service channels differ significantly more from one another (1.38) than the four commercial channels from each other (1.07).

This might seem contradictory to the trend in YLE's strategy emerging from the diversity analysis, the one that could be identified as "moderate specialization." However, the dissimilarity scores illustrate that the public service channel palette is broader than that of the commercial broadcasters and that the commercial channels compete with "more of the same." Given that Urheilukanava offers only sport programs (and thus, it differs greatly from all the other channels, increasing the dissimilarity scores notably for the total supply and for the commercial sector), it only underlines the fact that the other three commercial channels offer rather similar, fiction- and entertainment-oriented programming. The public service broadcasters, then, feature three full service channels (TV1, TV2, and FST–D) that do not distinguish themselves much from one another but that differ greatly from YLE24 and YLE Teema.

Universality—but How? Public Service Television and Strategies for the Digital Future

The program profiles of Finnish television channels in 2002 as well as the two measurements—of the breadth of programming and of the difference between channels—all support the generalist-meets-the-specialist approach taken by YLE: With this strategy, the Finnish public service television clearly both manages to remain universal in its total programe output as well as to counterbalance the commercial output with informative programming at the system level. Obviously, this tactic is not applied because of the virtues of diversity in itself but is justified also on grounds of maintaining the reach and popularity of public service broadcasting. Diversity through "dual strategy" serves as an approach to meet audience demand (Hellman, 1999b).

A good start with digital diversity does not necessarily define the future of YLE's television. In most public discussions, the traditional public service ethos is forgotten and replaced by criticism targeting the YLE-led digitalization (Aslama, 2003) in response to the numerous problems emerging during the process. To begin with, the launch of digital transmissions had to be postponed by 1 year partly because no MHP reception equipment was in the market for viewers to buy. In addition, the commercial channels were faced with stagnation of advertising revenues coupled with the expected fragmentation of audiences. This prompted the Finnish government, when granting commercial digital licenses, to favor applicants that based their business on pay TV. However, the Finnish pay-TV market has been and still is relatively undeveloped, the receivers were still unavailable by the launch date in 2001, and consequently four new channels had to give up their licenses in the very early stages of their operations (cf. Brown, 2002, 2003).

The Finnish Broadcasting Company, having invested heavily in digitalization, now faces the consequences of the trouble in the commercial sector. In the Communication Markets Act of 2002, the so-called operating license fees paid by commercial analogue broadcasters were halved, and the new digital channels get to broadcast free of charge for the first season of operations.[7] In contrast, the license fee paid by the viewers has been increased to provide additional funding for YLE. The company now operates five channels instead of two with a considerable loss, and according to its own estimates is expected to do so until the last years of this decade.

In respect to demand, the digital markets are small, if growing. At the end of the first digital year 2002, only 1.8% of Finnish households had digital accessory devices; in February 2004, the percentage had already risen to 14% (Finnpanel Oy, 2004a).[8] In spite of new television channels and improved picture quality, digitalization still faces major resistance among audiences. Symptomatically, parallel to the digitalization, the viewers' satisfaction with the licence fee has suffered during the last few years. Jääsaari, Kytömäki, and Ruohomaa (2004) interpreted that this discontent partly is a reaction against licence-fee raises caused by digitalization and partly reflects the general consumer uncertainty about the forthcoming switch off of the analogue service. Although YLE has "most to gain and least to lose from the transition," as Brown (2003, p. 30) put it, the truth is that in terms of popularity, YLE's new channels have remained extremely marginal, and it is unlikely that the company would manage to greatly increase its audience share. Rather, YLE24, FST–D, and YLE Teema may further fragment YLE's traditional viewership and weaken the company's capacity to invest in content on its main channels TV1 and TV2 (cf. Picard, 2000). This suggests that YLE's price for expanding its service, increasing the diversity of its supply, and approaching new viewer groups through digitalization is high. The digital channels almost double YLE's output: In 2002, this meant an additional 22 programming hours per day. Evidently, such expansion of program supply not only costs money but also harms, at least temporarily, YLE's legitimacy within society.

One of the most obvious and frequent criticisms of YLE's operations, brought about in political debates throughout the years, is whether there still exists a need for two full-service, Finnish-language channels in the multichannel digital era. YLE has begun to address this early on, as the TV1 and TV2 have gradually become different since the early 1990s (Hellman, 1999a). The goal of differentiation has recently been documented in the "channel commissions" designed by YLE in 2001. According to them, both channels should remain generalist, universal, and full-service channels with TV1, however, serving high quality demands and international orientation and focusing on news and current affairs, documentary, culture, heavy drama, and education; whereas TV2 should provide a more popular approach with its domestic and regional angle, comedy-oriented fiction, lifestyle programs, and entertainment and sports programs (Hujanen, 2002).

In light of the balancing act of generalist and specialist policies by YLE, it could be argued that public service television seems to face three—partly contradictory—demands. First, the question is of diversification system wide. It is clear that YLE does not intend to compete with its commercial competitors with more of the same but aims at filling in the gaps. When new channels enter the digital market, YLE might even have to become more distinct to correct the "market failure." Second, public service needs to secure a universal service within the public service channel system. Unsurprisingly, the commercial companies claim that YLE's remit as a whole should exclude certain program types such as sports and entertainment. Yet the dawn of pay-TV services in the Finnish digital platform requires diversification by public service channels so that diverse programming is offered for free or is only minimally charged. Last, there are still proponents of the idea of a full-service channel to be maintained in the public service remit. A fragmented multichannel strategy, the argument goes, may transform television, the former medium of social cohesion, into a medium of fragmentation that leaves lone consumers to surf in specialized channels (cf. Ellis, 2000). It may very well be that while new, specialized digital channels find their respective audience segments, viewers will still appreciate strong generalist channels that offer them the entire palette of program types. Yet, if TV1 and TV2 continue their division of labor further, a traditional full-service supply provided by each of these channels may soon be history.

Whether and how YLE meets the challenges of its future programming is not decided by YLE alone. To some degree, its prospects depend on the European-wide take on digitalization that, according to Näränen (2003), might be slightly shifting from market orientation to more supportive regulation for public broadcasters. Even more important, the key to the extremely high system-wide diversity of television content has so far, at least in Finland, been the successful market entry policy as realized by the government's choice of the licensees for commercial analogue broadcasting (Aslama et al., 2004). However, when channel proliferation continues in the digital environment, structural regulation might not suffice. Accordingly, there are signs that certain kinds of public service monopolies are being reestablished, for instance, in the UK and Norway; and some degree of reregulation is underway in most European countries (e.g., Syvertsen & Aslama, in press).

European-wide experience also suggests that the mere act of programming cannot remain as the main strategy of the survival for public service television in the digital era. For example, Born (2003) described the strategic rationales developed by the BBC and Channel Four executives ranging from increasing the revenue streams and branding public service to utilizing digital channels as sites of experimenting for the analogue main channels, building cross-platform and interactive operations, and developing new service for new platforms. It can be suspected that YLE is considering many of the tactics taken up in Britain, although many new revenue strategies would be restricted by law.[9]

More generally, the Digital Strategy Group of the EBU (EBU, 2002) argued that the traditional idea of universality must at present be seen as a twofold concept. The concept still entails universality of the content but also involves universality across the full portfolio of services, some of them specialized or tailored for specific audiences. A broad understanding of universality has to some extent already been adopted by the Finnish Broadcasting Company and political decision makers: YLE is active in the Internet as well as in mobile services. Besides, to ensure universal access, the Communications Market Act even obliges YLE to provide new services when they are developed in the digital TV environment. As YLE and other European public broadcasters encounter the complex challenges of providing diversity in program content, the universality of services may gain strategic importance for public service television in the digital era.

Minna Aslama
(minna.aslama@helsinki.fi)

is a doctoral candidate in Communication Studies at the University of Helsinki. She has participated in several research projects and has conducted a series of studies of Finnish program supply for the MINTC of Finland. She has also authored several articles for Finnish and international publications.

Heikki Hellman
(heikki.hellman@sanoma.fi)

has a doctorate in communication studies and is Culture Editor on the daily newspaper Helsingin Sanomat. He has authored or coauthored several articles on broadcasting policy, television programming, and the video market in, among others, the Journal of Media Economics, European Journal of Communication, and Media Culture and Society.

Tuomo Sauri
(tuomo.sauri@stat.fi)

is Senior Researcher of media and culture statistics for Statistics Finland. He has conducted studies and written articles on television supply (with Heikki Hellman). He has also written extensively on the Finnish mass media system including Mass Media in Finland: Structure and Economy *and* Finnish Mass Media.

Endnotes

1. For a detailed account on Finnish digitalization policies, see Brown (2003).
2. The extension of the DTV network should be completed in Autumn 2004. As of April 1, 2004, the rearrangement of the multiplexes is as follows:

   Multiplex A: TV1–D, TV2–D, FST, YLE24, YLE Teema
   Multiplex B: MTV3, Sub-TV, Nelonen, MTV3+, Nelonen Plus
   Multiplex C: CANAL+, CANAL+ Gold, CANAL+ Blue, Urheilukanava, Viisi

3. For a full (unofficial) English translation, see Finnish Broadcasting Company (n.d.).

4. Categorization used here is the following:
    1. News.
    2. Current affairs.
    3. Information and documentary.
    4. Cultural programming.
    5. Personal interest program.
    6. Sports.
    7. Domestic fiction.
    8. Foreign fiction.
    9. Movie.
    10. Children's program.
    11. Education.
    12. Entertainment.
    13. Other programs.

   The unit of analysis is the individual program, each of which is measured by its length.

5. To calculate the Relative Entropy Index, one needs first to measure the absolute (abs) entropy, H_{abs}, of the program output. This is done according to the following formula:

$$H_{abs} = \Sigma - p_i \log_2 p_i, \qquad (a)$$

   where p_i stands for the percentage devoted to each program category. Relative entropy H is then obtained by dividing the value of H_{abs} with the maximum (max) value possible ($H_{max} = \log_2 N$), where N is the number of program categories used:

$$H = \frac{H_{abs}}{H_{max} = \log_2 N} \qquad (b)$$

   The measure has been earlier used in similar studies by, for example, Wakshlag and Adams (1985); Ishikawa et al. (1996); Hillve, Majanen, and Rosengren (1997); van der Wurff and van Cuilenburg (2001), and Hellman (2001).

   Relative entropy H varies between 0 and 1, with 0 expressing minimum diversity (all content in one category) and 1 expressing maximum diversity (all categories equally large). Due to the logarithmic character of the measure, the closer one comes to the maximum score, the more difficult it becomes to increase its value (Hellman, 2001).

6. The index for dissimilarity is derived by subtracting the percentage of time p per program category i by one broadcaster A (p_{iA}) from the corresponding figure by another (p_{iB}) and summing up the differences:

$$D = \Sigma \, |p_{iA} - p_{iB}|$$

   The higher the sum of differences, the higher the dissimilarity between the channels and vice versa, the lower the dissimilarity index score, the more homogenous the output. The mathematical maximum of this index is 2 and the minimum is 0. In calculating the index, it plays no role whether the result of subtraction is positive or negative; only the extent of deviation matters. This measure has earlier been used by Hellman and Sauri (1994) and Hellman (2001).

7. It is envisioned that the operating license fee will be abolished entirely in 2007.

8. In 2002, the DTV's transmission area covered 70% of the Finnish households, and by autumn 2004, the coverage is envisioned to be some 90%.

9. A recent addendum on the Act on YLE states that the company may not broadcast television or radio advertising or other content services that are provided in various telecommunications networks, and when offering mobile and other multimedia services, YLE may charge only the amount required by the teleoperator (Finnish Broadcasting Company, n.d.).

References

Aslama, M. (2003). Digikansalainen kadoksissa? Katsojien roolit digitaalitelevisiosta käydyssä keskustelussa [Loosing digital citizen? Viewers' roles in the public debate on digital television]. In N. Malmelin (Ed.), *Välittämisen tiede. Viestinnän-näkökulmia yhteiskuntaan, kulttuuriin ja kansalaisuuteen. Ullamaija Kivikurun juhlakirja* (pp. 246–262). Helsinki, Finland: Publications of the University of Helsinki, Department of Communication.

Aslama, M., Hellman, H., & Sauri, T. (2004). Does market-entry regulation matter? Competition in television broadcasting and programme diversity in Finland, 1993–2002. *Gazette, 66*, 113–132.

Aslama, M., & Wallenius, J. (2003). *Suomalainen tv-tarjonta 2002* [Finnish television programming 2002]. Helsinki, Finland: Ministry of Transport and Communications.

Blumler, J. G. (1991). In pursuit of programme range and quality. *Studies of Broadcasting, 27*, 191–206.

Born, G. (2003). Public service broadcasting and digital television in the UK. The politics of positioning. In G. F. Lowe & T. Hujanen (Eds.), *Broadcasting and convergence. New articulations of the public service remit* (pp. 205–221). Gothenburg, Sweden: Nordicom.

Brants, K., & De Bens, E. (2000). The status of TV broadcasting in Europe. In J. Wieten, G. Murdock, & P. Dahlgren (Eds.), *Television across Europe: A comparative introduction* (pp. 7–22). London: Sage.

Brown, A. (2002). Different paths: A comparison of the introduction of digital terrestrial television in Australia and Finland. *International Journal of Media Management, 4*, 278–287.

Brown, A. (2003). *Technology-driven industry restructure: The case of terrestrial television broadcasting in Finland.* Turku, Finland: Turku School of Economics and Business Administration, Business Research and Development Centre.

Ellis, J. (2000). *Seeing things. Television in the age of uncertainty.* London: I. B. Tauris.

European Broadcasting Union. (2002). *Media with a purpose. Public service broadcasting in the digital era* [Electronic version]. Geneva, Switzerland: EBU Digital Strategy Group.

European Commission. (2003, November 17). *Communication from the Commission to the Council, the European Parliament, the European Economic and Social Committee, and the Committee of the Regions on Transition from Analogue to Digital Broadcasting, SEC(2003) 992, COM(2003) 541 final.* Retrieved May 10, 2004, from http://europa.eu.int/information_society/topics/ecomm/doc/useful_information/library/c ommunic_reports/switchover/acte_en_vf.pdf

Finnish Broadcasting Company. (n.d.). *Act on Yleisradio Oy.* Retrieved May 10, 2004, from http://www.yle.fi/fbc/actyle.shtml

Finnpanel Oy. (2004a, April 15). *Helmi-maaliskuun vaihteessa digisovittimia 321 000 taloudessa* [In the beginning of March, digital set-top boxes in 321 000 households]. Retrieved May 10, 2004, from http://www.finnpanel.fi/tulokset/tiedotteet/tv_150404_2.html

Finnpanel Oy. (2004b, January 14). *TV:n katseluun käytetty aika keskimääräisenä päivänä kanavittain* [The average daily viewing time by television channel]. Retrieved May 10, 2004, from http://www.finnpanel.fi/tulokset/tv/vuosi/viimeisin/kanavittain.html

Harrison, J., & Woods, L. (2001). Defining European public service broadcasting. *European Journal of Communication, 16*, 477–504.

Hellman, H. (1999a). *From companions to competitors: The changing broadcasting markets and television programming in Finland.* Tampere, Finland: University of Tampere.

Hellman, H. (1999b). Legitimations of television programme policies: Patterns of argumentation and discursive convergencies in a multichannel age. In P. Alasuutari (Ed.), *Rethinking the media audience: The new agenda* (pp. 105–129). London: Sage.

Hellman, H. (2001). Diversity—An end in itself? Developing a multi-measure methodology of television programme variety studies. *European Journal of Communication, 16*, 181–208.

Hellman, H., & Sauri, T. (1994). Public service television and the tendency towards convergence: Trends in prime-time programme structure in Finland, 1970–1992. *Media Culture & Society, 16*, 47–71.

Hillve, P., Majanen, P., & Rosengren, K. E. (1997). Aspects of quality in TV programming: structural diversity compared over time and space. *European Journal of Communication, 12*, 291–318.

Hujanen, T. (2002). *The power of schedule: Programme management in the transformation of finnish public service television.* Tampere, Finland: Tampere University Press.

Hujanen, T. (2004). Implications for public service broadcasters. In A. Brown & R. Picard (Eds.), *Digital terrestrial television in Europe* (pp. 57–84). Mahwah, NJ: Lawrence Erlbaum Associates, Inc.

Ishikawa, S., Leggatt, T., Litman, B., Raboy, M., Rosengren, K. E., & Kambara, N. (1996). Diversity in television programming: Comparative analysis of five countries. In S. Ishikawa (Ed.), *Quality assessment of television* (pp. 253–263). Luton, England: University of Luton Press.

Jääsaari, J., Kytömäki, J., & Ruohomaa, E. (2004). *Yleisökertomus 03* [Audience research report 03]. Helsinki, Finland: Finnish Broadcasting Company.

Jakubowicz, K. (2003). Bringing public service broadcasting to account. In G. F. Lowe & T. Hujanen (Eds.), *Broadcasting and convergence. New articulations of the public service remit* (pp. 147–165). Gothenburg, Sweden: Nordicom.

McQuail, D. (1992). *Media performance: Mass communication and the public interest.* London: Sage.

Ministry of Transport and Communications of Finland. (2003). *Kohti digiaikaa* [Towards the digital era]. Helsinki, Finland: Author.

Ministry of Transport and Communications of Finland. (2004). *Julkisen palvelun televisio ja radiotoiminta 2010* [Public service television and radio broadcasting 2010]. Helsinki, Finland: Author.

Näränen, P. (2003). European regulation of digital television. The opportunity lost and found? In G. F. Lowe & T. Hujanen (Eds.), *Broadcasting and convergence: New articulations of the public service remit* (pp. 57–68). Gothenburg, Finland: Nordicom.

Österlund-Karinkanta, M. (2003). *Current media policy issues in Finland.* Helsinki, Finland: Finnish Broadcasting Company.

Picard, R. (2000). Audience fragmentation and structural limits on media innovation and diversity. In J. van Cuilenburg & R. van der Wurff (Eds.), *Media and open societies. Cultural, economic and policy foundations for media openness and diversity in east and west* (pp. 180–191). Amsterdam: Het Spinhuis.

Syvertsen, T., & Aslama, M. (in press). Marginalization or re-monopolization? Public service broadcasting in the new media era. In E. de Bens (Ed.), *Media between culture and commerce.* Bristol, England: IntellectBooks.

van der Wurff, R., & van Cuilenburg, J. (2001). Impact of moderate and ruinous competition on diversity: The Dutch television market. *Journal of Media Economics, 4*, 213–229.

Wakshlag, J., & Adams, W. J. (1985). Trends in program variety and the prime time access rule. *Journal of Broadcasting & Electronic Media, 29*, 23–34.

Bundling in Cable Television: A Pedagogical Note With a Policy Option

Keith Brown and Peter J. Alexander
Federal Communications Commission, USA

Bundling can be a pricing mechanism by which monopolists capture economic surplus from consumers. We suggest that given the cost structure of media markets, channel bundling in the cable and satellite market could also emerge in a competitive environment. A la carte channel pricing on cable television may or may not increase consumer welfare and could decrease total welfare. Because bundling may create other problems, policymakers may consider allowing cable and satellite networks to sell packages of channel space to viewers at a given price, allowing viewers to choose which channels they want in their packages. We term this option quasi-bundling.

Speaking before Congress on issues relating to indecency in broadcasting, Commissioner Kevin Martin (*Protecting Children*, 2004) of the Federal Communications Commission stated that perhaps "cable and DBS operators could offer programming in a more a la carte manner. For example, they could permit parents to request not to receive certain channels and reduce the package price accordingly."[1] Concurring, Senator John McCain, Chairman of the Commerce Committee, noted that an "a la carte suggestion sounds ... more persuasive than ever in providing parents control over their television sets."[2]

Although the views of Commissioner Martin and Senator McCain are more expansive and comprehensive that what we have quoted here, their comments point to an interesting and important policy question relating to bundling of channels on cable television. *Bundling* refers to the grouping of a collection of products together in a single package that is then sold to final consumers. Thus, rather than selecting a few of the products offered on an individual or a la carte basis, the consumer has the choice of buying the bundle or nothing. With the exception of some channels, most consumers of cable must buy their programming in bundles.[3]

In this article, we employ a simple analytical structure and explore two related questions. First, why do domestic cable and satellite television services offer many channels only in bundles, and second, what are the implications of this bundling for consumers and policymakers? As we suggest, the results of our analysis are somewhat counterintuitive and imply that certain types of bundling can be a competitive response by cable providers that is welfare enhancing for consumers.

Economic Rationale for Channel Bundling

As Spence and Owen (1977) first observed, cable channels are differentiated products with high fixed costs and constant marginal costs.[4] Certain individual channels that attract strong interest from a small group of viewers[5] and face high fixed costs would not be produced in a pay television regime despite the fact that the total consumer surplus produced by these channels outweighs their fixed cost of production.[6]

Using some simple examples, we show how bundling helps solve this problem when viewers place divergent values on channels. Essentially, as Stigler (1963) pointed out, bundling acts as a price discrimination mechanism.[7] Price discrimination at least partially solves the aforementioned problem posed by Spence and Owen (1977) because it allows the seller to capture a larger fraction of a channel's surplus. Our final example, however, will illustrate a case in which bundling increases consumer economic welfare, decreases producer economic welfare, and increases total economic welfare.

As we suggest, a monopolist would not engage in the type of bundling that we illustrate in our final example, and thus, this type of bundling logically must be a consequence of actual or potential competition (which satel-

Address correspondence to Peter J. Alexander, 4517 Roxbury Drive, Bethesda, MD 20814. E-mail: peter.alexander@fcc.gov

lite providers or cable overbuilders might provide, respectively). This finding runs counter to the common intuition that bundling acts as a monopolist's mechanism for extracting surplus from consumers. However, the industry's desire to avoid a la carte pricing requirements may indicate that this latter type of bundling is not currently taking place on a large scale.

In the examples that follow, we use two channels and two viewers to illustrate our logic. This simplification, like many simplifications and assumptions used in economic modeling, clearly illustrates and isolates an idea that enables the reader to understand a world with many channels and many different viewers, abstracting away from other important details.[8] As we show, bundling may well have important implications for consumers and public policy.

Example 1

Assume there are two viewers, Moe and Lisa, and two channels, Itchy and Scratchy. Moe and Lisa value the programming as shown in Table 1. The fixed cost of producing either of the programs, Itchy or Scratchy, equals $11.

Without bundling and absent, first-degree price discrimination, neither program would be produced. To see this, suppose that the operator priced the Scratchy channel and the Itchy channel independently.

Looking only at the Scratchy channel, we observe that Lisa and Moe are willing to pay $10 and $2, respectively, whereas the fixed cost of producing the Scratchy channel is $11. Lisa would be willing to pay $10 for the Scratchy channel, so the provider could price the Scratchy channel at $10, reach one subscriber, and obtain $10, which would not cover the Scratchy channel's fixed cost of $11.

Moe is willing to pay $2 for the Scratchy channel, so the provider could sell the Scratchy channel to Lisa and Moe at $2 each, obtaining a total revenue of $4 (i.e., $2 from Moe and $2 from Lisa). However, once again, the total revenue ($4) does not cover the Scratchy channel's fixed cost of $11.

As is seen from Table 1, the same analysis would hold for the Itchy channel (only the names Lisa and Moe would

be reversed). Neither show will be produced independently. Under what conditions might they be produced?

In this case, the provider can produce and bundle both programs profitably, because Lisa and Moe have the "right" type of preferences. Referring back to Table 1, we recall that Moe is willing to pay $10 for the Itchy Channel and $2 for the Scratchy Channel, whereas Lisa is willing to pay $2 for the Itchy Channel and $10 for the Scratchy Channel. This means that Lisa and Moe's valuations move opposite one another because the channel that Lisa strongly prefers is the channel that Moe only weakly prefers and vice versa.[9]

Therefore, a cable operator could profitably produce both the Scratchy channel and the Itchy channel by producing both and selling the bundle for a price of $12. Because Lisa is willing to pay $10 for the Scratchy channel and $2 for the Itchy channel, Lisa is willing to pay $12 for the two bundled channels. Similarly, because Moe is willing to pay $10 for the Itchy channel and $2 for the Scratchy channel, Moe is also willing to pay $12 for the two bundled channels. In this case, Lisa and Moe obtain a consumer surplus of 0, and the seller makes a profit of $2.

Note that under a perfectly contestable market in which the monopolist faces the threat of immediate entry at any moment, the seller would bundle the two channels and price the bundle at $11.[10] Then, Lisa and Moe would each receive $1 of consumer surplus for a total consumer surplus of $2, and the seller would receive 0 economic profits. However, in both cases, bundling increases total economic welfare from 0 to 2. The split between consumer and producer surplus depends on the competitiveness of the market.

Example 2

Bundling can also reduce consumer surplus, increase producer surplus, and increase total economic welfare (as the standard economic analysis of price discrimination implies). We still employ Lisa and Moe and the Itchy and Scratchy channels; however, we modify the valuations from the original example to those shown on Table 2. As before, the fixed cost of producing either of the programs equals $11.

Table 1. Consumer Valuations of Programing, Example One

Valuation	Itchy	Scratchy
Moe	$10	$2
Lisa	$2	$10
Total	$10 + $2 = $12	$2 + $10 = $12
Maximum Combined Price, Each Channel	$2 + $2 = $4	$2 + $2 = $4

Table 2. New Consumer Valuations

Valuation	Itchy	Scratchy
Moe	$10	$7
Lisa	$5	$10
Total	$10 + $5 = $15	$7 + $10 = $17
Maximum Combined Price, Each Channel	$5 + $5 = $10	$7 + $7 = $14

In this case, the Itchy channel would not be produced on its own. The provider could either sell the Itchy channel to (Moe) for $10 or to two consumers (Moe and Lisa) for $5 each. In either case, the total revenue from the Itchy channel would be $10—clearly not enough to cover the fixed costs of $11.

The cable provider can, however, sell the Scratchy channel by itself. The cable provider can sell the Scratchy channel to Moe and Lisa at $7 each, generating $14 in total revenue, enough to cover the $11 fixed cost and make a profit of $3. Lisa also obtains $3 in consumer surplus because she pays $7 for a channel for which she would be willing to pay $10. Moe obtains no consumer surplus because he pays his exact valuation of $7. The total surplus is $6: $3 in producer surplus and $3 in consumer surplus.

However, the cable provider could make an even larger profit by bundling the two channels and selling the bundle for $15. In this case, both Moe and Lisa buy the bundle, so the cable company makes $30 in revenue while incurring fixed costs of $22 (the total cost of producing both the Scratchy and the Itchy channel).

Moe gains $2 in consumer surplus because he pays $15 for a bundle that he values at $17. Lisa gains no consumer surplus because she pays $15 for a bundle that she values at exactly $15. The total surplus is $10, higher than the total surplus of $6 under a la carte pricing. Consumer surplus, however, is lower: $2 instead of $3. Profits are higher: $8 instead of $3.

Essentially, in this example, bundling allowed the cable provider to capture more of the value from programming, which led them to produce the economically efficient amount of programming. However, because the provider captures more of the value from the programming, consumers are slightly worse off. The monopolist, however, is much better off. Consumers lose $1 of surplus, whereas the provider gains $5, for a total gain in economic welfare of $4. We summarize these results in Table 3.

It may seem that we have reached a final conclusion: Bundling likely increases total economic welfare but may leave consumers worse off mainly because it acts as a price discrimination mechanism, which tends to increase total economic welfare,[11] decrease consumer welfare, and increase producer welfare. As we show in the next example, this need not be the case.

Example 3

We employ one last example to illustrate a case in which bundling can increase consumer welfare, decrease producer welfare, and increase total welfare. As before, we employ Lisa and Moe and the Itchy and Scratchy channels, with new valuations for the channels. As before, the fixed cost of producing either of the programs equals $11.

As in the previous example, the provider could sell the Scratchy channel to both Lisa and Moe for $7 each, making a profit of $3 and generating a consumer surplus of $3.

However, if the cable provider bundles the two channels, the provider can sell the bundle for $12 to each Moe and Lisa. This generates revenues of $24. Given the fixed cost of $11 for each channel, this generates a profit of $24 − [2 × ($11)] = $2. Moe is willing to pay $17 for the bundle but pays only $12, receiving $5 in consumer surplus. Lisa is willing to pay $12 for the bundle and pays $12, receiving no consumer surplus. Therefore, bundling increases total consumer surplus from $3 to $5, decreases producer surplus from $3 to $2, and increases total welfare from $6 to $7 (see Table 4 and Table 5).

However, as Adams and Yellen (1976) demonstrated, the provider can increase their profits by engaging in mixed bundling, which consists of combining bundling with a la carte pricing. Let us say the provider prices the bundle at $17 and sells the Scratchy channel on an a la carte basis for $10. Moe purchases the bundle for $17 and Lisa buys only the Scratchy channel for $10. The provider gains a surplus of $27 − $22 = $5. Moe and Lisa both realize a zero consumer surplus. Total economic welfare is less than either under unbundling or under pure bundling, as is seen from Table 5.

Thus, pure bundling can increase consumer welfare and decrease producer welfare, whereas mixed bundling can increase producer welfare while reducing both con-

Table 4. New Consumer Valuations for Programming

Valuation	Itchy	Scratchy
Moe	$10	$7
Lisa	$2	$10
Total	$10 + $2 = $12	$7 + $10 = $17
Maximum Combined Price, Each Channel	$2 + $2 = $4	$7 + $7 = $14

Table 3. Unbundled Versus Bundled Surplus

Surplus	Unbundled	Bundled
Moe	$0	$2
Lisa	$3	$0
Producer	$3	$8
Total	$6	$10

Table 5. New Unbundled Versus Bundled Surplus

Surplus	Unbundled	Bundled	Mixed Bundle
Moe Surplus	$0	$5	$0
Lisa Surplus	$3	$0	$0
Producer	$3	$2	$5
Total	$6	$7	$5

sumer welfare and total economic welfare. Essentially, mixed bundling allows the monopolist to price the bundle very high, to capture the consumers with a high total valuation of all the channels, and still capture some consumers with a very high valuation of particular channels. Clearly, we would only expect to see welfare-enhancing pure bundling as a result of competition in the market because a monopolist could make higher profits by not bundling, and absent competition would therefore not have the incentive to bundle. When we observe the industry's apparent eagerness and willingness to incur costs to avoid unbundling rules, it seems unlikely that this competitive type of bundling currently takes place on a significant scale because requiring unbundling would then increase providers' profits.

However, our mixed bundling result does generate a somewhat counterintuitive insight. If the market is not sufficiently competitive, then an economic welfare-maximizing regulator may wish to consider forbidding a la carte pricing if the regulator also allows bundling. Conversely, the regulator may wish to forbid bundling. The combination, however, of bundling and a la carte pricing (termed mixed bundling) may be welfare reducing.

The Problem With Bundling

Even though bundling may confer welfare-increasing benefits on producers and even (under certain conditions) consumers, the current industry bundling practice may still have drawbacks beyond the possible reduction of consumer welfare through price discrimination. Recent work by Nalebuff (2004) raises the possibility that bundling may be a tool that incumbents use to foreclose entry. Although the Chicago School demonstrated that bundling could not be used to leverage monopoly power into a perfectly competitive market, a monopolist could use bundling to leverage monopoly power into an imperfectly competitive market. Thus, bundling has some very undesirable properties, and some of these properties arguably could contravene flow of programming to final viewers.

One Possible Solution

Can this problem be resolved? One might prefer a regulatory rule that preserves many of the efficiency enhancing price discrimination characteristics of bundling whereas eliminating many of the undesirable entry-blocking characteristics of bundling. One possibility emerges: Allow the cable operators to sell bundled packages of channel space to consumers at a given price, and then allow consumers to choose which channels they put on that space. For example, cable operators could

sell a package of 25 channels for $30 and a package of 50 channels for $55, but consumers would then choose what those 25 or 50 channels would be. Consumers would then self-select in such a way so that the final equilibrium would be identical to the price discrimination bundling equilibrium. Looking back at a few of our examples, one can see how such an arrangement would work. In Example 1, a cable operator could simply offer any 2 channels for $12, and Moe and Lisa would then select their preferred channels. As was shown, Moe and Lisa would each select both the Itchy and Scratchy channels. In Example 2, a cable operator would offer any two channels for $15, whereas Moe and Lisa would each select Itchy and Scratchy. In Example 3, the outcome depends on the level of competition. A provider with sufficient market power would simply not carry the Itchy channel and sell only one channel (the Scratchy channel) for $7. If the regulator also permitted a la carte programming, the provider with sufficient market power would sell the bundle for $17 and the Scratchy channel for $10, which, as Table 5 demonstrates, would lower both consumer welfare and total economic welfare. Thus, allowing a la carte pricing may lower economic welfare under this quasi-bundling scheme. In a competitive market, a provider would offer a package of any two channels at $11, and Moe and Lisa would choose the Itchy and Scratchy channels.

Thus, even our suggested bundling of channel space may lead to the loss of some worthwhile channels,[12] at least in a less competitive environment. A worthwhile channel could get dropped if it possesses all of the following features:

1. These channels would generate strong preference from a relatively small group of viewers and weak preference from the vast majority of viewers, that is, the demand for the channel would be convex.
2. The viewers who strongly preferred these channels would less strongly prefer another channel, and that other channel would attract relatively strong interest from all viewers, that is, the demand for the other channel is concave.

This possible channel loss, however, would not be as large and as severe as the channel loss that would occur under complete unbundling. In addition, any channels lost might be restored in a more competitive environment unlike under complete unbundling.

Cost is another important issue. In this article, we do not address the technical costs of either unbundling or the selling of channel space, but we do point out that cable systems in Canada offer a la carte channels and packages of channel space in which the viewer can purchase any 5, 10, and so forth channels for a given price. Therefore, we know that it is technically feasible for at least some systems to offer unbundled channels and/or packages of channel space to consumers, although we still do not necessarily know the cost of doing so and thus do not make any final policy recommendations in this article.

Conclusion

The issue of bundling in cable channels does not yield a clear answer. In this article, we clarify some of these issues using simple and accessible models and manage to generate another option for policymakers, the idea of selling bundled channel space in which viewers have to buy packages of channel space, but they choose which channels go in their package. This quasi-bundle approach, along with a la carte pricing, may also deal with policymakers' concern about so-called indecent material and how to allow consumers to avoid unwanted indecent material.[13] The quasi-bundling approach has the advantage of allowing consumers to opt out of viewing or paying for indecent material and avoid some of the disadvantages of pure a la carte pricing illustrated in this article. We also note that this quasi-bundling approach may benefit consumers the most when the regulator actually forbids a la carte pricing.

We stress, however, that we cannot (yet) determine which policy approach toward channel bundling is "correct" because that would require knowledge that we do not yet have. If a la carte pricing and/or quasi-bundling would be particularly costly for cable operators to implement, then the status quo may be the economic welfare-maximizing policy choice. If policymakers weight consumer welfare more heavily than producer welfare and believe that the industry is not competitive and will not be competitive in the near future, it then becomes possible that a la carte channel pricing maximizes the relevant economic welfare. If policymakers weight consumer and producer economic welfare more equally and/or believe that the industry is or is becoming fiercely competitive, then the quasi-bundling approach that we explore here may maximize economic welfare. In this article, we point out, however, using Adams and Yellen's (1976) mixed bundling example, that requiring a la carte pricing and allowing flexible bundling may actually lower both consumer and total economic welfare relative to requiring a la carte pricing and not permitting bundling or requiring flexible bundling and not permitting a la carte pricing. Because of the interaction between the a la carte price and the price of the bundle, policymakers should remember that more contractual flexibility is not necessarily better in the context of cable bundling.

Keith Brown
(Keith.Brown@fcc.gov)

is an Economist at the Federal Communications Commission. His publications cover broadcast media, telecom, and academic labor markets.

Peter J. Alexander
(Peter.Alexander@fcc.gov)

is an Economist at the Federal Communications Commission. His publications cover media industries and topics in product diversity, bargaining theory, and vertical integration.

Acknowledgments

The views and professional opinions expressed in this article are those of the authors and do not necessarily reflect the views of the Media Bureau, Commissioners, or any other Commission staff member or organizational unit within the Federal Communications Commission.

Endnotes

1. "Protecting Children From Violent and Indecent Programming," Wednesday, February 11, 2004, 9:30 a.m. The testimony of Honorable Kevin J. Martin, Commissioner, Federal Communications Commission, before the Committee on Commerce, Science and Transportation, United States Senate.
2. "Protecting Children From Violent and Indecent Programming," Wednesday, February 11, 2004, 9:30 a.m. The testimony of Honorable Senator John McCain before the Committee on Commerce, Science and Transportation, United States Senate.
3. In cable and satellite markets, these different bundles are commonly referred to as "tiers."
4. With no loss of generality, we can assume marginal costs are zero.
5. Spence and Owen (1977) demonstrated that convexity of the demand curve lowers the percentage of a channel's surplus that a single-price provider can capture.
6. Waldfogel (2003) expressed a similar idea using the concept of "preference externalities." Because many media products face high fixed costs and low, constant, marginal costs, an individual media consumer is made better off by other media consumers with similar preferences—hence, the term preference externalities.
7. Stigler (1963) also exploded the oft-repeated but incorrect cliché that "bundling makes people pay for products they don't want."
8. One important abstraction is to keep subscriber fees, an important source of revenue for cable providers, constant. It is

possible that unbundling might have an impact on the number of subscribers a cable operator can attract.

9. Moe's and Lisa's channel valuations are negatively correlated.

10. We abstract from the issue of the new entrant's effect on programming costs because the new entrant and incumbent could now share the fixed costs of programming.

11. Except possibly in the case of so-called hurdle price discrimination.

12. By "worthwhile," we mean those channels whose total consumer valuation is higher than their fixed cost of production.

13. For that matter, a la carte pricing and quasi-bundling may allow other viewers to avoid unwanted decent material.

References

Adams, W. J., & Yellen, J. L. (1976). Commodity bundling and the burden of monopoly. *Quarterly Journal of Economics, 90*, 475–498.

Nalebuff, B. J. (2004). Bundling as an entry barrier. *Quarterly Journal of Economics, 118*, 159–188.

Protecting children from violent and indecent programming: Hearing before the Senate Committee on Commerce, Science and Transportation, 108th Cong., 2 (2004).

Salinger, M. A. (1995). A Graphical Analysis of Bundling. *Journal of Business, 68*, 85–98.

Spence, A. M., & Owen, B. M. (1977). Television programming, monopolistic competition, and welfare. *The Quarterly Journal of Economics, 91*, 103–126.

Stigler, G. J. (1963). *United States v. Loew's, Inc.:* A note on block booking. *Supreme Court Review*, 152–157.

Waldfogel, J. (2003). Preference externalities: An empirical study of whom benefits whom in differentiated product markets. *RAND Journal of Economics, 34*, 557–568.

Managing Competition Through Barriers to Entry and Channel Availability in the Changing Regulatory Environment

■

Robert G. Picard
Jönköping University, Sweden

Bum Soo Chon
Korea National Open University, Korea

In this article, we explore factors that influence the number of broadcasters in a market and the achievement of optimal outcomes in broadcast markets. We explore a range of barriers to entry and means of overcoming those barriers in broadcast markets. We argue that choices regarding and influences on barriers to entry and channel availability act as forms of competition management in broadcast markets. Policymakers and regulators indirectly influence markets by altering the effects of those barriers and directly influence market activities by making decisions regarding the number of competitors, market structures, and—indirectly—the financial performance of broadcasters. We argue that barriers to entry can be controlled to produce competition levels and market outcomes that promote optimal social and economic outcomes.

Throughout the history of broadcasting monopoly and oligopoly, competition structures have existed worldwide because of spectrum scarcity, technological limitations, and political choices. During the past two decades, liberalization of broadcasting policy has permitted the expansion of broadcasting and the increasing reliance on commercial channels to provide additional services (Council of Europe, 1998; Davis, 1999; Dunnett, 1990; Silj, 1992).

Developments in cable and satellite television have concurrently increased the number of channels and programs available (*Cable and Satellite Yearbook*, 2002; Parsons & Frieden, 1998). Platform interconnectivity and interoperability between terrestrial broadcasting, cable, and satellite have developed, leading viewers to increasingly conceive them all as a single thing called "television." Because of technical ease of moving between channels on each, substitutability of the services has been increasing among consumers who have terrestrial receivers and cable and/or satellite set-top boxes. Advertisers also are increasingly addressing the various broadcast platforms as a single entity with different channels and audience char-

acteristics and now tend to make purchases across all three platforms as part of their television advertising expenditures.

Legislative bodies and administrative regulators worldwide have set and continue to determine the number of terrestrial broadcasters authorized within the constraints of the frequencies made available to them through the World Administrative Radio Conference. In some cases, determinations are made nationally; in other cases, they are regionally determined and nationally implemented, the latter being the case in Europe where joint spectrum management has existed since the 1961 Stockholm frequency planning agreement (International Telecommunications Union, 1961). Similar determinations are involved in determining satellite placement and frequency uses, but these are primarily international determinations.

Policymakers play a significant role in determining competition levels by allocating frequency to nations, by determining how much of the useable frequency will be used for broadcasting, and by determining the locations and broadcast power of broadcast licences. In doing so, they determine the number of competitors permitted, affect the willingness of capital sources to fund new entrants, and create advantages and disadvantages for some entrants. The policymakers' actions are a form of competition

Address correspondence to Robert G. Picard, Media Management and Transformation Centre, Jönköping International Business School, Box 1026, 551 11 Jönköping, Sweden. E-mail: robert.picard@jibs.hj.se

management, with regulators making decisions regarding the number of competitors, market structures, and—indirectly—the financial performance of broadcasters.

In this article, we address questions about factors that influence the number of broadcasters in a country or market and how regulators can determine the optimal number. We do not address the question of whether the number of broadcast competitors should be regulated by policymakers or the market itself. That question lends itself to political and economic debate that is not yet on the agenda in most nations.

The fundamental issue at the heart of government regulation today is the assumption of broadcasting market failure. Some spectrum limits remain in terrestrial broadcasting, and access of all potential competitors to satellite and cable distribution channels does not exist. The degree to which these impediments to open markets are present varies from country to country. Similarly, regulators worldwide have required content genre coverage and behavioral requirements designed to ensure performance they believe absent due to market failure. Management of competition levels through channel availability and entry barrier control is used by policymakers and regulators to promote outcomes they believe the market itself would not produce.

Managing competition is difficult because multiple broadcast markets are involved. It can be debated whether free-to-air broadcasting and paid broadcasting exist in the same economic market because their technologies, programming, demand characteristics, and consumption differ. Clearly, however, there is demand for both by some consumers, although significant numbers reject the paid form of broadcasting. There are also differences in the geography of markets involved. Some broadcasters serve local markets; others serve provincial markets. Some serve national markets, whereas others serve regional markets.

The interest of producers in different broadcast markets varies depending on factors such as market size, company and market resources, frequencies available, and alternative choices. Thus, broadcasters do not fully compete in a unified market, and regulators address different competition levels and issues in the different markets. Policymakers must consider questions about the optimal number of broadcasters and the type of service they wish to achieve overall and in given markets.

Despite differences in market conditions, there has been a general increase in number of competitors throughout the world in recent decades. The success of new entrants into established broadcast markets in the past two decades, however, has varied because of differences in the size and strength of barriers and the entrants' resources, capabilities, entry methods, and strategies. Their abilities to provide optimal service, meet public service obligations, and produce quality content is to a large extent determined by balance achieved between those fac-

tors and the levels of regulatory barriers maintained by policymakers and regulators.

In this article, we explore barriers to entry to broadcasting markets (both terrestrial and satellite), the effects of barrier reductions on markets, and we suggest optimal policies for reducing barriers and increasing competition.

Barriers to Entry and Mobility

Barriers to entry are factors that halt or make it difficult for new competitors to successfully enter a market in which they have not previously competed.

There are two main types of entrants. The first are firms entering the market for the first time, that is, those establishing new businesses. An example of this type of firm is a newly established company that wishes to operate a television channel. The second type of entrant is pre-existing firms entering the market by expanding their markets or moving into a new type of market. Examples of this type of firm may be a radio broadcaster that enters television broadcasting, a television channel operator that is expanding its operations by establishing a channel in another geographic market, or a satellite channel that spins off a new but related channel.

New businesses encounter barriers to entry, and established business encounter what are called *barriers to mobility*. The barriers are typically the same in both cases (van Kranenburg, 2002). There are many types of barriers to entry and mobility. Among the major barriers are government policies, capital requirements, economies of scale, product differentiation, switching costs, limited access to distribution channels, and other types of competitive advantages.

Government policies can create barriers to entry. In broadcasting, the classic cases are the licensing and franchising regulations that may provide barriers to new broadcasters and cable casters. If a ministry of communication has only 12 available terrestrial frequencies, a company that is not granted use of one of those frequencies will not be able to operate a television station no matter how much it wishes to do so. National governments have a far stronger ability to control entry and competition levels in terrestrial television than they do in satellite television. In addition, competition policies, general media policies, and other regulatory controls may limit some firms from entering specific markets. For example, a newspaper firm may not be able to operate a television station if regulations prohibit such cross-ownership, or the operator of a television channel may not be permitted to operate additional channels.

Capital requirements involve the financing needed to establish operations and pay start-up losses. Capital becomes a barrier when insufficient capital is available or when it is available only to certain firms or at preferential rates to certain firms. A firm may have the knowledge and desire to establish and operate a television channel but not have the capital required to purchase the necessary equipment or pay initial operating costs. Similarly, the assessment of capital sources about the desirability of providing funding for additional competition will affect the availability of the capital, the terms for capital rent, and—ultimately—the development and speed of development of the new market.

Economies of scale are created when unit costs decline as volume used or produced increases. Existing firms with high volumes will thus operate at a lower cost per unit than a new firm entering the market and create competitive conditions that can make entry unprofitable and undesirable (Scherer & Ross, 1990; Teece, 1980). Because broadcasting produces nonphysical, public goods, economies of scale generally are not a significant entry barrier in radio and television. However, large established broadcasting firms can achieve economies of scale in the cost of purchasing supplies and programming, technical operations, and administration that provide them competitive advantages not available to competitors. This is especially true in the operation of multiple channels under single ownership.

Product differentiation creates consumer loyalties and identification with existing products and services. These loyalties create barriers to entry that are difficult for a new firm to overcome.

Switching costs are consumer costs associated with changing from the use of one product to another. Consumers who switch from one satellite television operator to another typically must make substantial investments in set-top boxes or pay higher subscription costs to cover equipment rental or purchase. This issue makes it more difficult for another operator to compete or for providers of new communication technologies that offer substantially the same benefits as existing technologies to enter markets. Switching costs can also be psychological as well as financial because there is some psychological discomfort when changing products with which one is familiar, and many consumers tend to evidence inertia when new products become available.

Limited access to distribution channels creates barriers that keep companies from distributing their product or service. In cable TV and satellite TV, for example, this type of barrier occurs when channel capacity is not high enough to make space available for additional channels or when a company controlling the system chooses not to make space available to a company that offers competing channels to its own.

Other competitive advantages are factors inherent in some firms that provide advantages over their competitors. These arise from factors such as patents, trademarks, reputation, experience, preferred locations, better employees, or innovations. If two firms are considering entering a new market, the better known will be likely to have more success because it already has recognition when it enters the market or if it offers a new product (Galbi, 2001; Todreas, 1999). Thus, a programmer such as "Canal +" may be able to enter a new cable market more easily than a smaller, less internationalized firm with less experience in foreign markets. Similarly, firms with experience in broadcasting may be more likely to receive an available broadcasting license than firms without broadcasting experience.

Entry barriers exist to varying degrees in all media industries (Picard, 2002), but the broadcasting and newspaper industries are generally recognized as the most difficult to enter. In a study of entry barriers to newspaper markets, Gustafsson (1994) argued that audience and advertiser inertia, capital requirements, revenue structure, and economies of scale are the main factors that entrants must break through to succeed. Three are directly related to economic issues, but the fourth involves behavioral issues of audience preferences and inertia that limits changes to their behavior and trying new entrants.

Entry into the broadcasting market faces the variety of types of barriers previously discussed, but there are differences in the import of various barriers to potential entry. Entrants face six critical barriers into broadcasting markets (Figure 1).

The primary barrier is governmental policy. As noted previously, through the granting of broadcasting licenses government regulators determine the markets that are served and the number of competitors. Decisions regarding licenses involve spectrum availability, but they also are based on a variety of economic, political, cultural, and social factors. Decisions may not be fully rational in economic terms because of these other factors.

The second most important barrier is the presence of dominant existing broadcasters. These broadcasters usually have significant experience in the market and established relationships with audiences and—in some cases—

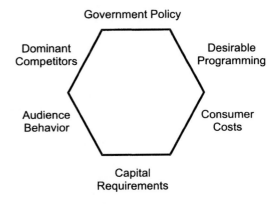

Figure 1. Primary barriers to broadcasting entry.

advertisers that must be challenged by entrants and are difficult to overcome. In many cases, existing broadcasters have historic, special relationships with the government, and regulators may fashion policies to protect them or give them additional advantages when new entrants are permitted. This barrier means that entrants must compete with a dominant competitor that enjoys significant advantages unavailable to new broadcasters. It can be argued that the dominant rival itself is not a barrier but a representation of the barriers created by consumer inertia, economies of scale, and government preferences. The presence of such a favored broadcaster—a protected public service broadcaster, for example—creates a significant impediment for entry of other players.

A third significant barrier is availability of suitable programming. Access to and reasonable prices for desirable programming in film and program libraries and to studios, directors, writers, actors, and technical personnel needed to produce attractive programming are necessary for successful entry. These critical resources can be controlled by competitors by various rights and licensing arrangements, contracts, or capacity utilization of scarce facilities.

The fourth barrier is audience behavior and the necessity for entrants to overcome long-established uses of television and set patterns of viewing and channel choice. This inertia, discussed previously, creates adherence to use patterns that change slowly, and entrants need to change the patterns rapidly to acquire audiences that are interesting to advertisers who fund commercial operations. Although new entrants may induce some audience members to alter their patterns and use preferences, experiences worldwide over the past two decades indicate that the largest audiences typically remain with the preexisting channels.

The fifth significant barrier is that of consumer costs. In many cases, entry into broadcasting markets is not available in a simple free-to-air situation and involves entry through cable or satellite activities or—in the contemporary environment through digital terrestrial television—it requires consumers to make significant expenditures for hardware and service to receive the entrants' channels. In such cases, entrants immediately face demand issues that result in smaller potential audiences than available in the free-to-air setting.

As previously noted, capital requirements for entry and operations before profitable operation are a significant barrier but not as critical for broadcasters as the previous barriers because of the potential for joint ventures and other financing arrangements that spread the amount needed and timing of capital contributions.

Technology also can pose a barrier in a technologically based industry. In terrestrial broadcasting, however, the general absence of proprietary basic technologies keeps it from becoming a significant issue, although it is more of an issue in satellite broadcasting and cablecasting.

Overcoming and Reducing Barriers

Barriers to mobility can sometimes be overcome by the ability of existing firms to invest sufficient resources over a longer period of time. A well-funded firm may be able to postpone returns in the short term to mid term to achieve long-term returns. Small and start-up firms rarely have this option.

Firms introducing new techniques and methods of operations that avoid traditional cost structures can sometimes overcome barriers to entry. They also can be overcome by the introduction of products that are sufficiently innovative that they surmount the traditional barriers.

Joint ventures can be entered with existing firms in the market or in related markets or with firms that have resources needed to overcome the barriers. Such tactics allow one to lessen the risk borne by a single company and to pool competencies in various firms. For example, a magazine with no online experience or with personnel unfamiliar with the tasks needed to start an online magazine might enter a joint venture with a firm that provides online design and management services and telecommunications access.

Government policies can help reduce barriers as a means of increasing competition and the number of firms in an industry (Gustafsson, 1993). One mechanism is guaranteed and subsidized loan funds that provide venture capital or capital for technology acquisition. Operation subsidies that provide another source of revenue and reduce operating losses in start-up firms can also be provided in some settings. Preferential awarding of licenses and franchises so that small companies have advantages in entering broadcasting or telecommunications is another mechanism of overcoming barriers for new firms.

Companies can create strategies to overcome the various barriers by providing different content, seeking different audiences, or entering with large operations that overcome economies of scale but require even more capital than the basic capital requirements, Gustafsson (1993) argued.

Effects of New Broadcasting Competition

Introducing or increasing competition in broadcast markets produces both beneficial and harmful effects. Regulators need to balance the beneficial effects with the accompanying harmful effects to achieve an optimal outcome. An optimal outcome is created when the market structure maximizes social welfare. This is usually conceived in economic terms as the sum of consumer surplus and producer surplus. In policy and media terms, it is often conceived as achievement of desirable content availability, behavioral performance, and industry stability.

Beneficial Effects of New Broadcasters

The introduction of additional broadcasters to a market produces several beneficial outcomes. First, it increases the overall supply of programming. Each new channel adds additional broadcast hours to the total hours broadcast in the market, increasing the availability of programming offered to consumers. The supply increases linearly, assuming each additional channel offers a similar number of hours of programming as illustrated in Figure 2. In many cases, however, the introduction of competition has been accompanied by an increase in the average number of hours broadcast per day by broadcasters, with many preexisting broadcasters increasing their broadcast days by 6 to 12 hr. This, of course, increases the total hours broadcast even more dramatically.

The increased hours of programming concurrently increases viewers' choices. This benefits consumers because it tends to provide them with a wider range of programming and more variety of programming at any given time. This occurs because when a limited number of suppliers exist, they tend to adopt programming strategies that narrow the range of programming offered, following Hotelling's (1929) theoretical notion of the rationality of similarity in products offered. Indeed, program choice theory in oligopolistic broadcasting markets is based on providing a similar mix of programming with the primary differences being sought through the times that programs are offered and counter-programming strategies (see Eastman, Head, & Klein, 1989; Owen & Wildman, 1992). As the number of broadcasters increases beyond only a few competitors, broadcasters and other media tend toward product differentiation and niche strategies that find a location in which they can successfully operate, which tends to increase the overall diversity and variety of programming offered (Dimmick, 2003; Wolf, 1993).

When commercial funding is involved, the introduction of new broadcasting channels places downward pressure on advertising prices that tends to remove any excess profits generated in monopoly or near-monopoly broadcasting markets. This reduces the costs of purchasing advertising and has the effect of increasing demand for advertising time and bringing new advertisers to the television market. This ultimately helps smaller retail firms grow, contribute to the national economy, and compete more effectively with larger retail firms.

Another benefit of increased competition is that it tends to remove inefficiencies in the operations of monopolist or oligopolistic firms in the market. Because such firms are able to generate excess profits, they tend toward inefficiency and reduced productivity. Increasing competition by adding new broadcasters forces existing broadcasting firms to manage themselves more effectively to remove the inefficiency. This tends to increase productivity and value added to the national economy.

An additional benefit of increased channels is that it tends to promote the introduction or development of independent program production capabilities. Increased demand for programs across all channels combined with the inability of many preexisting channels to increase their production capabilities concurrently with increases in their broadcast hours and their need to seek efficiencies leads broadcasters to seek programs from independent producers. This promotes the development and growth of independent production companies that increase national employment and economic growth as well as introduce new ideas, content, and formats to the programs available.

Harmful Effects of Introducing New Broadcasters

Significantly increasing the number of broadcasters creates instability in the market by altering audience and advertiser use patterns and reducing financial resources to existing broadcasters. These have significant financial and quality effects.

Increasing the supply of channels and hours of programming tends to fragment the audience rather than significantly increasing consumption. This occurs because it does not affect the number of households with television and the average amount of viewing time. This has the effect of reducing the average size of the audience for each channel and thus the desirability of each channel's advertisers. Demand for broadcasting does not grow proportionally with supply, so reducing entry barriers tends to create oversupply (Picard, 2001).

Audience fragmentation is also related to the amount of choice and broadcasters' program choices. Because of program choice models used in broadcasting, each channel tends to provide a range of programming, and the range of types of programs offered among channels tends to be similar. It has been observed that "where a country

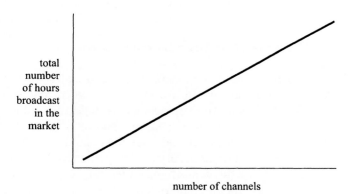

Figure 2. Relationship between number of channels and total hours of programming broadcast.

R. G. Picard and B. S. Chon

has several channels, each tends to be watched by many people for a part of their viewing time. Smaller channels not only have fewer viewers but also attract less of these viewers' viewing time than the larger channels" (Barwise & Ehrenberg, 1988, p. 63). This situation leads to competition among channels to draw viewers from their competitors (Owen & Wildman, 1992). Ultimately, situations emerge in which three to four channels dominate viewers' time, and other channels receive relatively low levels of viewership. If this structure produces anticompetitive effects in the economic market or harms welfare by reducing levels of diversity and plurality desired in a society, it may be seen as a form of market failure.

If channels added are dependent on commercial financing, the ability of the advertising market to support additional channels is crucial. Although new advertisers may enter the market, and existing advertisers may somewhat increase their expenditures, the growth of advertising expenditures does not equal the growth of advertising time available and thus reduces average income per channel (Picard, 2001). This reduces industry profitability and value added to the national economy and may lead to reductions in the overall workforce in the industry.

If the competition levels introduced are high, it can become ruinous to existing market structures, harm existing broadcasters, and make it impossible for new entrants to survive. Brown (2000) noted that "competition among channels will eventually result in each market determining the number of channels it can support with some channels incurring losses and ceasing operations and/or declining profits deterring further entry" (p. 4).

Because available revenue is split across channels, the average amount of expenditures for programming per channel declines (including that at preexisting stations). Heavily increasing competition forces broadcasters to reduce programming costs, and this is typically done by relying on inexpensive programming formats, imported programming, and reruns. Thus, significantly increasing the number of broadcast competitors reduces the overall quality of programming offered.

If the market were funded directly by consumers, quality reductions would reduce their willingness to pay and thus create an incentive for broadcasters to improve quality to benefit in the long run. However, because funding for free-to-air broadcasting does not emanate directly from viewers, this market-righting mechanism is very sluggish.

Because of the issues posed by revenues and costs, it is desirable to ensure that the entry of new competitors does not create such instability that firms already present in the market are mortally wounded and unable to survive, that the number of new entrants permitted is linked to the ability of the market to absorb them, and that the resources in the market are sufficient to maintain or achieve an acceptable level of program quality.

Optimal Structure of Broadcast Entry Barriers

Optimal policy for expanding broadcasting market offerings needs to be designed to reduce barriers to entry, to increase competition and choice, and to achieve the attendant economic benefits for consumers and society. While increasing competition, however, the policy needs to maintain sufficient barriers to ensure survival of existing and entrant firms so that the objectives and benefits of the policy-directed competition increases are achieved. This is necessary to achieve socially desirable content availability and quality levels as well as to create the economic benefits of increased competition. It is also a pragmatic necessity if policymakers are to avoid heavy political opposition by preexisting broadcasters to market entry policy proposals that clearly threaten their performance or survival.

These issues are illustrated conceptually in Figure 3. It shows that as the barriers are reduced to increase the number of broadcast channels, the threats to the survival of existing firms and new entrants rises.

Because of this issue, regulators need to determine the appropriate equilibrium of reducing barriers to increase competition, choice, and well-being while simultaneously controlling the reduction of barriers to avoid unreasonable economic harm to existing broadcasters, new broadcasters, consumers, and society. Additionally, regulators may wish to consider constructing advantages for domestic broadcasters to help maintain national identity and culture. If the reductions in barriers produce or can be expected to produce negative effects on quality of programming, regulators may wish to simultaneously introduce quality of programming initiatives including grants or subsidies for production of high-quality offerings or program quality requirements and monitoring.

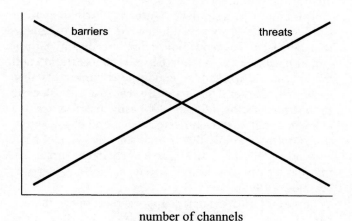

Figure 3. Effects of barrier reduction on threats to survival of broadcasters.

Because lowering barriers to entry creates market instability, it is useful that the barriers be incrementally reduced so that entry of new broadcasters is staggered to avoid sudden market shocks that are harmful both in the short term and long term.

Discussion

Until recently, the broadcasting industry throughout the world was structured as a concentrated and regulated market. Because the fixed costs and large investments needed for broadcasting companies make economies of scale feasible for the industry, the majority of broadcasting markets are dominated by oligopoly (Motta & Polo, 1997a; Organization for Economic Cooperation and Development, 2003). However, given the fact that the barriers to entry have been justified for public interests, many factors are involved, and it is difficult in practice to determine the optimal number or size of broadcasters in the industry. Therefore, it is not easy to choose the best approach in regulating the level of market concentration and competition in the broadcasting market.

Recent works (Motta & Polo, 1997a, 1997b) have emphasized the need for stability in the level of concentration in the broadcasting industry. According to Motta and Polo (1997b), "competition among TV companies is based not only on the choice of the program varieties broadcast, but also on the attractiveness (or quality) of program schedules" (p. 296). The key point is that rivalry among broadcasting programs can be explained in terms of investment for the programs, not by the variety of programs alone. This gives a key advantage to established broadcasters in securing their ability to compete in terms of investment. Thus, due to these higher fixed costs, there are a limited number of broadcasters in a market that can finance the costs of making and distributing programs with optimal quality and public service.

This argument is similar to Sutton's (1991) explanation that dominant firms have higher fixed costs and maintain persistent concentration. More specifically, Sutton emphasized that the relation between concentration and market size is weaker for endogenous sunk costs that grow with market size. As a result, because of sunk costs in the broadcasting industry, decreasing barriers to entry alone does not effectively decrease the level of concentration (Motta & Polo, 1997b). Additionally, as has been shown in the radio industry, free entry in the broadcasting market can also lead to social inefficiency (Berry & Waldfogel, 1996).

Some empirical evidence supports these views. In measuring the relation between structure and variety in the music recording industry, Alexander (1997) argued that high and low levels of concentration result in lessened variety, and maximum variety is promoted by a moderately concentrated structure. Goldfarb (2003) also maintained that less differentiated markets are more concentrated and that markets with higher sunk costs are more concentrated. Van der Wurff, Van Cuilenburg, and Keune (2000) emphasized that moderate competition improves content but that high competition results in ruinous competition that produces excessive sameness and diminishes the quality of media products. As a result, the barrier for entry should not be set too high or too low in regulated media markets.

Theoretically, the optimal degree of program differentiation can be determined. Mangàni (2003) conducted an analysis concerning quality and variety competition between commercial television broadcasters competing in a duopoly market, and summarized the main point as follows:

> Under certain circumstances, the firm providing the lower quality program faces no demand. This occurs because the high quality firm has the strategic opportunity to move towards the centre of consumer distribution along the horizontal characteristic (variety dimension). Therefore, when competition takes place between broadcasters, a "natural oligopoly" result can be obtained even if we are considering products (programs) defined by more than one characteristic. This seems relevant because it is impossible, when modelling product (not broadcasting) markets, to obtain a "finiteness property" result. The finiteness property can thus be restored when we consider broadcasting or similar markets. (Mangàni, 2003, p. 314)

A central question faced by regulators today is how broadcasting firms and markets should be organized to promote economic efficiencies and encourage variety and plurality in programs. In this article, we show that competition policy alone does not guarantee achievement of the basic social objectives for the broadcasting industry such as maintaining a pluralism of views or providing greater variety in programs. Given that broadcasting companies are social, cultural, economic, and political institutions, they need to be examined in terms of their social, cultural, and political contexts as well as their economic efficiencies.

Because competition alone does not ensure plurality or diversity of programming, merely lowering barriers to entry in the broadcasting market will not produce optimal outcomes. Achieving optimal public service outcomes will require maintaining some barriers to entry so that an oligopolistic market structure is maintained as well as behavioral regulation to constrain possible monopolistic abuses that such a concentration of power may bring and to ensure effective investments in program quality and diversity.

Robert G. Picard

(robert.picard@jibs.hj.se)

is Hamrin Professor of Media Economic and Director, Media Management and Transformation Centre, Jönköping International Business School, Jönköping University.

Bum Soo Chon

(ccblade2@yahoo.co.kr)

is a full time Lecturer at Department of Media Arts & Sciences, Korea National Open University. His research focuses on economic aspects of the media and entertainment industry.

References

Alexander, P. J. (1997). Product variety and market structure: A new measure and a simple test. *Journal of Economic Behaviour & Organization, 32*, 207–214.

Barwise, P., & Ehrenberg, A. (1988). *Television and its audience.* Newbury Park, CA: Sage.

Berry, S., & Waldfogel, J. (1996). Free entry and social inefficiency in radio broadcasting. *NBER Working Papers* (No. 5528).

Brown, A. (2000, October). *Commercial free-to-air television with unrestricted channel numbers.* Paper presented to Communications Research Forum 2000, Canberra, Australia.

Cable and Satellite Yearbook 2002. (2002). London: Information Media Group.

Council of Europe. (1998). *Radio and television systems in the EU member states and Switzerland.* Strasbourg, France: Council of Europe Publishing.

Davis, W. (1999). *The European TV industry in the 21st century.* London: Informa Publishing Group.

Dimmick, J. W. (2003). *Media competition and coexistence: The theory of niche.* Mahwah, NJ: Lawrence Erlbaum Associates, Inc.

Dunnett, P. (1990). *The world television industry: An economic analysis.* New York: Routledge.

Eastman, S. T., Head, S. W., & Klein, L. (1989). *Broadcast/cable programming: Strategies and practices.* Belmont, CA: Wadsworth.

Galbi, D. (2001). The new business significance of branding. *The International Journal on Media Management, 3*, 192–198.

Goldfarb, A. (2003). *Concentration in advertising-supported online markets: An empirical approach.* Retrieved from http://www.rotman.utoronto.ca/~agoldfarb/infohwy.pdf

Gustafsson, K. E. (1993). Government policies to reduce newspaper entry barriers. *The Journal of Media Economics, 6*(1), 37–43.

Gustafsson, K. E. (1994). Newspaper industries in Estonia, Latvia, and Lithuania: Comparative study of forces of change. *Nordicom Review, 1*, 129–136.

Hotelling, H. (1929). Stability in competition. *Economic Journal, 39*, 41–57.

International Telecommunications Union. (1961). *Final acts of the European VHF/UNF Brodcasting Conference, 1961.* Geneva, Switzerland: Author.

Mangàni, A. (2003). Profit and audience maximization in broadcasting markets. *Information Economics and Policy, 15*, 305–315.

Motta, M., & Polo, M. (1997a). Beyond the spectrum constraint: Concentration and entry in the broadcasting industry. (Working Paper 115). IGIER, Università Boconni.

Motta, M. & Polo, M. (1997b). Concentration and public policies in the broadcasting industry: the future of television. *Economic Policy, 25*, 295–334.

Organization for Economic Cooperation and Development. (2003). *Media mergers.* Paris: Author.

Owen, B. M., & Wildman, S. S. (1992). *Video economics.* Cambridge, MA: Harvard University Press.

Parsons, P., & Frieden, R. (1998). *The cable and satellite television industries.* Boston: Allyn & Bacon.

Picard, R. G. (2001). Expansion and limits in EU television markets: Audience, advertising, and competition issues. *Discussion Papers C2/2001*, Business Research and Development Centre, Turku School of Economics and Business Administration.

Picard, R. G. (2002). *The economics and financing of media companies.* New York: Fordham University Press.

Scherer, F. M., & Ross, D. (1990). *Industrial market structure and economic performance* (3rd ed.). Boston: Houghton Mifflin.

Silj, A. (1992). *The new television in Europe.* London: John Libbey & Co.

Sutton, J. (1991). *Sunk costs and market structure: Price competition, advertising, and the evolution of concentration.* Cambridge, MA: MIT Press.

Teece, D. J. (1980). Economics of scope and the scope of the enterprise. *Journal of Economic Behaviour and Organization, 1*, 223–247.

Todreas, T. M. (1999). *Value creation and branding in television's digital age.* New York: Quorum Books.

Van der Wurff, R., Van Cuilenburg, J., & Keune, G. (2000). Competition, media innovation and broadcasting. In J. Van Cuilenburg & R. Van der Wurff (Eds.), *Media and open societies* (pp. 119–157). Amsterdam: Het Spinhuis.

van Kranenburg, H. (2002). Mobility and market structure in the Dutch daily newspaper market segments, *Journal of Media Economics, 15*(2), 107–123.

Wolf, M. (1993). In search of market niches. *The Journal of Media Economics, 6*(1), 45–51.

Diversity in Broadcast Television: An Empirical Study of Local News

Peter J. Alexander
Federal Communications Commission, USA

Brendan M. Cunningham
United States Naval Academy, USA

The relation between the structure of a market and the diversity of its product offering has been extensively explored by theorists. We develop 2 measures of diversity and explore the content of local news for 60 stations and 20 designated market areas (DMAs) in the United States. Using a relative station-level diversity metric, ordinary least squares (OLS) estimates imply that relative diversity of local news content decreases as market concentration increases. This result is not, however, robust to an instrumental variables specification. Using a total market diversity metric, the Herfindahl–Hirschman Index (Hirshman, 1964) is significant in OLS and robust to instrumental variable estimation. Because the total market diversity metric is arguably superior to the incremental metric as a measure of overall diversity, this result is useful—it suggests that the total diversity of local news content within a DMA is sensitive to the level of concentration.

The relation between the structure of a market and the extent to which the products of the market are differentiated has generated a substantial theoretical literature that has produced a wide range of predictions. Although it was once conventional wisdom that competition would maximize diversity, theory has shown that the incentives to differentiate may plausibly imply a welfare maximizing structure that consists of a single firm. Empirically speaking, evidence for either of these positions is scant, although there are some suggestive contributions.

In what follows, we use an archive of broadcast news and categorize the number of unique seconds of local news broadcasts. From this data, we construct two measures of local news broadcast diversity—one station level and one designated market area (DMA) level. We then econometrically relate our measures of diversity back to structural and demographic characteristics.

Broadcast Media Literature

In commercial broadcast media industries, the essential theory can be partitioned into the early literature and the more recent.[1] Thus, for example, Steiner's (1952) seminal contribution to this literature demonstrated the plausibility of a welfare enhancing monopoly structure in broadcast television because a monopoly structure may internalize the business stealing effects of competition. Steiner's work was extended by Beebe (1977) who demonstrated that optimal structure depends on the distribution of preferences and the extent of channel capacity. Spence and Owen (1977) showed that the fixed costs associated with program production often result in underprovision of certain types of programming because the broadcast revenues of such programs do not exceed the costs. Spence and Owen noted that this bias is reduced under a pure pay-television framework relative to an advertiser supported structure. More recent contributions to this theoretical literature have included Gal-Or and Dukes (2003); Anderson and Coate (2001); Nilssen and Sorgard (2001); Gabszewicz, Laussel, and Sonnac (2001); and Cunningham and Alexander (2004). In particular, the works of Gal-Or and Dukes and Gabszewicz, Laussel, and Sonnac have predicted that market concentration and program diversity are inversely related in television broadcast marketplaces.

Empirical literature related to the relation between structure and diversity in commercial media is practically nonexistent. In a study that used the Telecommunications

Address correspondence to Peter J. Alexander, 4517 Roxbury Drive, Bethesda, MD 20814. E-mail: peter.alexander@fcc.gov

Act of 1996 to control for endogeneity of structure in the radio broadcast industry, Berry and Waldfogel (2001) showed that concentration is positively associated with the number of radio formats.[2] Goettler and Shacher (2001), taking structure as given, showed that television broadcasters differentiate within given time slots but cluster on program type across time slots.

Moreover, the importance of a relation between the structure (broadly defined) of mass media (e.g., television, radio, newspapers) and the diversity of output is not purely academic and has implications beyond simple product differentiation (strategies). Rather, embedded in these explorations is an issue of some political, social, and economic importance, for example, the relevance of diverse information to voters.

As suggested by Demsetz (1989), there may exist a large "amenity" benefit (e.g., political influence) from control of the media, and recent work by Besley and Burgess (2002) and Djankov, McLiesh, Nenova, and Shleifer (2001) has provided empirical evidence of such a benefit. Besley and Burgess suggested that political incumbents may be able to successfully circumscribe the content of media ("capture theory"), in part via distribution of rents determined by regulatory agencies, and presented econometric evidence that does not contradict their hypothesis. Moreover, Stromberg (2004b) found that the expansion of radio in the 1930s helped rural Americans capture an increasingly greater percentage of government transfers, whereas Stromberg (2004a) suggested that advertiser supported, increasing returns to scale technology (e.g., television) induces the production of news targeted to large groups that are valuable to advertisers while ignoring smaller fringe groups. George and Waldfogel (2002) documented a similar phenomenon for newspapers in which consumption reflects strong preference externalities. Because these media are the means by which politicians convey information to voters, preference externalities can introduce bias into public policy.

Additional contributions relating to ownership structure of the media include Coase (1974), Besley and Burgess (2002), and Besley and Pratt (2002), all of whom have suggested that a competitive market structure induces greater accuracy in the reporting of news. Mullainathan and Shleifer (2003) suggested that competition in media does not produce greater accuracy in reporting (one can think of competition as being a necessary but not sufficient condition); rather, a taste for content heterogeneity among consumers (within a competitive market environment) produces a convergence to some "average truth."

This broad literature can be partitioned, somewhat crudely, into three categories: (a) differentiated products in two-sided markets with welfare effects, (b) strategic interaction, and (c) political and economic. In this work, we contribute mostly to the second branch and hint at implications for the third.

Our Approach

We used an archive of broadcast news and catalogued and categorized the number of unique seconds of local news broadcasts across the "Big Three" (CBS, NBC, and ABC) network affiliates covering over 60 stations in 20 DMAs.[3] From this data, we constructed our measure(s) of local news broadcast diversity at both the station and DMA level because these results may be expected to vary. We then econometrically related our measure(s) of diversity back to structural and demographic characteristics including number of broadcast stations, cable penetration, total market revenues, average income, and market structure (as measured by both the Herfindahl–Hirschman Index [HHI; Hirshman, 1964] and the number of stations in the market).

We cannot, from this data, shed any light on the Steiner (1952) hypothesis because current broadcast television ownership rules preclude merger to monopoly. We can, however, provide some empirical evidence regarding the effect of firm-level and market-level concentration on the diversity of local news offerings. Thus, we may be able to contribute some insight to the strategic interaction literature branch noted previously. Finally, although we offer no direct hypothesis, this work might also provide modest interest relative to the political-economic literature. Specifically, if local news influences voting outcomes and hence the flow of funds to states, counties, cities, and towns (see Stromberg, 2004b, for an excellent study on the penetration of radio into rural America in the 1930s) and if the fraction of voter relevant information is constant for any level of output, greater diversity might imply a greater level of information relevant to voters.

Summary of Main Results

Our ordinary least squares (OLS) results suggest that market concentration as measured by the HHI has a negative impact on local news diversity, whereas the total number of stations in a market has a positive impact on local news story diversity. In short, our estimates suggest that increasing concentration appears to diminish diversity in local broadcast news both at the firm and market level. This result is robust to the measure of diversity used in estimation and emerges after controlling for possible endogeneity in market structure. Moreover, there is an apparent link between broadcast news and substitutes (broadly defined) for local broadcast news—the number of broadcast firms at the market level and the presence of cable have a strong positive effect on local news diversity. This might suggest that potential competition and the availability of substitute programming stimulates greater diversity in the offerings of local news broadcasts.

This article is organized as follows. First, we describe our data and methodology. Second, we detail our regression specifications and results. Third, we discuss the results. Finally, we make some concluding remarks.

Data and Methodology

Diversity implies difference, but as a practical matter, diversity is difficult to define with any precision let alone measure. However, assuming one has a plausible measure of diversity (which assumes one has an adequate definition of diversity) it may be enlightening to relate this measure back to media market structure as well as various demographic variables.

In this section, we describe our technique for measuring diversity in the content of broadcast news using an archive of local news content and relate the resulting diversity measure back to market structure and market level characteristics. The broadcast news archive (10,600 individual news stories from 20 DMAs across 60 stations from 1998 local broadcasts) was obtained from the University of Delaware and was originally gathered by the Project for Excellence in Journalism (hereafter PEJ).[4]

The use of DMA-level data in determining markets is appropriate. According to Nielsen (Schwartz-Leaper, 2003)

> In designing the DMA regions, Nielsen Media Research uses proprietary criteria, testing methodologies and data to partition regions of the United States into geographically distinct television viewing areas, and then expresses them in unique, carefully defined regions that are meaningful to the specific business we conduct.[5] (p. 3)

In Table 1, we list the sampled DMAs and their market size ranking. From Table 1, it is clear that our database sampled media content from a broad variety of markets.

Two Measures of Diversity

We employed two distinct, but related, measures of diversity.

First, for all local broadcast content within a particular DMA, we counted the total seconds of local news coverage that are unique to the three major network affiliates (CBS, ABC, and NBC) within the DMA as contributing to diversity. We refer to this measure as *relative* or *marginal station-level diversity* because this measure captures each network's incremental contribution to the total amount of coverage of unique stories. In this measure, if any two or more local news broadcasts cover the same story on the same day, only the seconds beyond the collective average of the respective overlapping broadcasts are counted as adding to diversity.[6]

Table 1. Markets and DMA Rank

DMA	Rank
New York	1
Los Angeles	2
Chicago	3
Boston	6
Washington, D.C.	8
Atlanta	10
Seattle	12
Minneapolis/St. Paul	14
Pittsburgh	20
St. Louis	21
Buffalo	44
Louisville	48
Albuquerque	49
Jacksonville	52
Wichita	65
Tucson	72
Burlington	91
Evansville	98
Lansing	107
Tallahassee	109

Note. DMA = designated market areas.

Our marginal station-level diversity measure may not adequately capture the collective output of diverse content by the broadcasters in a DMA because it is measured on a relative basis. To investigate the robustness of our findings, we employed a second measure of diversity that counts the total time devoted to all unique stories covered by the three networks. This variable, which measures each network's contribution to the total amount of news coverage, is referred to as *total DMA diversity*. We found that the raw correlation between these two measures was .18, implying that the distinction between relative and total diversity is more than conceptual.

Specification and Results

In this section, we discuss our specification and present our OLS regression results. Before discussing our specification and results, we give a brief discussion regarding our prior expectations for the signs of the regression coefficients. Our independent variables include HHI, number of firms within DMA, industry revenue, cable penetration rate, average household income, computer ownership rate, population density, and fraction of the population over age 65.

Structure

Because market structure is often difficult to measure, we employed two measures of structure, the revenue HHI and the number of broadcast stations in the market. Loosely, one can think of the HHI as reflecting the state of actual competition within a market, whereas the number of firms reflects potential competition.[7]

It is possible that the (increasing) relative cost of producing diverse output may lead to a reduction in diversity as the market becomes more concentrated; moreover, ownership structure may influence diversity if the within-market stations are owned and operated by large broadcast networks. In this case, given the scale economies inherent in national program distribution, diverse output may become relatively more costly (although the output within any given DMA might still be diverse in one sense). Thus, we might expect that increasing concentration might lead to lower diversity. On the other hand, actual, emergent, or potential competition might promote greater diversity in content (such as the type found by Goettler & Shacher, 2001).

Total Industry Revenue

The total revenue of all stations is meant to capture the size of the television market. A large DMA may experience greater or lesser diversity; we did not have a strong prior expectation for the sign of the coefficient.

Cable Penetration Rate

The cable penetration rate measures the extent to which consumers within DMAs have access to cable broadcasting in addition to over-the-air signals. Ex ante, we expected that as consumers have access to a broader set of broadcast choices, broadcast firms may have incentives to diversify their respective outputs to counter new entry.

Average Household Income

As average household income increases, consumers tend to diversify the items they purchase, generally speaking. Simply, rising income allows consumers to indulge their underlying "taste for diversity." Thus, we anticipated that as incomes grow, broadcast content may also become more diverse. Note the possible endogeneity problem inherent in this measure (see, e.g., Stromberg, 2004a).

Computer Ownership Rate

The computer ownership rate proxies for access to additional sources of news content. If consumers can access broad news content via the Internet, local broadcast stations may have an incentive to produce news that is more local in content (i.e., they become more locally special-

ized), especially if Internet news is broadly substitutable for local broadcast news. Or possibly, the content accessed by consumers via the Internet complements the output of broadcast news stations, leading to a greater overall content diversity. Thus, we did not have an expectation regarding sign for the coefficient on this variable, ex ante.

Population Density

If population density implies heterogeneity among consumers, we expected that the output of broadcast news would become more diverse. On the other hand, a large population that is concentrated in a small "footprint" may encounter a uniformity of events, thereby leading to uniformity in news coverage. For example, there is not much room for diverse perspectives on the weather in Manhattan. The same may not be true of an equally sized population spread across a broader area, such as the greater Los Angeles metropolitan area.

Population Over 65

Given that the population over 65 years old tends to be more homogeneous than a cross-section of the entire population, we expected that this cohort might reflect a "mass point" that induces greater homogeneity and hence less diversity in local broadcast news content. Thus, we expected the sign of the coefficient to be negative.

In light of the previous discussion, we estimated two OLS regressions given by

$$
\begin{aligned}
Diversity = \alpha_0 &+ \alpha_1 \ln HHI + \alpha_2 \ln IndustryRevenue \\
&+ \alpha_3 CablePenetration + \alpha_4 \ln Income \\
&+ \alpha_5 ComputerOwnership \\
&+ \alpha_6 \ln PopulationDensity \\
&+ \alpha_7 FractionOver65 + \varepsilon
\end{aligned} \tag{1}
$$

and

$$
\begin{aligned}
Diversity = \alpha_0 &+ \alpha_1 NumberofFirms \\
&+ \alpha_2 \ln IndustryRevenue + \alpha_3 CablePenetration \\
&+ \alpha_4 \ln Income + \alpha_5 ComputerOwnership \\
&+ \alpha_6 \ln PopulationDensity \\
&+ \alpha_7 FractionOver65 + \varepsilon
\end{aligned} \tag{2}
$$

In Table 2 we list the results from OLS estimation.

Discussion

As can be seen from Table 2, columns 2 and 5 report OLS results using the relative station-level diversity measure as a dependent variable (giving 60 observations). Columns 3 and 4 report OLS results using the total diversity measure

Table 2. OLS Results, Local News Data

Variable	Firm-Level Diversity	Total Diversity	Total Diversity, Income Dropped	Firm-Level Diversity, Alternative Concentration Method
HHI (log)	−16.81 (.047)	−56.45 (.135)	−56.82 (.074)	−
Number of stations	−	−	−	0.66 (.013)
Total industry revenue (log)	−6.76 (.002)	−12.533 (.212)	−12.69 (.087)	−5.81 (.000)
Cable penetration rate	0.47 (.000)	−0.62 (.211)	−0.62 (.200)	.367 (.001)
Average household income (log)	31.58 (.002)	−1.20 (.974)	−	31.92 (.000)
Computer ownership rate	−0.33 (.046)	−0.53 (.381)	−0.54 (.283)	−0.41 (.005)
Population density (log)	−3.91 (.000)	4.74 (.142)	4.68 (.109)	−3.41 (.000)
% population over 65	−1.18 (.015)	0.60 (.782)	0.61 (.777)	−1.59 (.003)
Constant	−27.45 (.786)	692.45 (.057)	684.94 (.049)	−164.76 (.032)

Note. p values appear in parentheses. In columns 2 and 5, the dependent variable is the average number of seconds devoted to unique stories by a given station. In columns 3 and 4, the dependent variable is the average number of seconds devoted to unique stories by all stations within a designated market area. OLS = ordinary least squares; HHI = Herfindahl–Hirschman Index.

as a dependent variable (giving 20 observations). The only difference between columns 2 and 5 is that column 5 substitutes the number of firms for HHI. All of the independent variables for the OLS regression in columns 2 and 5 using the firm-level measure were significant at the 5% level.

Note that in column 4, average household income was dropped from the regression. In column 3, this variable was not significantly related to the total diversity measure (p = .97). When the total diversity measure was used as a dependent variable, there was a small sample of only 20 observations. Note that after dropping average household income (and hence gaining a degree of freedom), the signs of all the coefficients in columns 3 and 4 were identical, and the magnitudes of the coefficients were nearly identical. However, the additional degree of freedom allowed us to obtain more precise estimates of the coefficients on the remaining variables. Importantly, we observed statistical significance on two of the variables, HHI and total industry revenue, in column 4.

Market Structure

Looking at the data in Table 2, there is a prima facie case to be made that market structure influenced the total and relative diversity of the product offerings in local broadcast news. More precisely, according to these OLS results, HHI was significantly negatively related to firm-level diversity in column 2 and total diversity in column 4. This result is robust to redefining our measure of market structure: In column 5, the number of firms exhibits a significant positive impact on relative firm-level diversity.

Total Industry Revenue

Total industry revenue had a significant negative effect on relative news diversity, implying that as industry revenue

increased, relative diversity in the content of local broadcast news diminished. The result in Table 2, column 4 using total news diversity is also significant.

Cable Penetration Rate

In specifications in Table 2, columns 2 and 5, the cable penetration rate has a strong positive relation with diversity. More generically, the presence of an outside viewing option (by which we mean alternative programming of a variety of types) is associated with increased diversity in the offerings of broadcast news outlets at the firm level. This might imply that firm-level broadcast news is responsive to the presence of alternative programming choices available to potential viewers. Thus, diversification of content may be one means by which local news broadcasts fight for viewers. Although the sign is reversed for specifications in Table 2, column 3 and 4, the results were not significant.

As can be seen in Table 2, various demographic variables including age, population density, average household income, and computer ownership were also significantly related to firm-level, but not DMA-level diversity.

Income

Average household income was positively related to diversity, implying that as incomes within a DMA increase, diversity increases. This does not contradict the idea that consumers' taste for diversity is increasing in income growth.

Computer Ownership

Computer ownership exhibited a small but significant negative relation with local news broadcast diversity, which implies that the Internet may be more complementary than substitutable for local broadcast news.

Population Density

Population density was also negatively associated with diversity. This implies that the greater the population density, the lower the overall level of diversity.

Age

The fraction of the population over 65 was negatively related to diversity, possibly the result of a homogenizing cohort or mass point effect.

Instrumental Variable Analysis

There is a possibility that the results reported in Table 2 are not reliable because in all likelihood, the level of broadcast news variety has an impact on industry structure and cable penetration. In other words, it is likely that uniformity in news coverage may induce lower concentration and higher cable penetration rates due to viewer response. In the presence of such "reverse causality," standard OLS estimation can lead to biased coefficients. We employed an instrumental variables technique to reduce this bias using lagged values of the HHI and Cable Penetration variables as instruments for market structure and the availability of outside media options. These results are given in Table 3. Column 2 reports lagged values of HHI and cable penetration using the relative diversity measure, whereas columns 3 and 4 report the total diversity measure. Note that in column 4, we dropped average household income in response to the small sample associated with the total diversity measure.

In this specification, nearly all of the independent variables for the relative diversity measure (Table 3, column 2) were significant at the 10% level—however, the HHI was in-

significant. This finding suggests that endogeniety plagued the OLS results given earlier or indicates weakness in the chosen instrument.[8] For this reason, caution should be used in interpreting the previous findings pertaining to market structure. However, when the total diversity measure is employed as a dependent variable in Table 3, column 4, the lagged value of HHI was significant at the 10% level. This finding is consistent with the earlier OLS results and suggests robustness in the negative relation between market concentration and diversity in local television news broadcasts.

Conclusions

The relation between the structure of a market and the diversity of its product offering has been extensively explored by theorists, and these theories have generated competing hypothesis. In this article, we developed two simple measures of diversity and explored the diversity of local news content for 60 stations and 20 DMAs. The relevance of the project derives largely from the strategic interplay between competing firms as well as the political-economic implications of variations in the diversity of news content. Because of ownership rules preventing merger to monopoly, we were not able to test the Steiner (1952) hypothesis directly.

Using a simple OLS framework, our preliminary findings suggest that market-level structure may influence the output of firms. Specifically, using the relative station-level diversity metric, we found that as the structure of the market became more concentrated, relative diversity of local news content was diminished. Importantly, this result was not robust to an instrumental variables specification. However, using the total market diversity metric, HHI was significant in OLS and robust to instrumental variable transformation. Because the total market diversity metric is arguably superior to the incremental metric as a measure of overall diversity, this result is use-

Table 3. Instrumental Variables, Local News Data (Lagged Values of HHI, Cable Penetration as Instruments)

Variable	Firm-Level Diversity	Total Diversity	Total Diversity, Income Dropped
HHI (log)	−5.04 (.610)	−55.92 (.162)	−56.54 (.094)
Total industry revenue (log)	−4.06 (.098)	−12.41 (.232)	−12.64 (.108)
Cable penetration rate	0.50 (.000)	−0.63 (.220)	−0.62 (.208)
Average household income (log)	25.75 (.022)	−1.51 (.966)	—
Computer ownership rate	−0.27 (.100)	−0.53 (.355)	−0.54 (.274)
Population density (log)	−3.86 (.000)	4.76 (.135)	4.69 (.116)
% population over 65	−1.39 (.012)	0.60 (.793)	0.61 (.785)
Constant	−90.10 (.400)	690.20 (.074)	682.35 (.059)

Note. p values appear in parentheses. In column 2, the dependent variable is the average number of seconds devoted to unique stories by a given station. In columns 3 and 4, the dependent variable is the average number of seconds devoted to unique stories by all stations within a designated market area. HHI = Herfindahl–Hirschman Index.

ful—it suggests that total diversity within a DMA is sensitive to the level of concentration.

Future research using this data suggests several plausibly enlightening extensions. First, ownership structure may be a significant influence on diversity—perhaps as important as overall concentration. Specifically, we wonder whether stations that are part of a national broadcast chain might overutilize national broadcast feeds. This technique for creating content is relatively less expensive than gathering news independently.[9] Because this option is not available to single-station owners, gathering local news is relatively less expensive for those stations associated with a national organization. Providing the overlap between national stories and local news is modest (as might be expected for most DMAs), single-station owners might contribute more to diversity than owned-and-operated chain stations.

Peter J. Alexander
(Peter.Alexander@fcc.gov)

is an Economist at the Federal Communications Commission. His publications cover media industries and topics in product diversity, bargaining theory, and vertical integration.

Brendan Cunningham
(bcunning@usna.edu)

is an Assistant Professor, Department of Economics, United States Naval Academy.

Acknowledgments

We are grateful for the many helpful comments of two referees and Keith Brown. All views expressed in this paper are our own; they do not necessarily reflect the opinion or views of the Federal Communications Commission or any of its commissioners.

Endnotes

1. See also Hotelling (1929). Although Hotelling's work was not focused on commercial media, his theoretical apparatus has been widely applied by those who study the industry. It is also important to note that although Hotelling suggested that concentration would lead to minimum differentiation, the more recent work of d'Aspremont, Gabszewicz, and Thisse (1979), under different assumptions regarding (preference) costs, suggests that firms would maximally differentiate.

2. Alexander (1997) used sheet music to back out characteristics (e.g., harmonic structure, melody, etc.) of hit songs and then related them back to structure. These results suggest

mid levels of industry concentration promote the highest levels of diversity in the product offerings of the music recording industry.

3. Given our database covers the year 1998, the penetration of other broadcast networks was practically nil. Thus, our sample consists of only CBS, NBC, and ABC affiliates.

4. For more information on this database, visit http://www.localtvnews.org

5. Geographic continuity is a standard feature of all 210 DMAs except 3.

6. We did not explore intrastory diversity given the highly subjective nature of this task.

7. HHI refers to the sum of squared market shares of all firms in the market and is calculated on a revenue basis.

8. There are two reasons to believe this is an unlikely but feasible explanation for the findings in Table 3. First, a variable is a poor instrument when it is not tightly related to endogenous or caused variables. We have found that lagged values of the HHI are very highly correlated with current values of the HHI. In addition, lags of variables have been viewed as inappropriate instruments when a variable is by its nature forward looking and caused by future values of the dependent variable (so that the lag is not truly exogenous). Although this is often the case in financial markets, we believe it is a very remote possibility in broadcast media markets. For example, it is hard to believe that a viewer in Atlanta decides to subscribe to cable because she or he expects that next year, local broadcast news will be less diverse.

9. Federal Communications Commission rule makings and public information given by television and radio broadcasters during merger applications often include programming efficiencies as a motivating factor. We are simply taking this explanation at face value.

References

Alexander, P. (1997). Product variety and market structure: A new measure and a simple test. *Journal of Economic Behavior and Organization, 32*, 207–214.

Anderson, S., & Coate, S. (2001). *Market provision of public goods: The case of broadcasting.* Unpublished manuscript. University of Virginia, Charlotte, and Cornell University, Ithaca, NY.

Beebe, J. (1977). Institutional structure and program choice in television markets. *Quarterly Journal of Economics, 91*, 15–37.

Berry, S. & Waldfogel, J. (2001). Do mergers increase product variety: Evidence from radio broadcasting. *Quarterly Journal of Economics, 116*, 1009–1025.

Besley, T., & Burgess, R. (2002). The political economy of government responsiveness: Theory and evidence from India. *Quarterly Journal of Economics, 117*, 1415–1451.

Coase, R. H. (1974). The lighthouse in economics. *The Journal of Law and Economics, 17*, 357–376.

Cunningham, B., & Alexander, P. (2004). A theory of broadcast media concentration and commercial advertising. *Journal of Public Economic Theory, 6*, 557–575.

d'Aspremont, C., Gabszewicz, J., & Thisse, J. F. (1979). On Hotelling's "Stability in Competition." *Econometrica, 47*, 1145–1150.

Demsetz, H. (1989). The amenity potential of newspapers and the reporting of presidential campaigns. In H. Demsetz (Ed.), *Efficiency, competition and policy* (pp. 245–262). London: Basil Blackwell.

Djankov, S., McLiesh, C., Nenova, T., & Shleifer, A. (2001) Who owns the media? *NBER Working Paper 8288*, 341–381.

Gabszewicz, D., Laussel, J., & Sonnac, N. (2001). *TV-broadcasting competition and advertising*. Discussion Paper No. 00/6 CORE, Universite Catholique de Louvain, Louvain-la-Neuve, Belgium.

Gal-Or, E., & Dukes, A. (2003). Minimum differentiation in commercial media markets. *Journal of Economic and Management Strategy, 12*, 291–325.

George, L.,& Waldfogel, J. (2002). *Does the* New York Times *spread ignorance and apathy?* (Working Paper). University of Pennsylvania.

Goettler, R. L., & Shacher, R. (2001). Spatial competition in the network television industry. *RAND Journal of Economics, 32*, 624–656.

Hirshman, A. O. (1964, September). The paternity of an index. *American Economic Review, 54*, 761.

Hotelling, H. (1929). Stability in competition. *Economic Journal, 39*(153), 41–57.

Mullainathan, S., & Shleifer, A. (2003). *The market for news*. Retrieved October 30, 2004, from http://ssrn.com/abstract= 485724

Nilssen, T., & Sorgard, L. (2001). *TV advertising, programming investments and product-market oligopoly* (Working Paper). University of Oslo, Oslo, Norway.

Schwartz-Leaper, D. A. (2003, April 3). *Letter to Federal Communications Commission Chief of Wireless Telecommunications Bureau and General Council*. Washington, DC: Federal Communications Commission. Retrieved from http://hraunfoss.fcc.gov/edocs_public/attachmatch/FCC-03-85A2.pdf

Spence, M., & Owen, B. (1977). Television programming, monopolistic competition and welfare. *Quarterly Journal of Economics, 91*, 103–126.

Steiner, P. (1952). Program patterns and preferences and the workability of competition in radio broadcasting. *Quarterly Journal of Economics, 66*, 194–223.

Stromberg, D. (2004a). Mass media competition, political competition and public policy. *Review of Economic Studies, 71*, 265–284.

Stromberg, D. (2004b). Radio's impact on public spending *Quarterly Journal of Economics, 119*, 189–221.

Pie Sharing or Food Fight? The Impact of Regulatory Changes on Media Market Competition in Singapore

■

Marc Edge
University of Texas at Arlington, USA

The media market in Singapore was deregulated to a limited extent in 2000 when the government there announced the introduction of "controlled competition." Newspaper publisher Singapore Press Holdings (SPH), which for 16 years had enjoyed a government-sanctioned print monopoly, was granted licences for 2 television stations and began broadcasting in both English and Chinese. Government-owned MediaCorp, which formerly held a broadcasting monopoly, was issued a newspaper publishing licence and began publishing a free commuter tabloid titled Today *in competition with SPH's broadsheet* Straits Times. *The start-up losses brought by competition in both media have resulted in heavy financial losses for both firms and have led to government signals that a return to monopoly media might be considered. Some in the Singapore media, along with some scholars there, have argued that the island nation of 4 million is too small as a market to support competing media outlets, particularly in newspaper publishing. This article is an analysis of the Singapore situation in which I argue for a rationalization of media competition there rather than its elimination.*

The Singapore government loosened its iron grip on mass media in the Southeast Asian city state ever so slightly in 2000, introducing what was called "controlled competition" to a market that had for decades seen mandated monopolies in both newspaper publishing and television broadcasting (Ang, 2002, p. 246). Granting a newspaper publishing licence to government-owned broadcaster MediaCorp and television licences to newspaper publisher Singapore Press Holdings (SPH) was intended to allow those firms to take advantage of the synergies believed to be inherent in media convergence (Ong, 2000). Three years later, not only had the expected benefits of convergence failed to materialize, but heightened competition for advertising had cut sharply into the profits of both SPH and MediaCorp. This financial squeeze caused many Singaporeans to wonder whether media competition was desirable or even possible in a market of 4 million in population. Before 2003 was over, the government had signaled its willingness to allow a return to the old system of media monopolies, sparking heated public debate both in the media and in scholarly circles.

"If you ask me, the limited media liberalization of recent years has been an expensive experiment," wrote *Straits Times* columnist Fernandez (2003, p. H15) in responding to the government signals. "The bleeding of the two local media companies has done little good" (Fernandez, 2003, p. H15). The foreign editor of SPH's flagship broadsheet argued that the benefits brought by media competition in 21st-century Singapore had been outweighed by the financial difficulties that accompanied market liberalization:

> The undercutting of advertising rates has meant less [*sic*] resources to recruit, train, and retain much-needed talent. Newsrooms are now doing much more with much less and the strain often shows. ... Will the market sort out these difficulties? I doubt it. To my mind, these are not matters best left to a market free-for-all. (Fernandez, 2003, p. H15)

The signals given by the government brought speculation that a consolidation of media operations was imminent in Singapore, but many in the city state resisted the move, including MediaCorp. Some Singaporeans had long advocated for the introduction of media competition not just to allow market pricing for advertisements but to also bring a more vibrant public sphere than had been seen under the system of monopoly. "Something more impor-

Address correspondence to Marc Edge, Department of Communication, University of Texas at Arlington, Box 19107, Office 118 Fine Arts Building, Arlington, TX 76019-0107. E-mail: mail@marcedge.com

tant [is] at stake than the fate of these business units," wrote author and former journalist George (2003, p. 32) in a rebuttal to Fernandez published in the *Straits Times*. "It is Singapore's comfort with competition that is being tested" (George, 2003, p. 32). Arguing in favor of continued competition, the Singapore media critic instead made a case that the new-found freedom had been bungled by media managers:

> Let's be blunt about this: Singapore's partially liberalised media industry basically amounts to a duopoly run by chief executives with no prior experience in media management ... whose recent track records in growing new businesses could not be described as confidence-inspiring. (George, 2003, p. 32)

In this article, I examine the competing analyses of the media market in Singapore including those offered in the academic arena. I examine the deregulation debate there in historical and theoretical context and offer recommendations for redressing some of the difficulties encountered with the introduction of media competition.

Background

Singapore is a 648 km² island nation of 4 million in population situated near the equator at the tip of the Malaysian peninsula in Southeast Asia. Its small size and lack of natural resources make it dependent on trade, including with Malaysia for its domestic water supply, which is supplied by a pipeline across the narrow Straits of Johor that separate the countries. Singapore and Malaysia were briefly united in the mid-1960s after colonial Malaya received independence from Great Britain in the late 1950s, but the marriage did not last due to ethnic and political incompatibility. The *Straits Times*, which had expanded from its base in Singapore following World War II to distribute in Malaysia as well, moved its headquarters to Kuala Lumpur in 1959 after Lee Kuan Yew of the People's Action Party (PAP) was elected Singapore's first prime minister. The newspaper's relationship with Lee, whose policies it had opposed editorially, had been tense from the earliest postcolonial days of the PAP (Turnbull, 1995, p. 213). When the 1963 merger between Singapore and Malaysia fell apart 2 years later, the *Straits Times* found itself in an even more precarious position—headquartered in a foreign country. The newspaper was forced to return its offices to the city state in 1972 after Malaysia limited foreign ownership of its media, leading to the creation of a new Malaysian-owned daily published in Kuala Lumpur titled the *New Straits Times* in which the *Straits Times* retained the 20% interest allowable under the new law (Turnbull, 1995, p. 294). Circulation of each country's newspapers in the other's territory has long been prohibited in Singapore and Malaysia.

Licensing of newspapers was a legacy of colonialism Singapore inherited from Great Britain, but the authoritarian model of press regulation was even more harshly applied under home rule in the city state after Singapore gained independence (Ang, 2002, p. 244). The early 1970s were a watershed era of press repression in Singapore, with several publications stymied by imprisonment of their editors, revocation of work permits for some expatriate journalists, and ultimately cancellation of the embattled Singapore *Herald*'s publishing license in 1971 amidst allegations of foreign influence (Seow, 1998, p. 85). The following year, Lee Kuan Yew issued a stern warning in a speech to the annual Press Club dinner:

> Every morning my task begins by reading five—four now—newspapers. And it's a tiresome business. I note the scurrilous, the scandalous. I can live with that. But when any newspaper pours a daily dose of language, cultural, or religious poison, I put my knuckle-dusters on as the first stage. If you still continue, then I say here are the stilettos, choose your weapons. (Seow, 1998, p. 106)

Within months, the government announced the Newspaper and Printing Presses Act (NPPA) under which all newspaper companies were required to convert to public ownership, with only Singaporeans and corporations approved by the government eligible to hold management shares, which controlled editorial policy. A percentage of management shares was also required to be held by government-controlled companies, which placed representatives on the newspapers' boards. In 1977, the act was amended to restrict ownership of shares by any one person to 3% (Y. S. Tan & Soh, 1994, p. 37).

The early 1980s saw a series of forced mergers that led to the creation of SPH as a government-controlled newspaper monopoly. In 1982, two competing Chinese dailies were required by the government to join forces under a single holding company, Singapore News and Publications Ltd. (SNPL), which was also handed the *New Nation*, an afternoon daily that the *Straits Times* had recently begun publishing. According to Turnbull (1995), who wrote the official history of the *Straits Times* for its 150th anniversary, the government at first wanted the *Straits Times* to hand over both its *Business Times* and the *New Nation* to SNPL along with their staffs. Such corporate sacrifice was deemed necessary by the government in its quest to promote multiculturalism because it was considered in the national interest that the Chinese-language newspaper group also publish dailies in English. A compromise was finally reached in which only the *New Nation* was ceded to SNPL without its staff. "In return the [*Straits Times*] group would be guaranteed freedom from competition in the English-language morning market for three years," according to Turnbull (1995), "and would be permitted to publish its own Chinese-language newspaper" (pp.

342–343). In 1984, a merger between the *Straits Times* group and SNPL was announced, leading shocked journalists to demonstrate against the consolidation of all newspapers in Singapore into one publishing company. The government denied it was behind the creation of SPH, but according to former Singapore solicitor general Seow (1998), "Lee's fingerprints could be seen all over the merger agreement" (p. 123). SPH went on the Singapore stock exchange as the country's sixth-largest listed company, its largest industrial group, and its only monopoly.

The foreign press has similarly been targeted for attitude adjustment by the Singapore government, which has severely restricted the circulation of—or "gazetted"—publications whose coverage it has considered unfavorable or even overly political, such as *Time*, the *Economist*, the *Far Eastern Economic Review*, and *The Asian Wall Street Journal*. Others, such as the *International Herald Tribune*, have been hit with stiff monetary damages following legal actions commenced for libel after criticizing the Singapore government (Wallace, 1995). The PAP's tight grip on media in the city state has helped it to retain political power continuously since 1959 in a de facto, one-party system. This harsh press repression has earned Singapore not only international scorn but also annual rebuke in the form of press freedom rankings. Freedom House regularly rates the city state near the bottom of its scale, grouped in the "not free" category with countries such as Russia, Colombia, and Sierra Leone. Singapore's score in recent years has been 66 out of 100, based on three criteria of constraints on each of which it scores almost equally poorly: legal environment (24); political influences (21); and economic pressures (21; Karlekar, 2003, p. 135).

Market Liberalization

In mid 2000, the Singapore government decided to loosen slightly its restrictions on the island nation's media at least in terms of economic constraints. In June of that year, it announced that limited media competition would henceforth be allowed, granting a newspaper licence to MediaCorp, which is controlled by the government through its private-sector arm Temasek Holdings, and radio and television licences to SPH (Ang, 2002, pp. 246–247). Almost immediately, MediaCorp announced it would begin publishing by year's end a free commuter tabloid titled *Today* in partnership with local transit companies (Ong, 2000). Four months earlier, SPH had been granted a licence to publish as an 11th newspaper a morning tabloid titled *Project Eyeball*, which was aimed at "younger, Net-savvy readers" and included a continuously updated Internet edition (Khalik, 2000). However, even before it began publishing in August, the promised new competition from MediaCorp put SPH in a quandary with *Project Eyeball*, which had been priced at 80 cents compared with only 60 cents for the thick broadsheet *Straits Times* (Edge, 2004b). MediaCorp's free commuter tabloid promised to rob *Project Eyeball* of much of its market, so 2 days after *Today* was announced, SPH management decided it would begin publishing its own giveaway tabloid titled *Streats*. The decision effectively doomed *Project Eyeball*, which achieved a circulation of only about 20,000 before folding in June 2001 after only 10 months of publication (Edge, 2004b). Despite conceiving it after MediaCorp announced it would begin publishing *Today*, SPH hit the streets with *Streats* on September 2, 2000, more than 2 months before its new competition appeared in November due largely to the publishing giant's advantage of having an extensive newspaper staff and plant already in place. MediaCorp countered SPH's first-mover edge, however, by giving away *Today* at stations along Singapore's extensive light-rail transit line operated by Singapore Mass Rapid Transit, its largest partner in the new publication.

In early 2001, the first financial results in the media war of attrition were reported, with SPH's first-half profits falling $19 million Singapore dollars (S$; approximately U.S.$10 million) due largely to start-up losses of S$2.9 million for *Streats*, S$4.8 million for *Project Eyeball*, and S$9.5 million for its MediaWorks television arm (Low, 2001). By the time SPH announced the closure of *Project Eyeball* in June, it had lost a total of S$13.3 million on the start-up daily (Rajeev, 2001). When SPH's financial year-end results were announced in October, the losses had increased to S$42.5 million for MediaWorks—which chalked up revenues of only S$16.6 million—and S$5.6 million for *Streats*. The resulting 18.7 % drop in its profits to S$340.8 million prompted SPH to embark on a S$35-million cost-cutting program including wage cuts for two thirds of its 4,300 employees (Teh, 2001b). *Today* was also debilitating the financial fortunes of its investment consortium by an estimated S$22.2 million in its first 11 months of operation ("*Today* Drags Down Profits," 2001).

After a year of competition, *Streats* held the advantage in readership, as surveys by AC Nielsen estimated it had captured 14% of the market with 408,000 readers compared with 346,000 readers and 11% coverage for *Today* (Teh, 2001a). However, by 2002, according to AC Nielsen, those positions had been reversed, with *Today* enjoying a readership of 16% and *Streats* only 11% ("Consumption of Media," 2002). *Streats* then underwent a revamp to make it more of an up-market product and thus more similar to *Today*, and 6 months later, in March 2003, SPH published figures that claimed its readership had leapt by one half to 554,000 (Quah, 2003). Two months after that, in mid-May, SPH claimed that readership of *Streats* had almost jumped by one half again to 800,000, which amounted to almost three readers for every one of the 280,000 copies it printed (W. Tan, 2003). MediaCorp questioned the survey's methodology, which SPH and market research firm Synovate refused to disclose, insisting only that it adhered to "professional research standards" (Divyanathan, 2003). *Streats* trumpeted the 800,000 figure on its front page until Nielsen's revised estimate of its readership came in at the end of June at less than half that number—392,000 (Yap, 2004). MediaCorp was similarly accused by SPH of fudging the figures when it claimed that a readership of 580,000 made it the "undisputed second most widely read daily English newspaper in Singapore" (Ng, 2003, p. H7). *Today* executives quickly amended that claim to "second-highest morning daily" (p. H7) when SPH pointed out that its tabloid *The New Paper*, which it had started in 1988, had an average readership of 456,000 (Ng, 2003).

Competition between the commuter tabloids for advertising was also fierce, with *Today* almost bending over backward to attract business onto its pages. According to the industry magazine *Media*, advertisers appreciated the "flexibility" offered by the MediaCorp tabloid. "*Today* advertisers are allowed to run 'island' ads, ads at the top of the page, flags, wrap-arounds and advertorials. Other innovations *Today* has implemented include letting Dell computers run a front-page wrap around with 'Tomorrow' as the masthead [sic]" ("Dailies Bank On Facelifts," 2002, p. 10). In its quest for advertisers, *Today* even sold its entire issue of March 24, 2003 to HP for use in the computer company's "Everything is possible" branding campaign, turning its tabloid pages broadsheet for a day and printing its front-page "flag" in HP blue instead of its regular red (Said, 2003). By the end of that month, increased advertising revenues had helped *Today* trim its yearly loss to S$10 million from S$18.8 million ("MediaCorp Posts," 2003).

In broadcasting, SPH was on the other side of the uphill climb inevitably faced by new entrants to a market. The channels broadcast by its subsidiary MediaWorks immediately gained solid viewership, with its Channel U actually outdrawing MediaCorp's Chinese-language Channel 8 by July 2002, according to AC Nielsen. Its English-language Channel i, however, lagged far behind MediaCorp's flagship Channel 5, with only 25% of viewership. More important, MediaCorp's dominant position in the market allowed it to retain more than 85% of television advertising sales. However, due to a deepening recession, even MediaCorp's local television operations (it also operates the regional network Channel News Asia) showed a S$65-million loss in 2002 compared with a S$35-million profit the previous year (Low, 2002). Competition for broadcast advertising was also fierce, fuelled by a protracted demand slump. In late 2003, HSBC Bank issued a report estimating the average discount rate for advertising in the city state that year had been 37% (Leng & Pek, 2003).

In an attempt to level the uneven playing field of media competition between the entrenched players and the new entrants, the Singapore government introduced a competition code in 2003, which had been lobbied for by MediaCorp in response to rate cutting by SPH for advertising in *Streats* (Siow, 2002). Under the code, archived editorial material had to be shared by the established media outlets with their new competition, and the dominant player in each medium was prohibited from undercutting advertising rates. "Predatory pricing," which was defined as selling products below cost to stymie emerging competition, was expressly forbidden under the new code but only of the established companies, not the new entrants, which brought protests from SPH (T. H. Tan, 2003).

Cooling Competition

SPH first began signaling its desire for a cease fire in the Singapore media war in late 2002, suggesting it would be willing to get out of the television business if MediaCorp left the newspaper field. SPH executive chairman Lim Kim San said, "We are bleeding. Both *Streats* and *Today* are bleeding. And in TV we are also bleeding. So we are wasting our resources" (W. K. Wong, 2002, p. 8). In June 2003, SPH announced the layoff of 111 employees to save S$5.7 million annually. It was the third mass layoff in as many years for SPH, following downsizings of 97 in 2002 and 116 in 2001 (Khalik, 2003). In October, the company's annual report showed that although the losses incurred on its MediaWorks television operations had narrowed to S$40.2 million from S$44.6 million in the previous year, the red ink spilled by *Streats* over the previous year had increased to S$5.8 million from S$5.2 million (Koh, 2003).

In mid-November, the government signaled that it would be willing to allow a return to monopoly operations in the media after 3 years of costly competition. Minister for Information, Communications and the Arts, Lee Boon Yang, indicated in a speech to the Singapore Press Club that the government would be open to allowing consolidation between SPH and MediaCorp to reduce the competitive environment. "Wherever we can, we will try to promote and encourage competition, but we are also realistic and if competition does not work, then, well, we have to accept that the market itself is just too small to accept more than one significant player" (Lim, 2003, p. 1). Founding prime minister Lee Kuan Yew, who was still active in the government at age 80 as Senior Minister, said in an interview broadcast on television that evening that he had doubted from the beginning whether media competition would be possible in Singapore due to the small size of the market. The officially expressed doubts were enough to spark widespread speculation that a media consolidation was imminent in the micromanaged city state. The pronouncement by Lee Kuan Yew particularly led many to believe it was a fait accompli, so great was his influence in the fledgling nation he personally shepherded from third-world to first-world status through three decades of leadership. As political analyst Seah Chiang Nee told Reuters, "When Kuan Yew says something, traditionally he is not offering an opinion" (Espina, 2003).

However, SPH denied it was negotiating to acquire MediaCorp ("SPH says," 2003). Its chairman, Lim Chin Beng, also declared the media giant had no intention of getting out of the television business, saying SPH was in TV for the long term, calling it a "strategic" platform given the waning influence of print (W. K. Wong, 2003). For its part, MediaCorp insisted it was not about to merge with or sell out to SPH, nor did it intend to fold *Today*, although its CEO did express an interest in taking over the television assets of SPH if it decided to bow out of the medium (A. Tan, 2003). The influence of shareholders and investment analysts also began to be felt by SPH, with discontent expressed at its annual general meeting in December about the idea of buying more broadcasting assets. Complained one shareholder: "Broadcasting is cash draining. If you buy another broadcasting business, you'll be carrying an albatross around your neck" (W. K. Wong, 2003, p. 1). A survey of investment analysts taken by the *Business Times* showed that most believed there was room for competing players in each medium, but that some of the behavior seen so far in the Singapore media war had been anticompetitive:

> What investors really want, the analysts said, is an end to the severe price discounting in the media industry. They said the main hurdle to commercial viability is not the capacity of the market but severe price wars, especially in broadcasting. ... "In markets like the U.S., it would be an anti-trust situation, where you're operating at a loss to drive someone out of competition," [one] said. "The pie is big enough to go around, but they'd rather have a pie fight than share the pie." (W. K. Wong & Lim, 2003, p. 2)

The poor financial results led many to question whether the formerly entrenched monopolists possessed the acumen required to compete in a market environment. The trade journal *Media* even asked, "Have the two incumbents done their sums right? ... Do both sides have the necessary top and middle management talent, with enough media experience, to exploit growth opportunities presented by a deregulated environment?" ("Has Time Come," 2003, p. 4). The model some critics claimed should have been followed in deregulating the Singapore media market in 2000 was the one followed successfully there in 1997 in telecommunications. From a government-run monopoly dominated by SingTel, a more orderly introduction of competition was seen from the outset due to rules that ensured a level playing field. "The free-for-all in mobile telephony has also spurred innovation," noted *The Edge* (Leng & Pek, 2003, p. 5), a Malaysian business weekly. "And when it comes to calling overseas, prices have never

been cheaper. According to government data, international direct dial rates to popular destinations around the world have fallen by up to 80% since the telecoms market was fully liberalized" (Leng & Pek, 2003, p. 5). The difference, according to George (2003), was that in telecommunications, the competition came from multinational companies, which are prohibited from investing in Singapore's mass media:

> Foreign investors will enter only on condition that government policies are transparent and former government-linked monopolies do not exercise an unfair advantage. ... The government may have felt less pressure to carry out media liberalization with the same nurturing touch it had applied to telecoms. (p. 32)

Some called for foreign ownership to be allowed into the media market as well. Mused *Media:* "Perhaps the time has come to take deregulation a step further. If the Government is serious about media competition, the time is right to consider opening the media door to foreign players with the ability to inject investment dollars into the industry" ("Has Time Come," 2003, p. 4). *Today* even ran an analysis by Australian scholar Backman (2003), headlined "Is Singapore Paranoid," in which he called for an end to licensing of newspapers under the NPPA and for foreign competition to be allowed into the market, referring to the city state's government control over media as "the old fashioned, outmoded trappings of a Third World dictatorship" (p. 3).

In November 2003, SPH reported that its first quarter print revenues had slipped another 3%, and that its broadcasting losses had widened to S$10 million from S$6.3 million for the quarter. In an attempt to stem the tide of red ink arising from competition in both the newspaper and broadcasting fields, SPH announced in January 2004 a cover price increase for 9 of its 11 newspapers, including Sunday editions. The newsstand price of its flagship *Straits Times,* which in 2002 had a paid circulation of 385,000, was increased 33% to 80 cents (Paul, 2004).

Economic Theory

In early 2004, the media competition debate in Singapore took to the academic arena, and theorists in the city state also disagreed on whether the island nation was large enough to sustain competing media players. Ang and Fu (2004a, 2004b) published a two-part analysis in the *Straits Times* in which they argued that the problems brought by media competition were behavioral in television but structural in newspapers. As a result, Ang and Fu (2004a) concluded that television broadcasting in Singapore was well capable of supporting more than one player and that eventually an equilibrium position would be reached between the competing firms. MediaCorp and SPH were bleeding red ink in television only in the short term, Ang and Fu (2004a) argued, due to their "overly enthusiastic behaviour in pricing and bidding" in a "frenzied market-share battle" (p. 12). In the newspaper business, however, Ang and Fu's (2004b) analysis was reversed. Higher start-up costs and lower marginal costs meant that *Today* would never be able to compete with SPH due to the "circulation spiral," which sees advertisers and then readers and then more advertisers gravitate to the largest daily in a market:

> To defy this downward spiral, a paper like Today needs to pour in a fearsome amount of money, which may not be recovered if market fundamentals do not change favourably. ... The Singapore newspaper market will probably not develop into a truly competitive market without some structural intervention. (Ang & Fu, 2004b, p. 16)

Part of the problem in the Singapore media war, Ang and Fu (2004a) added, was that "perhaps unexpectedly" the battle for television advertising had spilled over into the newspaper business, which had an unintended effect when competition on price turned predatory. "Under-priced advertising airtime siphoned off sizeable newspaper advertising sales from SPH. ... No market is ever large enough to be profitable if companies undercut each other's price below costs" (Ang & Fu, 2004a, p. 12). To redress the imbalances in newspaper competition, Ang and Fu (2004b) offered three possible solutions:

- A U.S.-style Joint Operating Agreement between SPH and MediaCorp Press, under which *Today* could benefit from the same vertical integration and economies of scale enjoyed by the SPH dailies while still competing editorially.
- Dividing the newspaper market linguistically between SPH and MediaCorp, with one taking the English-language market and the other the Chinese newspapers.
- Enlarging the MediaCorp stable of publications in other ways, such as with a chain of weekly magazines, to increase its economies of scale.

A dissenting scholar (Edge, 2004a) argued that Singapore was large enough as a market to sustain competing players even in newspaper publishing given the demonstrated success of tabloids as second-place newspapers in other countries. Citing the success of the Toronto *Sun* chain of morning tabloids in his native Canada, Edge (2004a) argued in an analysis published in *Today* that the natural monopoly theory of newspapers had been effectively repealed there and replaced by a paradigm of product differentiation and niche marketing. By appealing to a younger readership, the *Sun* tabloids had proven profit-

able, Edge (2004a) pointed out, by reaching a demographic that was not being served effectively by broadsheets and was coveted by advertisers for its disposable income. Giveaway commuter tabloids in particular had proven in many countries to be a viable model for differentiated newspaper competition, Edge (2004a) added, as seen with the worldwide success of Sweden's Modern Times Group, which had provided the template for both *Today* and *Streats*:

> The solution to the media problem in Singapore is not more government regulation, but less. Media businesses must be allowed to manage their own affairs, or mismanage them as the case may be. Left alone, market forces will sort things out. A market approaching four million in population is more than large enough to support at least two newspapers, but neither will be as profitable as a monopoly daily. Get used to it. (p. 17)

Politics and Culture

Economic theory is only one level on which media competition must be considered in postcolonial Singapore, as normative considerations must also be taken into account. Politics are an inescapable reality in a nominal democracy that has not seen a change in its ruling party since gaining independence in 1959. Culture is another crucial variable in the multiethnic republic, which saw race riots in the 1950s and 1960s result from tensions, sometimes fanned by the press, between the country's Malay Muslim minority and its Chinese majority. Media competition in Singapore must be viewed as a kind of multilevel chess game with economic considerations constituting only the most apparent variables and political and cultural factors playing themselves out on underlying levels. In this article, I deal explicitly only with economic issues, as normative considerations of press freedom must be left to Singaporeans to reconcile. The complexity of political and cultural issues in Singapore must be recognized at least implicitly, however, even by the economist.

In an attempt to foster the twin goals of ethnic harmony and economic growth, the Singapore government has historically taken an interventionist hand in the nation's press to a point where some scholars have considered that it qualifies as an authoritarian regime under the old four theories of the press (Hachten, 1996, p. 17). Others have felt it conforms more closely to the "development" model due to the explicit onus placed on the press to contribute to nation building. Some scholars, however, have doubted the applicability of the development press model to Singapore because its expectations of uncritical journalism are supposed to lapse after a nation grows into adulthood, and as one of the leading "Tiger economies" of Asia, the city state graduated to developed nation status decades ago. As Bokhorst-Heng (2002) noted, "The use of the term 'development model' suggests that at some higher stage the press in Singapore will move to a more advanced press model" (p. 564). Another model offered to explain press performance in Singapore has been the "Asian values" paradigm under which the media are expected to demonstrate respect for authority, foster harmony, and build consensus in contrast to Western models that expect the press to perform a "watchdog" function in a more adversarial system. One study (Massey & Chang, 2002) of online newspapers in the region, however, found that Asian values in journalism (as reflected by a lack of conflict as a central story-telling device) correlated more closely with measures of press freedom than with geography. Countries with a press rated not free, such as Singapore and Malaysia, also had a press that was more supportive of the government in contrast with neighboring nations with a freer press, which demonstrated fewer Asian values (Massey & Chang, 2002, p. 999).

Analysis

Straits Times columnist Fernandez (2003) engaged in some disingenuousness when he claimed that the assumption on the part of many that SPH is state owned and controlled is mistaken because "the bulk of its shares is owned not by Singaporeans, but foreigners, mainly institutional players" (p. H15). The truth is that non-Singaporeans are prohibited from owning management shares in SPH, which carry 200 times the voting power of common shares, and that the holders of these "golden" shares must be approved by the government under the NPPA. As George (2000) noted in his book *Singapore: The Air-Conditioned Nation*, this provision in the law allows the government to actually determine the composition of SPH's board of directors:

> It [the NPPA] has been so effective in fulfilling its objective of behind-the-scenes control that most Singaporeans are not even aware of it, even though it is the main instrument shaping how the press operates. ... With this mechanism in place, the government needs neither to post its officials directly into top newsroom positions, nor to nationalize the press. (p. 66)

George (2000) noted that the quid pro quo for press acquiescence to controls on its freedom in Singapore was monopoly profits. "A press allowed to make money out of a system will support that system [as] publishers value their bottom line more highly than they do their editorial freedom" (George, 2000, p. 67). If competition is to be allowed at all in the Singapore press, monopoly profits will no longer be made, and the press will thus less likely to accept restrictions on its editorial freedom and thus its pursuit of commercial success.

K. K. Wong (2001) identified the fundamental contradiction of postcolonial Singapore as the city state's openness to foreign commerce through duty-free trade policies at the same time as it restricts the flow of information in the domestic media. K. K. Wong developed a theory of "controlled commodification" to explain media and culture in Singapore and claimed that the pursuit of economic prosperity in the city state has been at the expense of "depoliticization" of the public sphere in Singapore. State control of media through its controlling corporations has seen a mandated "political-economic separation" under which the media are proscribed from covering politics in the pursuit of the nation's economic ends. "PAP state control has been legitimized and internalized in the industry as part of the country's press policy, which is largely to serve PAP economic control in the name of Singapore's survival" (K. K. Wong, 2001, p. 96). When Mahbubani's provocatively titled book, *Can Asians Think?*, was first published in Singapore in 1998, it caused a stir not only in the city state but also regionally and even worldwide. A more appropriate question to ask in considering media competition in Singapore, however, might be "Can Asians think critically?" Mahbubani, who is Singapore's ambassador to the United Nations, challenged the "end of history" view that sees the American empire as the pinnacle of human advancement, and his book has since been republished around the world. The fact that his question sparked the discussion it did amply demonstrates the importance of asking critical, even insulting, questions in the search for useful answers.

Singapore's economic achievements have proven beyond doubt the financial acumen of its leaders, but the success has come at a considerable social cost due to government micromanagement not only of industry but also of the public sphere. Dissent to the government's economic and social policies has not been permitted under a controlled press, but when the former policies fail, all that is lost is financial. Misguided social policies that go unchallenged can result in long-term structural problems such as the city state's current "baby bust," which is a result of government admonitions against having large families in the 1960s. Constructive criticism of and even vigorous disagreement with government policies is essential for a healthy democracy and would be a social good in and of itself in addition to a needed critical counterbalance to the city state's traditional tendencies toward "groupthink." For effective reform of media competition to take place in Singapore, the draconian restrictions of the NPPA must first be abolished. Micromanagement of the market by the issuing and revoking of newspaper licenses creates an artificial barrier to entry and through self-censorship has the effect of turning the nation's press into less of a critical watchdog and more of a government lapdog. The requirement for government representation on newspaper boards of directors similarly should be dropped for Singapore to free the press from official oversight.

However, there is good reason not to push the limits of cultural flexibility too far. The suggestion that allowing foreign ownership of Singapore media can cure what ails it is unrealistic given the cultural and political constraints facing the city state. The suggestion of Backman (2003) and others is bound to fail given not only some considerable xenophobia extant in the city state but also due to its small size and precarious position geopolitically. Control of any nation's press is a privilege that is rightfully reserved for nationals only, despite the fact that some countries, such as the United States, allow newspapers to be owned by foreigners. The depth of resistance in Singapore to Backman's (2003) suggestion can be seen in the official reaction to it. In the same speech in which he bruited an end to media competition, Minister for Information, Communications and the Arts Lee Boon Yang declared the government's opposition to foreign ownership of media in no uncertain terms. "By attacking the Government's media policy and urging the adoption of the Western model, he had clearly crossed the line and engaged in our domestic politics" (Lee, 2003). The twin topics of foreign ownership and the possible return of monopoly media dominated press coverage in and about Singapore for days, with the question of media competition proving more enduring—and open. The importation of foreign expertise in media management should be considered in Singapore, however, beyond the ad hoc hiring of contract managers and consultants. Only through an ownership stake will multinational corporations lend their most self-interested expertise, but that equity position need not be a majority. Even minority ownership would no doubt help to attract foreign investment, and the resulting injection of outside perspective into media management could be beneficial.

Ang and Fu (2004b) were correct in their assessment that the newspaper market in Singapore will probably not develop into a truly competitive market without some structural intervention. However, following Ang and Fu's (2004b) suggestion of adding *Today* to what is undoubtedly already the largest jointly operating newspaper publishing company in the free world would likely do little to ameliorate the circulation spiral, which has been seen to continue in effect in joint operating agreements (JOAs) in the United States (Lacy & Simon, 1993, p. 99). Folding *Today* into the SPH stable of dailies in a JOA would mean an effective end to competition; and although it might preserve one editorial voice (although that is also unlikely, as SPH would doubtless close *Streats* under this scenario), it would inevitably see a return to monopoly price fixing for advertising, as has been seen in many United States markets (Picard, 1989, p. 81). The sharing of advertising revenues by SPH with MediaCorp under competition may mean that it no longer enjoys the monopoly profits it reaped for

16 years, but in the long term, it will benefit not only other media firms in Singapore but also advertisers by shifting that prosperity around.

Ang and Fu (2004b) noted that their suggestion of dividing the press in Singapore along linguistic lines suffers from the drawback of the decline in readership seen of Chinese newspapers recently, which would tend to disadvantage the company publishing them. However, it would also be a perilous move culturally and politically, as ethnic divisions are something the press in Singapore has historically been charged with reducing rather than enhancing. Ang and Fu's third way of solving the media competition conundrum in Singapore, by reducing the size disparity between the players in the newspaper field, perhaps holds more promise. However, adding a few weekly magazines to MediaCorp Press to allow it sufficient size to afford its own printing plant would hardly afford it the economies of scale enjoyed by SPH.

Conclusion

SPH is not only one of the world's largest newspaper publishing companies, it is also one of the wealthiest, due to the profit levels of 40% to 50% it often rang up during the 16 years it enjoyed a newspaper monopoly in Singapore. Even since deregulation and with its start-up losses in television and tabloids, SPH recorded a healthy 15.7% return on revenue before extraordinary items in its 2003 fiscal year (Koh, 2003). As a result, it has cash reserves estimated at S$450 million along with investments in foreign media companies and extensive holdings of valuable Singapore real estate including a shopping mall estimated to be worth S$1 billion (Paul, 2004). Its ability to continue waging the media war of attrition in Singapore is enormous, limited only by the will of its shareholders to endure lower earnings in the short term. As for MediaCorp, which does not report publicly, its cash reserves have been estimated at S$200 million as a result of the monopoly profits it reaped for decades in television (Paul, 2003). Thus, both players have the financial wherewithal to endure losses in their start-up media ventures for many years. The question becomes whether the government will intervene and rationalize media competition in Singapore. It has shown no hesitation to orchestrate the industry in the past, and its suggestions of November 2003 indicated to many that just such a reorganization was imminent. Yet rather than pull the plug on competition, a more effective way of meeting the needs and wants of all stakeholders, and not just the media players, might be to instead better level the playing field for competition.

Instead of a merger between SPH and MediaCorp Press, the advantages already seen of media competition—not only in the market for information but also in the market for advertising—can only be continued through an equalization in the size of the competitors. Instead of dividing the press in Singapore between English-language and Chinese newspapers, if MediaCorp were to be ceded some of the ethnic language dailies now published by SPH along with a serious broadsheet such as the *Business Times*, it may have a better chance of financial viability in the long term. Folding *Streats* might also help to balance the situation, as under fair competition rules from the outset, its publication might not have even been allowed. However, in the end, it is not Singapore politicians who will decide the fate of media competition in the city state but Singapore citizens. If Singaporeans decide to support *Today* by reading it and businesses decide to patronize its pages by placing advertisements, newspaper competition is bound to not only survive but thrive.

Marc Edge

(mail@marcedge.com)

is a Visiting Assistant Professor in the Department of Communication at the University of Texas at Arlington, Arlington, TX. He studies newspaper competition and is the author of Pacific Press: The Unauthorized Story of Vancouver's Newspaper Monopoly *(Vancouver, British Columbia, Canada: New Star Books, 2001).*

References

Ang, P. H. (2002). Media and the flow of information. In D. da Cunha (Ed.), *Singapore in the new millennium: Challenges facing the city-state* (pp. 243–268). Singapore: Institute of Southeast Asian Studies.

Ang, P. H., & Fu, W. (2004a, February 11). Singapore's TV market: One player or two? *Straits Times*, p. 12.

Ang, P. H., & Fu, W. (2004b, February 12). Newspaper publishing in S'pore: One player or two? *Straits Times*, p. 16.

Backman, M. (2003, October 8). Is Singapore Paranoid? *Today* (Singapore), p. 3.

Bokhorst-Heng, W. (2002). Newspapers in Singapore: A mass ceremony in the imagining of the nation. *Media, Culture & Society, 24,* 559–569.

Consumption of media boosted by deregulation. (2002, October 18). *Media*, p. 12.

Dailies bank on facelifts. (2002, October 4). *Media*, p. 10.

Divyanathan, D. (2003, May 26). SPH stands by Streats' 800,000 readership figure. *Business Times* (Singapore), p. 5.

Edge, M. (2004a, February 14–15). An enduring success story: The little newspaper that could. *Today* (Singapore), pp. 16–17.

Edge, M. (2004b). The failure of *Project Eyeball*: A case of product over-pricing or market over-crowding? *International Journal on Media Management, 6,* 114–122.

Espina, K. (2003, December 5). Singapore considers return of monopoly in media. *Reuters News Service*.

Fernandez, W. (2003, November 15). Media "golden age" looking tarnished. *Straits Times*, p. H15.

George, C. (2000). *Singapore: The air-conditioned nation*. Singapore: Landmark Books.

George, C. (2003, November 22). Give media competition a genuine chance. *Straits Times*, p. 32.

Hachten, W. A. (1996). *The world new prism: Changing media of international communication* (4th ed.). Ames: Iowa State University Press.

Has time come to open media door? (2003, November 28). *Media*, p. 4.

Karlekar, K. D. (Ed.). (2003). *Freedom of the press 2003: A global survey of media independence*. New York: Freedom House. Available at http://www.freedomhouse.org/pfs2003/pfs2003.pdf

Khalik, S. (2000, February 6). New SPH paper gets its licence. *Straits Times*, p. 2.

Khalik, S. (2003, July 1). SPH lays off 111 staff to stay lean. *Straits Times*, p. 4.

Koh, E. (2003, October 11). SPH earnings rise 23% to S$379m. *Straits Times*, p. A29.

Lacy, S., & Simon, T. F. (1993). *The economics and regulation of united states newspapers*. Norwood, NJ: Ablex.

Lee, B. Y. (2003, November 13). Media free-for-all? No, our values can't be sacrificed. *Straits Times*, pp. 20–21.

Leng, S. S., & Pek, T. G. (2003, November 24). Free to choose? *The Edge* (Singapore), p. 5.

Lim, K. (2003, November 15). Govt open to ending rivalry in media industry. *Straits Times*, p. 1.

Low, E. (2001, March 27). SPH interim net earnings slip 8.5% to S$204m. *Business Times* (Singapore), p. 4.

Low, E. (2002, September 27). MediaCorp loss widens to S$120m from S$19m. *Business Times* (Singapore), p. 2.

Mahbubani, K. (1998). *Can Asians think?* Singapore: Times Books International.

Massey, B. L., & Chang, L. A. (2002). Locating Asian values in Asian journalism: A content analysis of Web newspapers. *Journal of Communication, 52,* 987–1003.

MediaCorp posts S$134.4m net profit after SCV sale. (2003, August 5). *Business Times* (Singapore), p. 9.

Ng, J. (2003, October 9). ST is the No. 1 paper, now for the No. 2 ... . *Straits Times*, p. H7.

Ong, C. (2000, June 6). Broadcast licences for SPH, newspaper licence for MediaCorp. *Business Times* (Singapore), p. 1.

Paul, B. (2004, January 19). SPH – Between a rock and a hard place. *The Edge* (Singapore), p. 7.

Picard, R. (1989). *Media economics: Concepts and issues*. Newbury Park, CA: Sage.

Quah, M. (2003, March 4). Streats readership surges 50%. *Business Times* (Singapore), p. 4.

Rajeev, P. (2001, June 28). SPH to suspend operations of Project Eyeball—Singapore media firm cites market conditions. *Asian Wall Street Journal*, p. M2.

Said, S. (2003, March 24). S'pore Tabloid "Today" goes broadsheet. *Bernama Daily* (Malaysia), p. 4.

Seow, F. T. (1998). *The media enthralled: Singapore revisited*. London: Rienner.

Siow, D. (2002, April 11). Singapore tabloid girds to stir media competition. *Reuters News Service*.

SPH says it is not in talks to buy MediaCorp. (2003, November 15). *Business Times* (Singapore), p. 4.

Tan, A. (2003, December 9). MediaCorp CEO rules out merging with SPH or giving up Today. *Straits Times*, p. A15

Tan, T. H. (2003, January 11). OK, let's keep this media fight fair and clean. *Straits Times*, p. H18.

Tan, W. (2003, May 13). Sharp jump in readers, ads for revamped Streats. *Straits Times*, p.6.

Tan, Y. S., & Soh, Y. P. (1994). *The development of Singapore's modern media industry*. Singapore: Times Academic Press.

Teh, H. L. (2001a, October 3). Channel U now second in TV viewership—AC Nielsen. *Business Times* (Singapore), p. 10.

Teh, H. L. (2001b, October 17). Start-up losses drag SPH earnings down 18.7%. *Business Times* (Singapore), p. 4.

Today drags down profits. (2001, October 26). *Straits Times*, p. H11.

Turnbull, C. M. (1995). *Dateline Singapore: 150 years of the Straits Times*. Singapore: Singapore Press Holdings.

Wallace, C. P. (1995, November/December). Singapore's grip. *Columbia Journalism Review*, p. 19.

Wong, K. K. (2001). *Media and culture in Singapore: A theory of controlled commodification*. Cresskill, NJ: Hampton.

Wong, W. K. (2002, November 13). Competition hurting both media groups. *Business Times* (Singapore), p. 8.

Wong, W. K. (2003, December 6). SPH chairman—TV is a strategic platform for group. *Business Times* (Singapore), p. 4.

Wong, W. K., & Lim, K. (2003, November 13). Small media market worsened by price-cutting. *Business Times* (Singapore), p. 2.

Yap, J. (2004, March 26). Streats steps up free sheet fight with afternoon edition. *Media*, p. 8.

GENERAL RESEARCH ARTICLES

The Dual Structure of Global Networks in the Entertainment Industry: Interorganizational Linkage and Geographical Dispersion

■

Bum Soo Chon
Korea National Open University, Korea

In this article, I describe the contours of global media networks in terms of interorganizational linkages and spatial distribution of foreign direct investment in the entertainment industry. The results of multidimensional scaling revealed that there were significant differences in the positional structures of global networks in the entertainment industry. However, in the case of the structural relations between the interorganizational and geographical dispersion networks, the quadratic assignment procedure analyses revealed structural similarities between both networks in the entertainment industry. A multiple regression analysis also showed music and film industries played a significant role in explaining interorganizational and geographical dispersion networks. The findings indicate the benefit of distinguishing between interorganizational and geographic dispersion networks in understanding global media networks.

With the rapid progress of economic globalization and developments in information technologies, increased research attention has been devoted to the interorganizational alliances and mergers facilitating global expansion. For example, global strategic alliances have significantly increased over the last 10 years (Harbison & Pekar, 1998; Kang & Sakai, 2000). The basic purpose of these interorganizational linkages is to create value by sharing resources among firms in the global space (Doz & Hamel, 1998). All of these structural changes in industries and businesses may point to the economic consequences of globalization. Dunning (1998) suggested that current world economy can be characterized by the following three features:

> The first is the emergence of intellectual capital as the key wealth creating asset in most industrial economies. … Secondly, and even more transparent, is the increasing globalization of economic activity, made possible, inter alia, by advances in transport and communications technologies and the reduction in trade and investment barriers throughout the world. … The third feature of the contemporary global economy is the emergence of what may be called "alliance" capitalism. (pp. 47–48)

In Dunning's (1998) view, the development of the global economy may be based on the following two dimensions: geographical expansion and interorganizational linkages. This may be referred to as the global interdependence system through the network society (Castells, 1996). Castells (1996) characterizes the current society as spaces of flows based on a variety of networks. Interestingly, the three characteristics just mentioned can be found in the media industry. First, the media industry is primarily included in a service or intellectual category. Second, it is experiencing rapid geographical expansion (Swart, 2001). Finally, it is possible to witness a large number of interorganizational alliances in the media industry (Kang & Sakai, 2000). In this context, the media industry may be the appropriate context for examining global linkages among firms.

However, previous research has been mainly centered on interorganizational linkages such as global strategic alliances (Barley, Feeman, & Hybels, 1992; Contractor & Lorange, 1988; Gomes-Casseres, 1996; Nohria & Garcia-Pont, 1991), ignoring the spatial character of global industry networks. Little attention has been centered on how global media companies expand worldwide or how they construct the spatial network that is geographically dispersed through foreign direct investment (FDI). In reality, most media companies tend to partner with competitors in cross-border expansion rather than using risky FDI

Address correspondence to Bum Soo Chon, 169 Dongsung-dong, Chongro-gu, Seoul, 110–791, Korea. E-mail: ccblade2@yahoo.co.kr

(Leander, 1999). However, as Craig and Douglas (2000) contended, the spatial configuration of the firm's resources may be a significant element of its global strategy. In fact, every multinational corporation (MNC) can be considered as a spatial network (Ghoshal & Bartlett, 1991; Gupta & Govindarajan, 2001a). Moreover, it is not only a network-based organizational structure (Malnight, 1996) but also a kind of intrafirm network in that they link headquarters with foreign subsidiaries (Anderson & Forsgren, 2000).

In sum, little research has attempted to combine multidimensional characteristics in the global media networks. Thus, important questions concerning the global media may involve structural characteristics of interorganizational linkages and spatial expansion and the relation between them. That is, to understand the multidimensional characteristics of the global media network, it will be necessary to examine structural patterns in the interorganizational network and geographical expansion among global media firms. In this context, the starting point of much of this article is the observation that the structure of global media networks may be represented as two dimensions: interorganizational linkages and geographical dispersion. The overall goal of this research was to describe and to compare the preceding dual networks in the entertainment industry. In addition, in this article, I identify geographical, cultural, and industrial factors that have contributed to shaping the dual structure of global media networks.

Theoretical Background

Forms of Organizational Linkages

Although previous research on organizational networks has mainly focused on interorganizational alliances or mergers among organizations, the forms of organizational linkages may vary by the degree to which organizations are linked. Clearly, there are a variety of ways to define interorganizational networks in understanding the pattern of interorganizational linkages. To examine global strategic linkages in the auto industry, Nohria and Garcia-Pont (1991, p. 105) distinguished interorganizational linkages into nine types of networks: mergers, acquisitions, equity partnership, consortia, joint ventures, technology licensing and development agreements, supply agreements, manufacturing collaborations, and marketing agreements. It is a categorical classification using ordinal scales. Nohria and Garcia-Pont's classification is based on observations from the manufacturing industries. Thus, it may not be useful for studying service-based industries.

Barringer and Harrison (2000) classified those interorganizational linkages into several types in terms of tightness of coupling. Barringer and Harrison suggested that joint ventures, networks, and consortia are tightly

coupled relations based on the configuration of ownership. These interorganizational linkages imply that organizations intentionally interact with other organizations, thus they are involved with the relations of power exchange based on resource distribution. In contrast, nonequity-based linkages are considered as loosely coupled relations based on shared resources. Those loosely coupled relations have the purpose of getting or exchanging information.

In this article, interorganizational linkage refers to which different organizations in the entertainment industry are directly or indirectly linked through two ways of networking such as joint ventures and equity partnerships. Likewise, in this study, I limited the scope of interorganizational linkages as the equity network (joint venture + equity partnership) for the entertainment industry. It has the following purposes. Given that interorganizational linkages in the media industry have experienced significant structural changes due to industrial consolidation and the developments in communication technology, it is appropriate for using strong ties such as equity-based networks rather than using weak ties such as marketing agreements. I explore relatively stable ties among media firms because those organizations may be strongly embedded in the equity network.

From the theoretical perspective, equity-based linkages may be a type of relational embeddedness (Granovetter, 1973). Simply, it refers to strong tie linkage. The theory of relational embeddedness is based on the degree of cohesion among actors. As Gulati (1998) maintained, "relational embeddedness or cohesion perspectives on networks stress the role of direct cohesive ties as a mechanism for gaining fine-grained information" (p. 296). In relation to access to information, "strong ties are associated with trust and fine-grained information exchanges between partners. On the other hand, weak ties lead to novel information" (Rowley, Behrens, & Krackhardt, 2000, pp. 369–370). As noted previously, the interorganizational equity network is a strong linkage based on direct interaction between two firms. It is "broader and deeper in terms of investment and interaction than marketing joint ventures and technology licensing, which requires less coordination or understanding of partner's organizations" (Powell, 1990, p. 314).

Geography of FDI as Spatial Networks

Some entertainment companies are mapping out an aggressive strategy to expand globally. These trends show that for the entertainment industry, global reach is an important factor for gaining competitive advantage and expanding markets based on intellectual assets such as media content. In this context, one of most important motives for establishing operations in foreign countries is to seek competitive advantages (Porter, 1986). International expansion is "a strategic process that moves a firm beyond its domestic boundaries to positions in new markets" (Smith & Zeithaml, 1999, p. 34). In this context, previous research on multinational firms has increasingly emphasized that multinational firms tend to construct networks of foreign subsidiaries for making value chains at the global level (Bartlett & Ghoshal, 1989; Porter, 1990). Similarly, using multiple locations may be effective global strategies for MNCs (Dunning, 1993). International expansion of MNCs is closely related to firms' competitive advantages at the firm level (Porter, 1990).

Likewise, although several theories have been suggested to capture the process of internationalization through FDI, the Dunning's (1993) eclectic paradigm of ownership, location, and internalization receives much attention. In Dunning's (1993) view, those three factors all contributed to explain the pattern of companies' international expansion. Nevertheless, it is notable that Dunning's (1993) approach mainly focused on the specific location advantages. Moreover, in his recent study, Dunning (1998) argued that "more attention needs to be given to the importance of location per se as a variable affecting the global competitiveness of firms" (p. 60). In this respect, international expansion refers to the spatial distribution of firms' internal resources across countries for gaining global competitiveness.

In addition, the spatial distribution of FDI in the service industries has attracted much attention because they have different characteristics from traditional goods. The significant difference between a service and a manufactured good is intangibility such as brand names (Zeithaml, 1981). Moreover, as Fernandez (2001) argued, "the combination of intangibility and the need for proximity between producer and client are two characteristics which greatly determine the chosen mode of service provision abroad through exports, foreign direct investment (FDI), strategic alliances, [and] networking" (p. 6). In this context, firms that are mainly dependent on intangible resources in their profit structures tend to expand globally.

From the organizational perspective, the relations between headquarters and their international subsidiaries show intraorganizational governance structures. That is, "network form of governance in international business may be interpreted as the organizational forms and processes through which transnational activities are directed across different fields and geographic locations" (Wai-chung, 1997, p. 5). Simply, they are spatially connected intrafirm networks. Based on this idea, in this article, I describe the similarities in geographical structure of media companies' activities that are dispersed in foreign countries. I focus on how global media companies are similar in terms of the spatial spread of their multinational activities.

Because in this article I focus on the dispersion network, I measure the similarities in networking structures of

headquarters and international subsidiaries among global media companies. Thus, in this article, I do not focus on why media companies invested in foreign countries but on how they are similar in selecting foreign countries. This will allow for the comparison of the similarities in the behaviors of media companies. To determine if the distributions of international subsidiaries are similar across media companies, in this article, I use network analysis for exploring the similarities in the spatial spread of international activities by global media companies.

Research Questions

The arguments that have been developed up to this point suggest that both interorganizational linkages and geographical dispersion jointly contribute to form global media networks. Thus, two dimensions of global media networks have been identified. As discussed previously, the first dimension is the interorganizational linkage, which defines interorganizational ties among global media companies. The second dimension is the similarity in the geographical dispersion through FDI by global media companies. Jointly, these indicators represent the dual structure of global media networks in the entertainment industry. The specific arguments can be summarized in terms of the following research questions (RQs):

RQ 1: What is the structure of global networks in the entertainment industry? How are global media companies interlinked in terms of relational structure and geographical dispersion?

RQ 2: Are there any relations between interorganizational linkages and geographical dispersion networks? In addition, what are the relations between the preceding two networks and other shared attributes such as language, country of origin, regions, and industry similarities?

RQ 3: What factors have contributed to shaping the structure of global networks in the entertainment industry?

Method

The structure of global media networks in the entertainment industry may be examined with the network analysis method. Here, the purpose of doing network analysis is to identify global structures based on the relations among organizations (Barnett, Danowski, & Richards, 1993; Burt, 1992; Rogers & Kincaid, 1981). In Wellman and Bekowitz's (1988) view, "social or market structures can be represented as networks—as sets of *nodes* and sets of ties depicting their *interconnections*" (p. 4). In this sense, in this section, I describe the procedures used to gather the network data in detail.

Network Boundary

For the network analysis of the media industry, it is necessary to delimit the boundaries of the network, selecting which actors and types of relations should be included in the study (Laumann, Marsden, & Prensky, 1983). For the entertainment industry, the data include equity partnerships and joint ventures in terms of the forms of interorganizational relations (Nohria & Garcia-Pont, 1991). In terms of sampling, the 30 largest global entertainment firms were chosen for study because of both the availability and reliability of data. This way of sampling enabled me to examine the behavior of significant players in each industry. In addition, previous network studies on interorganizational linkages have focused on the leading firms (Gulati, 1995).

Entertainment Industry Network

The data on the entertainment industry were selected from the 30 leading global entertainment companies from *Variety* (Swart, 2001). The 30 global entertainment companies in the study are listed in Table 1. These data are based on the seventh annual list of the top entertainment companies around the world by *Variety*. Those companies in the list are ranked by total media revenues in dollars for 2000 to 2001, with revenues from newspapers, magazines, television, radio broadcasting, cable television, satellite broadcasting, film, and other media sources.

Data on interorganizational alliances for the entertainment industry were collected from multiple sources to verify the data. Some sources include the *Standard & Poor's Corporate Descriptions Plus News* for the U.S. corporations and the *Major Companies Database* for the international corporations. In this article, I focus only on fully or majority owned subsidiaries worldwide. Additional data for the entertainment industry were collected from the *Dow Jones News Retrieval Service* database, various annual reports, and 10-K financial reports. For geographical distribution of subsidiaries, foreign subsidiaries of entertainment companies were used for this study. The data on foreign subsidiaries were drawn from the preceding sources. Here, only majority owned subsidiaries were included in the study.

Constructing the Networks

The structure of global media networks was measured by two separate variables: interorganizational network and

Table 1. List of Companies Included in the Global Entertainment Network

Ranking	Company	Major Business	Country
1	AOL–Time Warner	Diversified group	USA
2	Walt Disney	Diversified group	USA
3	Viacom	Diversified group	USA
4	Vivendi–Universal	Diversified group	France
5	Bertelsmann	Diversified group	Germany
6	News Corp.	Diversified group	USA
7	Sony (Entertainment assets)	Film + music	Japan/USA
8	Comcast	Cable television	USA
9	AT&T Broadband	Cable television	USA
10	Cox Communications	Cable television	USA
11	NBC	Broadcasting	USA
12	Gannett	Newspaper	USA
13	Tribune	Newspaper	USA
14	Clear Channel	Radio broadcasting	USA
15	DirecTV	Satellite broadcasting	USA
16	Kirch Group	Television broadcasting	Germany
17	USA Networks	Television broadcasting	USA
18	Cablevision	Cable television	USA
19	NTL	Cable television	United Kingdom
20	Fuji Television	Television broadcasting	Japan
21	RTL Group	Television broadcasting	Luxembourg
22	EMI	Music	United Kingdom
23	Charter Communications	Cable television	USA
24	BskyB	Satellite broadcasting	United Kingdom
25	Globo	Television broadcasting	Brazil
26	Nippon Television	Television broadcasting	Japan
27	Carlton	Cable television	United Kingdom
28	EchoStar	Satellite broadcasting	USA
29	Tokyo broadcasting	Television broadcasting	Japan
30	Rogers	Cable television	Canada

geographical dispersion network. Other external factors such as geographical, cultural, and industrial variables were measured by constructing similarity matrices.

Interorganizational networks. This article is based on strong ties such as equity alliances and joint ventures that "have a higher level of resource commitment" (Rowley et al., 2000, p. 377). The basic network data set for the entertainment industry is an $n \times n$ matrix S in which n equals the number of nodes (firms) in the analysis. In this case, a node is a firm. Each cell, s_{ij}, indicates the strength of the relation. S is symmetrical because the purpose of this article was to identify the relational structure of media firms. If there was a joint venture or equity investment in the dyad, it is coded as 1. It is coded as 0 if no joint venture or equity investment existed. This network indicates the existence of linkages between two global media firms. The industry networks were constructed by constructing the 30 × 30 matrix.

Geographical dispersion network. The geographical dispersion network was constructed using the country × firm matrix.[1] The basic network data set for the network was an affiliation matrix A ($n \times k$) in which n equals the number of countries and k equals the number of global media companies. More specifically, an affiliation matrix of countries × firms was constructed to analyze the shared structure in similarities of geographical dispersion. Each cell in the matrix indicates if a firm is represented in the corresponding country. Then, a square firm × firm matrix was created from the original affiliation matrix by premultiplication of its transpose.

Industry similarity networks. Industry similarity networks between dyads were created. The four-digit standard industrial classification codes were used to classify business types. Data on the shared industry networks were obtained from the *Standard & Poor's Corporate Descriptions plus News* and 10–K financial reports for the year 2000. The industry similarity network measures similarities in industry types. For each of these variables, adjacency matrices of whether or not each pair of firms shared these attributes were created. If both corporations of the dyad shared an industry, their relation is coded as 1 and 0 if they did not.

Language similarity network. In the interorganizational networks, "greater cultural similarity improves inter-partner communication by sensitizing firms to nuances of language and/or non-verbal communication, thus circumventing language-based hazards" (Merchant, 2000, p. 116). Data on the primary languages spoken in the countries that include global media firms' headquarters came from the Linguasphere Observatory's *Linguasphere Table of the World's Major Spoken Languages*

1999–2000 (2001). An adjacency matrix of whether or not each pair of firms shared this attribute was created (with a 1 in the shared cell if the pair of firms shared in the same language and 0 if they did not).

Shared country of origin network. According to Gupta and Govindrajan (2000b), "country of origin has an important impact on the propensities of MNCs vis-à-vis the choice of global strategies and organizational structures" (p. 481). For this variable, adjacency matrices of whether or not each pair of firms shared this attribute were created (with a 1 in the shared cell if the pair of firms' headquarters are located in the same country and 0 if they are not).

Shared regional networks. Regions reflect the characteristics of geographical markets (Hoopes, 1999). In this study, based on the Hoopes' (1999) argument, regions were divided into six geographical parts: North America, Latin America, Asia, Europe, Africa, and the Middle East. For this variable, adjacency matrices of whether or not each pair of firms shared this attribute were created (with a 1 in the shared cell if the pair of firms are located in the same region and 0 if they are not).

Network Analysis

Multidimensional scaling (MDS). MDS identifies the spatial representation of the network (Barnett & Danowski, 1992; Barnett & Rice, 1985; Woelfel & Danes, 1980). According to Woelfel and Danes (1980), "MDS procedures construct a multidimensional space or map in which the objects scaled are arrayed such that the distances between any two objects in the map are functions of their measured distance from each other on the scaling instrument" (p. 334). In this article, the aim of scaling is to determine the dimensions underlying the structure of the global media network based on both interorganizational and geographical dispersion networks. For this article, the network is examined using the metric multidimensional algorithm from UCINET Version 5.0 (Borgatti, Everett, & Freeman, 1999).

Quadratic assignment procedure (QAP) correlation analysis. QAP correlation may be used to evaluate the strength of the relation between the two networks. QAP correlation is used to compare similarities between matrices (Krackhardt, 1987, 1988). More specifically, "the QAP is a nonparametric, permutation-based test that preserve[s] the integrity of the observed structures" (Krackhardt, 1987, p. 174). Using a QAP correlation analysis in this article, I evaluated the relations among several matrices including interorganizational and geographical dispersion networks, language similarity, shared country of origin, shared regions, and shared industry networks. Recent research indicates that QAP correlation can be useful to compare various networks (Barnett, Chon, & Rosen, 2001; Doelfel & Barnett, 1999).

Multiple Regression Analysis

In this study, I used multiple regression analysis to examine whether the inclusion of the geographical, cultural, and industrial variables significantly affected both interorganizational linkage and geographical dispersion. A series of regression analyses were run to find predictors of both networks. Here, independent variables were geographical variables such as shared country of origin, shared regions, cultural variables including language similarity, and industry similarities. Using the enter method, the independent variables were included in the equation.

Results

Structure of the Interorganizational Network

To examine the structural positions of the entertainment companies in more detail, MDS was performed. A two-dimensional solution produced a stress level of

0.198.[2] The two dimensions are displayed in Figure 1. Dimension 1 differentiated the Europe group from the non-Europe group. Europe-based companies—Bertelsmann (Germany), RTL (Luxembourg), Kirch (Germany), and EMI (United Kingdom)—were in the left, and they were closely grouped. Dimension 2 differentiated the cable group from the noncable group. Cable-related companies such as AT&T broadband, Charter Communications, Cox Communications, and Cablevision were in the upper space. In the lower were both noncable and Europe and Japan groups. In addition, diversified entertainment companies such as Vivendi Universal (France), BSkyB (United Kingdom), AOL–Time Warner (United States), and Sony (Japan) formed a relatively tight group. In contrast, other Japanese companies including Fuji Television, Tokyo Broadcasting, and Nippon Television were located around the periphery in the space.

Structure of the Geographical Dispersion Network

As mentioned before, MDS identifies the spatial representation of the network (Barnett & Rice, 1985). Using MDS, the dimensions underlying the structure of the global media network were identified in terms of geographical dispersion of global entertainment companies.

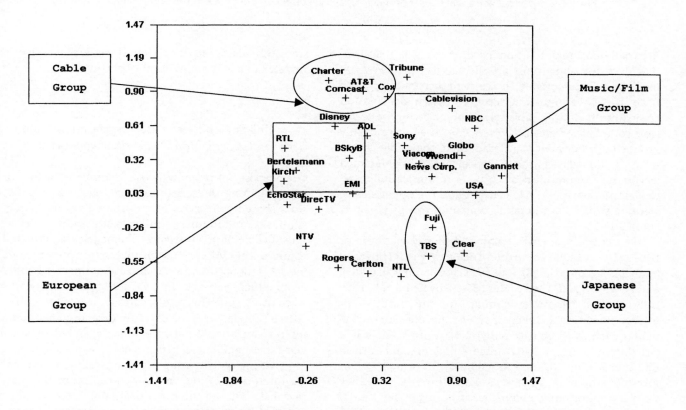

Figure 1. Multidimensional scaling of the interorganizational network in the entertainment industry.

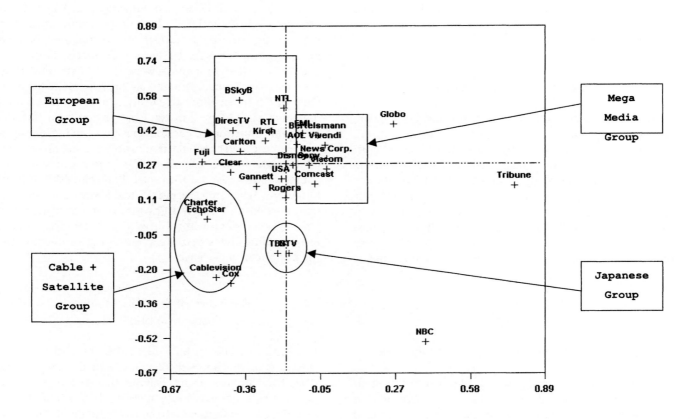

Figure 2. Multidimensional scaling of the geographical dispersion network in the entertainment industry.

A two-dimensional solution produced a stress level of .176. The two dimensions are displayed in Figure 2. Dimension 1 differentiated the content-distribution group from the content-making group. Content-distribution companies including cable television and satellite television companies were in the left, and they were closely grouped. Dimension 2 differentiated the cable group from the noncable group. Cable-related companies such as Charter Communications, Cox Communications, and Cablevision were in the lower space. In the upper sphere were most of entertainment companies except Japanese companies.

The central space was composed mostly of music or film industry-based companies such as Vivendi Universal (France), Viacom (United States), Bertelsmann (Germany), and News Corp. (United States). They formed a relatively tight group. However, similar to the results for interorganizational linkages, several Europe-based companies such as Kirch (Germany), NTL (United Kingdom), RTL (Luxembourg), BskyB (United Kingdom), and Carlton Communications (United Kingdom) also formed a tight group on the higher space. It can be inferred that they were Europe-oriented companies in terms of the spatial distribution of FDI. Other companies including NBC (United States), Globo (Brazil), and Tribune (United States)

were located around the periphery in the space. They have invested in a very small number of countries.

Relations Between Interorganizational and Geographical Dispersion Networks

The purpose of this analysis was to compare the overall relations among interorganizational, geographical dispersion, shared country of origin, shared region, language similarity, and industry similarities including television, music, cable, film, newspaper, theme park, and radio. The results of the QAP correlation analysis are presented in Table 2.[3] Data on the interorganizational network and the geographical network among the 29 companies were analyzed using QAP. This resulted in a statistically significant correlation of .307 (p = .001). The correlation between the interorganizational network and the shared region network was small but significant (r = .116, p = .042), indicating that region was a slightly significant determinant of the interorganizational network. In addition, the analysis revealed that the interorganizational network and the music industry network were the most strongly related (r = .312, p = .000) followed by the interorganizational net-

Table 2. The QAP Correlations Among Networks in the Entertainment Industry

	Interorganizational	Geographical	Country	Region	TV	Music	Cable	Film	News	Theme	Radio	Language
Interorganizational network	1.0											
Geographical network	r = .307 p = .001	1.0										
Country network	r = .106 p = .096	r = −.085 p = .227	1.0									
Regional network	r = .116 p = .042	r = −.033 p = .403	r = .754 p = .000	1.0								
Television network	r = .021 p = .387	r = .045 p = .336	r = .075 p = .226	r = .033 p = .327	1.0							
Music network	r = .312 p = .000	r = .528 p = .000	r = −.097 p = .120	r = −.060 p = .371	r = −.048 p = .445	1.0						
Cable network	r = .046 p = .296	r = .068 p = .292	r = .151 p = .131	r = .247 p = .013	r = −.220 p = .060	r = −.071 p = .403	1.0					
Film network	r = .239 p = .005	r = .496 p = .000	r = .014 p = .400	r = −.026 p = .485	r = .157 p = .110	r = .233 p = .032	r = .235 p = .050	1.0				
Newspaper network	r = −.062 p = .316	r = .013 p = .339	r = .108 p = .178	r = .058 p = .292	r = .166 p = .058	r = −.031 p = .728	r = −.091 p = .252	r = −.046 p = .510	1.0			
Theme Park network	r = .052 p = .339	r = .214 p = .017	r = −.008 p = .616	r = −.015 p = .797	r = .004 p = .548	r = .136 p = .098	r = .111 p = .215	r = .295 p = .012	r = −.014 p = .339	1.0		
Radio network	r = −.077 p = .184	r = −.088 p = .167	r = −.046 p = .401	r = −.014 p = .603	r = .329 p = .007	r = −.053 p = .459	r = −.192 p = .017	r = −.080 p = .193	r = .333 p = .016	r = −.023 p = .821	1.0	
Language network	r = −.015 p = .502	r = −.125 p = .242	r = .609 p = .000	r = .457 p = .000	r = −.030 p = .433	r = −.115 p = .254	r = .323 p = .040	r = −.056 p = .486	r = .037 p = .483	r = −.027 p = .716	r = −.071 p = .495	1.0

Note. QAP = quadratic assignment procedure.

work and the film industry network ($r = .239$, $p = .005$). However, a correlation between the interorganizational network and language similarity was not significant. The overall results suggest that some industry similarities such as film and music were correlated with interorganizational network in the entertainment industry.

With regard to the geographical dispersion network, the correlation between the geographical dispersion network and the music industry network was significant ($r = .528$, $p = .000$), indicating that the shared music industry was a significant determinant of the geographical dispersion network in the entertainment industry. The QAP analysis also revealed that the geographical dispersion network and the film network were strongly related ($r = .496$, $p = .001$) followed by the geographical network and the theme park network ($r = .214$, $p = .05$). The overall results suggest that although the geographical network was strongly correlated with industry similarities including film and music in the entertainment industry, it was not correlated with geographical factors such as shared country of origin or shared region.

Determinants of Global Media Networks

Two separate regressions provided the best predictions of the dual structure of the global media networks in the entertainment industry.[4] The dependent variable for the first regression was the interorganizational network, and the second one was the geographical dispersion network in the entertainment industry. First, the 11 independent networks were entered into a multiple regression to determine their combined impact on the interorganizational network. A standard multiple regression algorithm was employed using the zero-order QAP correlations. It enabled me to control for the lack of independence among the cells (Barnett et al., 2001).

The combined impact of the independent networks on the interorganizational network in the entertainment industry was .412 ($R^2 = .169$, $p = .000$). Three independent networks were significant. Among these networks, the music industry network was most strongly related ($\beta = .222$, $t = 4.040$, $p = .000$), followed by the geographical dispersion network ($\beta = .143$, $t = 2.334$, $p = .020$), and the film industry ($\beta = .115$, $t = 1.984$, $p = .048$). However, other geographical factors such as shared country of origin and shared region as well as other broadcasting or newspaper industry networks were not statistically significant. As a result, the best model to explain the interorganizational network was the combination of three of the independent variables, explaining almost 17% of the variance in the network. Specifically, they suggest that the more entertainment companies share content-related industries such as music or film, the greater would be the possibility to form interorganizational linkages.

Second, like the previous procedures, the 11 independent networks including the interorganizational network were also entered into a multiple regression to determine their combined impact on the geographical dispersion network in the entertainment industry. The combined impact of the independent networks on the geographical dispersion network in the entertainment industry was .670 ($R^2 = .449$, $p = .000$). Overall, like the previous results, the regression analysis showed similar patterns. Three independent networks were significant. Among these networks, the music industry network was the most strongly related ($\beta = .397$, $t = 9.667$, $p = .000$), followed by the film industry ($\beta = .362$, $t = 8.231$, $p = .000$), and the interorganizational network ($\beta = .143$, $t = 2.334$, $p = .020$). The results of the regression revealed that music and film industry networks played a significant role in explaining the geographical dispersion network in the entertainment industry. The results of the two multiple regression's are summarized in Table 3.

Discussions and Conclusions

In this article, I have attempted to describe the contour of the global media networks in terms of interorganizational and spatial networks in the entertainment industry. The results of MDS revealed differences of spatial groupings between two kinds of global media networks. That is, although the diversified entertainment companies such as Vivendi Universal, BskyB, AOL–Time Warner, and Sony formed a relatively tight group at the center, AOL–Time Warner and Disney were located at different positions from the central cluster in the geographical networks. Noticeably, Europe-based entertainment companies and Japan-based entertainment companies were extremely localized in both networks.

In the case of the relations between the interorganizational and geographical dispersion networks in the entertainment industry, the QAP analyses revealed structural similarities between both networks. Simply, the interorganizational network in the entertainment industry was significantly related to similarities in the spatial distribution of FDI. These results suggest that there was a similar relation between making linkages with other companies and the way in which they invest in other countries. The results of multiple regression analyses showed that music and film industry networks played a significant role in explaining interorganizational and geographical dispersion networks in the entertainment industry.

It is noticeable that although both networks in the entertainment industry were moderately correlated in terms of relational similarity, they showed structural differences in terms of the configurations of network positions. The findings show that although the two network's

Table 3. Multiple Regression Analysis of Determinants in the Entertainment Industry

Variable	B	SEB	β	t	p
Interorganizational network					
Constant	5.046E-02	0.030		1.692	.092
Geographical dispersion similarity	7.800E-03	0.003	.143	2.334	.020
Shared origin of country	0.107	0.061	.144	1.750	.081
Shared region	4.652E-02	0.050	.068	0.934	.351
Industry similarity (television)	9.213E-03	0.038	.013	0.245	.806
Industry similarity (music)	0.306	0.098	.222	4.040	.000
Industry similarity (cable)	9.213E-03	0.038	.013	0.233	.816
Industry similarity (film)	0.396	0.073	.115	1.984	.048
Industry similarity (newspaper)	8.927E-03	0.108	−.061	−1.239	.216
Industry similarity (theme park)	0.145	0.190	−.048	−0.999	.318
Industry similarity (radio)	−0.133	0.069	−.024	−0.470	.639
Language similarity	−0.190	0.042	−.088	1.432	.153
Geographical dispersion network					
Constant	3.019	0.422		7.161	.000
Interorganizational network	1.748	0.749	.095	2.334	.020
Shared origin of country	−1.725	0.912	−.126	−1.892	.059
Shared region	1.150	0.744	.092	1.545	.123
Industry similarity (television)	0.287	0.562	.021	0.510	.610
Industry similarity (music)	13.024	1.347	.397	9.667	.000
Industry similarity (cable)	8.337E-02	0.573	.007	0.146	.884
Industry similarity (film)	8.336	1.013	.362	8.231	.000
Industry similarity (newspaper)	3.043	1.606	.078	1.933	.054
Industry similarity (theme park)	3.491	2.838	.048	1.230	.219
Industry similarity (radio)	−1.663	10373	−.068	−1.604	.109
Language similarity	−0.380	0.624	−.031	−0.609	.543

Note. For the interorganizational network, $R = .412$; $R^2 = .169$; adjusted $R^2 = .146$; $F = 7.306$; $p = .000$. For the geographical dispersion network, $R = .670$; $R^2 = .449$; adjusted $R^2 = .434$; $F = 29.180$; $p = .000$.

clustering structures were similar, the configuration of the central group was different in both networks. As noted previously, there is evidence of differences in the dual structure in the entertainment industry. One possible explanation for this pattern of results is that the structure of the media industry may have been partly affected by two factors: geographical and industrial characteristics. Attributes including types of industries and geographical similarities among entertainment firms served as significant factors for constructing the dual structure of global media networks.

Clearly, industry-specific variables such as types of industries were found to be significantly related to the dual structure of global media networks. The structure of the interorganizational network was related to the music and film industries. Given that a few diversified media companies such as AOL–Time Warner, Disney, Fox Entertainment, Viacom, Sony, and Vivendi-Universal were major actors in the film entertainment sector, it is easily observed that they tend to use international joint ventures as their global strategy. More important, the entertainment industry is closely related to their market structures. In fact, a few media firms dominate global film and music markets. These trends indicate that the previous two industries have oligopoly market structures. In this context, market structures in the film and music industries may signifi-

cantly affect the formation of interorganizational linkages and firms' spatial dispersion behavior.

There were also important country-specific differences. The noticeable point is that Japanese companies had a small number of overseas subsidiaries and interorganizational linkages in the entertainment industry. That is, Japanese companies had unique positions in the global network space, showing that they were spatially localized. In this context, it is reasonable to infer that Japanese companies mainly paid particular attention to the Asian region. In contrast, some European companies including the United Kingdom, French, and German firms have expanded their foreign operations and have engaged in making ties with other global companies.

With regard to the cultural factors in forming global networks in the entertainment industry, the results indicated that language similarity was not a significant factor in the entertainment network. That is, contrary to the findings of previous research on the effects of cultural factors on the trade of cultural products (Straubhaar, 1997), the results of this article suggest that cultural factors may not be significant determinants in explaining the formation of interorganizational networks and behavior of cross-border investments within the entertainment industry. Although media content, production-based companies are identified as the most active actors in trading cultural goods including music and film, geographical expansion of global entertainment companies appears not to be limited to certain culturally bounded regions or partners. Rather, as noted earlier, the dual structure of global networks in the entertainment industries may be affected more by industry-specific factors than by any other cultural factors.

In relation to the previous discussion, there is another important point that should not be ignored: Trends in the interorganizational linkages and global expansion in the entertainment industry were closely related to regional integration. Overall, the results show the consistent patterns of regional configuration in the networks. Interestingly, regional groupings identified in this study were consistent with the regional focus of recent studies on international communication networks (Barnett, Salisbury, Kim, & Langhorne, 1999; Kim & Barnett, 2000). The spatial distribution of FDI tended to be regionally grouped in the entertainment industry.

There are several limitations of this study. First, in this study, I used mainly old media companies in analyzing the current entertainment industry. It may have a problem with boundary specification in selecting the specific media firms (Laumann et al., 1983). Simply, in this study, I did not focus on interactions between old media and new media based on developments in communication technologies. Thus, how Internet and data processing related companies are linked with communication companies within the broader media industries is still an open question. In relation to the preceding problem, in this study, I did not pay attention to direct interrelations among various media industries. In reality, it may be possible to observe media convergence or media consolidation through various strategic alliances among different kinds of media companies (Chan-Olmsted, 1998; Danowski & Choi, 1998).

The second limitation of this research is that by looking at global media networks at one point in time, only a static analysis was provided. Thus, in this article, I did not examine changing structures of interorganizational and geographical dispersion networks, excluding dynamics of interorganizational networks. Simply, there remains a need for examining "how networks evolve and change over time" (Nohria, 1992, p. 15). In this sense, the time period of study should be expanded.

The third limitation of this study is on the measurements of ties between two media firms. As shown earlier, limited types of ties were used for this study. For example, only strong ties between media companies were employed to analyze interorganizational relations for the entertainment industry, excluding weak ties. Consequently, in this study, I did not consider the strength of linkages among media firms at the various levels. Although Contractor and Lorange (1988) developed an ordinal scale for measuring the strength of linkages, schol-

ars have argued that it did not differentiate weak ties from strong ties (Rowley et al., 2000). Thus, there is a need to develop measurement scales to examine different interorganizational linkages.

These limitations suggest several directions for future research. Future research will have to pay attention to a number of factors that have not been discussed in this article. Further research efforts might attempt to incorporate variables besides regional and industrial factors into the research framework to improve our understanding of the global media networks. An important research topic concerning the structure of global media networks is the issue of the relations between network characteristics and organizational behaviors. For example, it is interesting to note that global interorganizational blocks can influence firms' behaviors (Gomes-Casseres, 1996; Nohria & Garcia-Pont, 1991). In addition, using the concept of isomorphism, it is possible to observe the relations between interorganizational networks and organizations' tendencies to follow strategic behaviors of other organizations (DiMaggio & Powell, 1983; Galaskiewicz & Wasserman, 1989). Finally, further research needs to include the effects of social structure such as interorganizational directorates (Gulati, 1995) on the structure of global media networks.

In conclusion, the findings indicate the benefit of distinguishing between interorganizational and geographic dispersion networks in understanding global media networks. On the one hand, in this study, I paid much attention to the point that interorganizational linkages can be formed by the coexistence of competition and collaboration among global media firms in parallel with key environmental events. The overall results of this study indicate that the spatial structure of global media networks may be affected by multiple factors including industry related variables, cultural similarities, and other regional factors.

Bum Soo Chon
(ccblade2@yahoo.co.kr)

is a full-time lecturer in the department of Media Arts and Sciences at the Korea National Open University. His research focuses on economic aspects of the media and entertainment industry.

Endnotes

1. Due to missing data (AT&T), $N = 29$ for the geographical dispersion network in the entertainment industry.
2. The stress index decreases as the number of dimensions increase (Young, 1987, p. 204) and stress values less than .20 are considered acceptable (Choi & Danowski, 2001).

3. The sample size for this analysis was 29. QAP was used to determine the correlation.
4. Because the matrices were symmetrical, the significance levels for the regression analyses were determined using 406 {the links [(n × n − 1)/2]} among 29 companies as the number of cases.

References

Anderson, U., & Forsgren, M. (2000). In search of centre of excellence: Network embeddedness and subsidiary roles in multinational corporations. *Management International Review, 40,* 329–350.

Barley, S. R., Freeman, J., & Hybels, R. C. (1992). Strategic alliances in commercial biotechnology. In N. Nohria & R. G. Eccles (Eds.), *Networks and organizations: Structure, form, and action* (311–347). Boston: Harvard Business School Press.

Barnett, G. A., Chon, B., & Rosen, D. (2001). The structure of the internet flows in cyberspace. *NETCOM, 15,* 61–80.

Barnett, G. A., & Danowski, J. A. (1992). The structure of communication: A network analysis of the international communication association. *Human Communication Research, 19,* 264–285.

Barnett, G. A., Danowski, J. A., & Richards, W. D., Jr. (1993). Communication networks and network analysis: A current assessment. In W. D. Richards & G. A.Barnett (Eds.), *Progress in Communication Sciences 12,* (pp. 1–19). Norwood, NJ: Ablex.

Barnett, G. A., & Rice, R. E. (1985). Network analysis in Rieman space: Applications of the Galileo System to social network. *Social Networks, 7,* 287–322.

Barnett, G. A., Salisbury, J. G. T., Kim, C., & Langhorne, A. (1999). Globalization and international communication: An examination of monetary, telecommunications, and trade networks. *The Journal of International Communication, 6*(2), 7–49.

Barringer, B. R., & Harrison, J. S. (2000). Walking a tightrope: creating value through interorganizational relationships. *Journal of Management, 26,* 367–403.

Bartlett, C., & Ghoshal, S. (1989). *Managing across borders: The transitional solution.* Boston: Harvard Business School Press.

Borgatti, S. P., Everett, M. G., & Freeman, L. (1999). UCINET Windows 5.0: Network Analysis Software [Computer software]. Columbia, SC: Analytic Technologies.

Burt, R. S. (1992). *Structural holes.* Cambridge, MA: Harvard University Press.

Castells, M. (1996). *The rise of the network society.* Cambridge, MA: Blackwell Publishers.

Chan-Olmsted, S. M. (1998). Mergers, acquisitions and convergence: The strategic alliances of broadcasting, cable television and telephone services. *Journal of Media Economics, 11*(3), 33–46.

Choi, J. H., & Danowski, J. A. (2001). *Making a global community on the Net-Global village or global metropolis?: A network analysis of Usenet newsgroups.* Manuscript submitted for publication.

Contractor, F. J., & Lorange, P. (1988). *Cooperative strategies in international business.* Lexington, MA: Lexington.

Craig, C. S., & Douglas, S. P. (2000). Configural advantage in global markets. *Journal of International Marketing, 8,* 6–26.

Danowski, J. A., & Choi, J. H. (1998). Convergence in the information industries: Telecommunications, broadcasting and data processing 1981–1996. In H. Sawhney & G. A. Barnett (Eds.), *Progress in Communication Sciences, 15* (pp. 125–150). Stamford, CT: Ablex.

DiMaggio, P., & Powell, W. W. (1983). The iron cage revisited: Institutional isomorphism and collective rationality in organizational fields. *American Sociological Review, 28,* 147–160.

Doelfel, M. L., & Barnett, G. A. (1999). A semantic network analysis of the International Communication Association. *Human Communication Research, 25,* 589–603.

Doz, Y. L., & Hamel, G. (1998). *Alliance advantage.* Boston: Harvard Business School Press.

Dunning, J. H. (1993). *Multinational enterprises and the global economy.* Don Mills, Ontario, Canada: Addison-Wesley.

Dunning, J. H. (1998). Location and the multinational enterprise: A neglected factor? *Journal of International Business Studies, 29,* 45–66.

Fernandez, M. T. (2001). Performance of business services multinationals in host countries: Contrasting different patterns of behavior between foreign affiliates and national Enterprises. *The Service Industries Journal, 21,* 5–18.

Galaskiewicz, J., & Wasserman, S. (1989). Mimetic processes within an interorganizational field: An empirical test. *Administrative Science Quarterly, 34,* 454–479.

Ghoshal, S., & Bartlett, C. A. (1991). The multinational corporation as an interorganizational network. *Academy of Management Review, 15,* 603–625.

Gomes-Casseres, B. (1996). *The alliance revolution: The new shape of business rivalry.* Cambridge, MA: Harvard University Press.

Granovetter, M. S. (1973). The strength of weak ties. *American Journal of Sociology, 78,* 1360–1380.

Gulati, R. (1995). Social structure and alliance formation patterns: A longitudinal analysis. *Administrative Science Quarterly, 40,* 619–652.

Gulati, R. (1998). Alliances and networks. *Strategic Management Journal, 19,* 293–317.

Gupta, A. K., & Govindarajan, V. (2001a). Converting global presence into global competitive advantage. *The Academy of Management Executive, 15*(2), 45–58.

Gupta, A. K., & Govindarajan, V. (2001b). *The quest for global dominance: Transforming global presence into global competitive advantage.* San Francisco: Jossey-Bass.

Harbison, J. R., & Pekar, P. (1998). *Smart alliances.* San Francisco: Jossey-Bass.

Hoopes, D. G. (1999). Measuring geographical diversification and product differentiation. *Management International Review, 39,* 277–292.

Kang, N., & Sakai, K. (2000). International strategic alliances: Their role in industrial globalization. *STI Working Papers 2000/5.* Paris, France: Directorate for Science, Technology, and Industry, Organization for Economic Cooperation and Development.

Kim, K., & Barnett, G. A. (2000). The structure of the international telecommunications regime in transition: A network analysis of international organizations. *International Interaction, 26,* 91–127.

Krackhardt, D. (1987). QAP partialling as a test for spuriousness. *Social Networks, 9,* 171–186.

Krackhardt, D. (1988). Predicting with networks: nonparametric multiple regression analysis of dyadic data. *Social Networks, 10,* 359–381.

Laumann, E. O., Marsden, P. V., & Prensky, D. (1983). The boundary specification problem in network analysis. In R. S. Burt & M. J. Minor (Eds.), *Applied network analysis* (pp. 18–34). Beverly Hills, CA: Sage.

Leander, T. (1999). Industry focus: That's entertainment. *Global Finance*, 43–45.

Linguasphere Observatory. (2001). *Linguasphere table of the world's major spoken languages 1999-2000*. Retrieved from http://www.linguasphere.org/major.pdf

Malnight, T. (1996). The transition from decentralized to network-based MNC structures: An evolutionary perspective. *Journal of International Business Studies, 27*, 43–65.

Merchant, H. (2000). Configurations of international joint ventures. *Management International Review, 40*, 107–140.

Nohria, N. (1992). Introduction: Is a network perspective a useful way of studying organizations? In N. Nohria & R. Eccles (Eds.), *Networks and organizations: Structure, form, and action* (pp. 1–22). Boston: Harvard Business School Press.

Nohria, N., & Garcia-Pont, C. (1991). Global strategic linkages and industry structure. *Strategic Management Journal, 12*, 105–124.

Porter, M. E. (1986). *Competition in global industries*. Boston: Harvard Business School Press.

Porter, M. (1990). *The competitive advantage of nations*. New York: Free Press.

Powell, W. W. (1990). Neither market nor hierarchy: Network forms of organization. *Research in Organizational Behavior, 12*, 295–336.

Rogers, M., & Kincaid, D. L. (1981). *Communication networks: Towards a new paradigm for research*. New York: Free Press.

Rowley, T., Behrens, D., & Krackhardt, D. (2000). Redundant governance structures: An analysis of structural and relational embeddedness in the steel and semiconductor industries. *Strategic Management Journal, 21*, 369–386.

Smith, A. D., & Zeithaml, C. (1999). The intervening hand: Contemporary international expansion processes of the regional Bell operating companies. *Journal of Management Inquiry, 8*, 34–64.

Straubhaar, J. D. (1997). Distinguishing the global, regional and national levels of world television. In A. Sreberny-Mohammadi, D. Winseck, J. McKenna, & O. Boyd-Barret (Eds.), *Media in global context: A reader* (pp. 284–298). New York: Arnold.

Swart, S. (2001, August 27). The Global 50. *Variety, 384*, 73–87.

Wai-chung, Y. H. (1997). Business networks and transnational corporations: A study of Hong Kong firms in the ASEAN region. *Economic Geography, 73*, 1–25.

Wellman, B. (1988). Structural analysis: From method and metaphor to theory and substance. In B. Wellman & S. D. Berkowitz (Eds.), *Social structures: A network approach* (pp. 19–61). New York: Cambridge University Press.

Wellman, B., & Bekowitz, S. D. (1988). Introduction: Studying social structures. In B. Wellman & S. D. Berkowitz (Eds.), *Social structures: A network approach* (pp. 1–14). New York: Cambridge University Press.

Woelfel, J., & Danes, J. E. (1980). Multidimensional scaling models for communication research. In P. Monge & J. N. Cappella (Eds.), *Multivariate techniques in human communication research* (pp. 333–364). New York: Academic.

Young, F. W. (1987). *Multidimensional scaling : History, theory, and applications*. Hillsdale, NJ: Lawrence Erlbaum Associates, Inc.

Zeithaml, V. A. (1981). How consumer evaluation processes differ between goods and services. In J. H. Donnelly & W. R. George (Eds.), *Marketing of services* (pp. 186–189). Chicago: American Marketing Association.

Market Competition and Cultural Tensions Between Hollywood and the Korean Film Industry

■

Eun-mee Kim
Yonsei University, Korea

The market shares of Hollywood movies in European and Asian markets are so large that policymakers around the world are concerned about the import domination not only in theaters but also in the subsequent windows. Media economists acknowledge that domestic producers have an advantage in terms of a "cultural discount," referring to the unavoidable disadvantage of imported films. However, expenditure on a film's production also determines the extent of popular appeal, thus creating an advantage for films that have a large and wealthy home market base such as Hollywood. In this article, I aim at understanding the dynamics of these 2 seemingly opposing forces in the motion picture market in Korea. I review the film market in Korea, explore the relation between performances of 2 windows, theaters and home video, over the two countries—the United States and Korea—and compare the determinants of performance of Hollywood and local films in Korean box offices. A strong hit orientation and preference for local content was empirically found.

Opening an Old Debate

The effect of exchanges of cultural products, such as motion pictures and television programs, on culture and cultural sovereignty has been at the core of debates over media imperialism, media hegemony, and the exercise of economic and cultural powers. Communication researchers tend to see this as a new problem that started with the advent of electronic media and mass communication. However, it is not hard to find examples of cultural influences, intentional or not, related to power throughout history before the advent of mass communication. Newcomb (1996) noted that throughout the history of conquest and subjugation, immigration and refugee movement, evangelism and education, issues have often been focused on matters of expressive culture, meaning, and art and entertainment.

Despite the repeated concerns about the potential peril of "undue" cultural influence, there has been little consensus not only about the possible resolution but also on the nature of the problem. Perhaps a part of the problem is the essential question on the definition of culture and where it resides and how it is formulated. When culture is

mixed with commerce, the matter gets even more complicated. Cultural products are heavily marketed as much as other kinds of industrial goods. Does culture "reside" in the cultural products?

Recently in Korea, confrontational negotiations are going on between local producers calling for the continued governmental protection such as screen quotas[1] and the governmental counterpart that is under the pressure of U.S. trade negotiators demanding the abolishment of such trade barriers. Those who are against screen quota policy are supported by the fact that the market share of local movies in Korea has been drastically rising over the recent years.[2] Despite such success of local productions over imports, local producers argue that such protective measures worked as the initial springboard for the consistent growth of the local movie industry and that continued protection is a must. The conflict stemmed from the dual nature of "motion pictures" (same for television programs or any other entertainment media products): motion pictures as a business product and as an agent of culture or identity formation. It makes the problem unique and interesting and at the same time difficult to sort out.

The dual nature of audiovisual products as cultural expressions and economic goods has also been reflected in previous research on the issue. It was the critical scholars who first noted the one-way flow of motion pictures from Hollywood to the rest of the world, concerned with the ho-

Address correspondence to Eun-mee Kim, Department of Communication, Yonsei University, Shinchon-Dong, Sudaemun-Gu, Seoul, Korea. E-mail: eunmee@yonsei.ac.kr

mogenizing effects of American culture on the indigenous one. They generally belong to the rubric of the "cultural imperialism" thesis. The concern has a long history from the postwar period when the Hollywood majors began to be active in the war-torn European countries.

One also sees the old debate getting renewed with *globalization* becoming the most popular term being used in intellectual, media, and other circles. As new media technologies make way for globalization that goes through diverse facets of modern society, the problem, it seems, gets complicated, and even worse, exacerbated. As the construction of information superhighways gets on the top agenda for virtually every country, policymakers are concerned that all sorts of foreign content might inundate their information superhighways.

Technological advances accompany the changes in media environments not only on global terms but also on the local level. The emergence of regional, transnational, or "proximate" television (Moragas Spa & Lopez, 2000); global diffusion of individual media such as the VCR; and increasing diffusion of multichannel television and broadband are some of the examples that have profound implication for the local cultural industries as well. The distribution bottleneck has been breaking fast, and the market is expanding. If there are indeed some changes in the distribution bottleneck of audiovisual products, how does this change affect the dynamics of the competition between a local cultural industry and a global force?

The Korean film industry is flourishing because, unlike Europe, it has an industry with an increasing portion of big commercial films. There seems to be growing interest and respect for the quality of films made in Korea nowadays. Korea is even regarded as an emerging regional cultural capital of East Asia, exporting movies and television programs to neighboring Asian countries including Japan.[3] At the same time, globalization is not bypassing Korea either. The Korean market seems to provide a venue for a case study on the current dynamics of a local industry and Hollywood in a growing media market. The market force of the local cultural industry has been growing at the same time that Hollywood has increased its global market influence over the world.

In this article, I focus on describing the competitive dynamics of Hollywood and local films distributed through the multiple windows of theaters and home video in the Korean market. What is unique about this study is that the competition between Hollywood and Korean (local) films that have a large difference in terms of home market size was the subject of the study, and I include the analysis of the intertemporal dimension of the competition. With the advance of communication technology and accompanying windowing strategy of a global media firm, the influence of the intertemporal dimension of competition should be taken in as a factor.

In the following section, I review the previous research concerning the competition between Hollywood and indigenous movies in the global marketplace. Cultural discount factors and economic efficiency factors sometimes become conflicting, not necessarily opposing, forces in predicting the competitive dynamics of local and Hollywood movie productions. I also discuss the literature on the competitive effect of windowing in this section. In the following section, I set out research questions and the methodology. In the next section, I present the results. First, I document the growth of local movie productions in Korea followed by the relation between box office performance and video rental business performance. I also present empirical evidence for local audience preference for local content. In the last section, I conclude with a discussion.

Literature Review: The Dynamics of Global Competition in Motion Picture Industries

Competition Between Hollywood and the Local Films in the Box Office

Researchers began noticing the one-way flow since as early as the 1960s (e.g., Guback, 1969; Schiller, 1969). It was the critical scholars who first noted the one-way flow of motion pictures from Hollywood to the rest of the world. There is no question that the United States is the world's economic superpower, but few industries parallel the entertainment industry in terms of the dominance of the United States over the world. Hollywood dominance in foreign theatrical markets began to be extended from a trade issue to a larger cultural sovereignty issue.

Microeconomic research has focused on the economic explanations of the U.S. dominance of the global motion picture trade. Researchers (e.g., Waterman, 1996; Wildman, 1995; Wildman & Siwek, 1988) have also noticed the trend of increasing market share of Hollywood films over the world and a steady decline for national productions, but they have proposed a different set of reasons. According to Waterman (1996), it was around the 1972 to 1974 period when the steady or somewhat declining market share of Hollywood films in the world theatrical market began to strike a sharp turn and start the steady increase ever since.

These scholars have attributed the one-way flow to the economic market forces that give films produced for larger or wealthier market a competitive advantage. Motion pictures are "public goods," and the investment on product quality (i.e., content) increases with the potential revenue. The products with higher quality investment tend to have stronger popular appeal, which wins not only the domestic but also the foreign audience.

Two common assumptions that economists have employed when they have studied the competition between foreign and domestic audiovisual products are first, domestic producers have advantage over foreign if all other conditions are equal. The term *cultural discount* refers to the fact that audience members, in general, have a stronger preference for film content originating from their own cultural background. Second, expenditure on a film's production costs determines the public appeal (attraction) of it, thus creating an advantage for having a large, wealthy home market base (Dupagne & Waterman, 1998; Wildman, 1994).

Furthermore, the existence of the cultural discount factor over the world marketplaces strengthens the advantage of the producers from larger markets because the English-language producers experience less loss in the value of their creations due to the cultural discount than do producers working in other languages (Hoskins, Finn, & McFadyen, 1996). Having a larger home market allows larger sales for Hollywood producers as they face cultural discounts in a smaller portion of the global market while the others face the similar discount in a larger part of the market (Wildman & Siwek, 1988).

Wildman (1995) concluded that the Hollywood films' public appeal is high enough to overcome the cultural discount because of the film's "public good" characteristics. Waterman (1996) attributed the increasing share of Hollywood films in the global market to (a) the faster development of domestic media infrastructure to support film production in the United States and (b) a "foreign feedback effect" whereby privatization and media market development in foreign countries simultaneously benefits the U.S. producers by enlarging their markets. Furthermore, market penetration of foreign countries would gradually reduce the value discount (Cho, 1999).

The concept of cultural discount is one of the key assumptions that these economic models are based on. Domestic audiences prefer domestically produced films, and the models also imply that increases in domestic market size—that is, increases in consumer spending on theatrical films through the box office, video rentals, subscription to pay channels, and so on—will increase the potential markets for film producers for all countries. Therefore, increases in film spending by local audiences will help local producers proportionately more than they will help Hollywood (Waterman & Jayakar, 2000).

The two economic assumptions, the effect of film budget on the audience appeal and the notion of a cultural discount, respectively, originate from the dual nature of the motion pictures: film as a business and film as a cultural embodiment. The cultural discount factor and the budgetary advantage (market size advantage) factor can be conflicting but not necessarily opposing forces influencing the competition between local and Hollywood movies in a local marketplace.

The size of the global market is increasing not through a physical expansion but because of the technological advancement that brings about multiplication of delivery media. Wang, Ku, and Liu (2000) noted that academics have paid much closer attention to the foreign and global than they have to the national and local dimensions of communication industries. National and local media are juggling for position in a market that has suddenly doubled and even tripled in size. They state that the end result is a communication ecology in which the role of the local and national vis-à-vis the transnational and global media is being redefined. Therefore, focusing attention of the globalization force of media conglomerates such as Hollywood industries would miss the half of the picture.

The seemingly expanding global market power of Hollywood is raising concerns over the world. Large market shares of Hollywood movies in European and Asian markets show that such concerns are indeed real. For example, the market share of Hollywood films in France, which is famous for its protective policy, is 53%; that of Canada, 87%; and in United Kingdom, 73.5% as of 2003 (European Audiovisual Observatory, 2004). In Korea, where the market share of domestic films has been growing at a record-breaking rate over the last few years, Hollywood films' market share is 43.2% (as of 2003; Korean Film Council, 2004a).

The meaning of something being global cannot be comprehended without regard to the other side of the meaning pair, being local. Global power can only be captured in the local market as it competes and interacts with the local. How local industry as well as global forces have been dealing with the local market expansion and new openings of opportunity deserves attention.

Intertemporal Dimension of Competition: Home Video as an After Market for Theatrical Films

In addition to geographic flows of media products from one country to another, there is a largely unidirectional flow of media products among the different distribution channels (Wildman, 1994). This intertemporal flow is referred as a windowing phenomenon. Theatrical films are usually released as a home video after their run in the theaters.

Not all movies are first seen at the theaters. In Korea, many imported movies move directly to the home video window without going through theatrical run. That means, many Hollywood (and other imported) movies, when they are exported to overseas markets, are released immediately as home videos.[4] Also, theatrical films are sure to be produced as home videos for rental and sell through. These films have gained a new window, initial or additional.

The video cassette recorder (VCR) used to be characterized as a mass medium that gives viewers the freedom of choice in terms of the content selection. The VCR was the first electronic medium that has brought a wide range of content, both domestic and foreign (Ogan, 1989). Unlike theater releases in which the number of screens and the period by which a title is screened are limited, the home video window remains "open" almost indefinitely. Rental or purchase of the films on home video remains available for years after the film is first introduced.

Of course, a theater gives a much better sound and screen. Moviegoers have a chance to watch a film much earlier than the others. However, it costs less to watch a film by renting a video than by visiting a theatre.[5] Waterman (1985) argued that an important advantage for home video's ability to compete with other media is the great product diversity it offers. Noble (1988) argued that the VCR was used to express a wide range of political views and to provide the kinds of content designed for a specific target group.

Despite such initial expectations on the medium, a gradual growth of hit orientation in the U.S. home video market was observed (Wasko, 1994). As the video rental industry developed, fewer stores needed to stock library materials and viewers became more and more interested in major hits (Wasko, 1994). Such hit orientation favored the major studios, which have blockbusters in their product lineup.

Wasko (1994) explained in detail how the hit orientation affected the industry structure. Majors began to squeeze out the independent distributors. They started to bypass wholesalers to directly distribute to large retail chains and to many foreign markets. Around the same time, large wholesale companies started to concentrate on the majors. By 1988, films grossing over $10 million at the box office (almost always distributed by major studios) represented 70% of wholesale video business. As a result, the market for "B" titles was specifically affected (Wasko, 1994). Wasko (1994, p. 158) emphasized the increasing interest by the entire home video industry in ordering and pushing big films. Shop owners have to basically guess the audience's choice of titles, and the safe bet would be to follow the popular appeal and box-office hits.

Waterman (1988) posited that adding a new delivery system of media content eventually expands a market, which in the long run increases the demand for programs. Video is an additional distribution window for theatrical films. However, if the hit orientation of the video market is an unavoidable path of development, video is not so much a new outlet for the distribution of new media products but rather an outlet that gives advantage to the proven products of the established producers by selectively expanding the market for them. The growth of the video market might have reduced the degree of diversity of film content by offering an added incentive for blockbuster hits with high production qualities such as Hollywood films with world-renowned stars vis-à-vis local films. Increasing penetration of home video in the world throughout the 1980s and 1990s would have been benefitting Hollywood producers as well as local producers.

Despite the fact that the video market is an important factor in considering motion picture industry, the video industry has not only been excluded in the discussion of motion picture trade but also has rarely been introduced as a variable in empirical studies. Home video is an important channel through which motion pictures are distributed. Multiple windows that follow the initial medium of distribution constitute an enlarged market on the intertemporal dimension, and the larger the total market size that a movie can target, the bigger investment a producer can put into the picture, which would increase the commercial appeal aside from the cultural discount factor.

Research Questions and Methodology

As discussed previously, an expanding global market brings a new set of market dynamics between Hollywood and local film industries, and such forces exert influences that are not necessarily unidirectional. There is a large home market advantage. Yet, the cultural discount factor can be advantageous to local producers (it can be also advantageous to Hollywood producers on a global level). Having a new window expands the home market for local producers. Yet, the hit orientation makes such market expansion disproportionately beneficial to Hollywood producers with big budget blockbusters.

During the past two decades, the total flow of revenue to U.S. distributors from the export of films has been growing even faster than their revenues from the domestic market. The result of foreign market growth has been a greatly increased feedback of commercial resources to support American film production (Waterman & Jayakar, 2000, p. 519). At the same time, in Korea, the market share of local films has been consistently increasing, and the VCR rental market also has been expanding very rapidly.

Based on the previous discussion, the research questions (RQs) are as follows:

RQ1: How are local and imported movies competing in the theaters of Korea over the years?

This first question is to describe how local films versus Hollywood films meet the demands of theatrical market expansion in Korea. I present the analysis of secondary data on market shares along with other statistics.

RQ2: Do local audiences have preference for local content?

RQ3: How is the size of a film's budget related to the box office performance?

RQ4: How is the size of a film's budget related to the video rental performance?

The following questions are to understand the implications of the home video market for theatrical films, especially when Hollywood films are distributed in a foreign market:

RQ5: Is there a "hit concentration" in the home video window in a foreign movie market?

RQ6: How are the performance figures of the two windows related to each other?

For research questions other than the first, data were collected and matched together from different sources. The movie titles, Hollywood and domestic (Korean) movies, released as home video in Korea between January of 1995 through February of 1999 along with the genre and revenue amount earned through sales of home video were acquired from a private company.[6] There are 2,933 films in the data set. Korean box office figures were acquired from the *Annual Review of Korean Films* (Korean Film Council, 1995–1999). U.S. box office figures and production budgets were acquired from the data set of Fu (1999). Out of 2,933 video titles released through video during the given period, 71.3% were Hollywood movies and 8.3% were domestic (Korean) movies.[7]

A linear regression model was run to capture the difference between Hollywood and local movies in terms of the home video performance (RQ2), and the Pearson correlation coefficients were computed for the rest of the research questions. The variables included are budget, U.S. box-office figure (USBO), Korean box-office figure (KRBO), U.S. video revenue (USVR), video revenue in Korea (KRVR), and movie genre dummy variables (comedy, animation, action/thriller, drama) for control purposes in the regression model.

Results: Market Competition in Korea

Growth of Local Film Industry

The purpose of this section is to review the status of market competition between Hollywood and indigenous cultural products in Korea. Within a local market boundary (in this case, Korea), both Hollywood and local cultural industries are competing to meet the expanded opportunities offered by regulatory changes (deregulation and privatization) and the diffusion of new technologies.

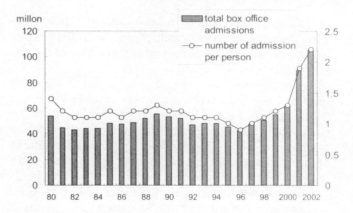

Figure 1. Theatrical market in Korea—Box office figures.

From Korean Film Council (1981–2003). *Annual Review of Korean Films*, Seoul, Korea: Jib-moon-dong.

Figure 1 and Table 1 show the steady expansion of total market size of the Korean theatrical market in the last decade or so. In Figure 1, one can see that the number of admissions is stabilized throughout much of the early 1990s. However, since 1997 and on, the market has been increasing steadily. In addition, Table 1 shows that the total revenues earned through box offices have been increasing throughout the 1990s and at an accelerating rate from 1999 and on.

A series of deregulations over 1990s eased the zoning restrictions for new theater constructions in the residential areas and allowed multiple prints of a title to be released simultaneously (which used to be banned). Large conglomerates saw business potential in audiovisual products, as penetration rates of VCR and cable television went up along with the increasing expectation and demand for other diverse media and started to enter the business and invested heavily as they competed with each

Table 1. Total Box Office Revenues

Year	Total Box Office Revenue (in U.S. $ Millions)
1991	13.72
1992	14.16
1993	15.50
1994	16.31
1995	16.67
1996	17.57
1997	20.65
1998	22.38
1999	24.79
2000	29.97
2001	45.36
2002	54.80

Note. From Korean Film Council (2004b). *Statistical data for the annual review of Korean film 2004.* Retrieved on July 5, 2004, from http://www.kofic.or.kr/attach/pds_attach/II-2,3,4,5.hwp

other to get the control of the new business. Theaters began to be reconstructed as multiplexes. Such effects began to show as box office figures and revenue toward the end of the year 2000.

Figure 2 shows how the expanding market is shared by local and foreign film producers. As can be seen in Figure 2, the audience market share kept increasing from the early 1990s. The ratio of local film titles, by the way, show a decreasing trend. This implies that the smaller number of local movie productions were attracting disproportionately larger audience shares.

One can see that the market share of Korean films was as high as 51.3% in 1983. The Korean government allowed direct distribution of foreign distributors in 1987 by making regulatory adjustments, and Hollywood majors have begun setting up their branch offices in Korea since then. The market share of local producers has been steadily decreasing up to 1993 in which the local share was a record low 15.9%. However, since 1994 and on, the trend has been reversed, and the local share has been steadily on the increase to close to 50% in 2002. There may be other reasons for market expansion such as the increasing leisure time and income level. However, some industry analysts have attributed increasing theater admissions to the quality commercial films produced by the local industry.

On the other hand, the situation is not so optimistic for the local film industry in terms of the number of films produced domestically vis-à-vis the number of films imported (including direct distribution of Hollywood distributors). Table 2 shows that the number of imported films has not decreased despite the fact that the theatrical market share of foreign films has been decreasing as shown previously.

It seems that increased communication channels (such as cable television and the VCR) have increased the demand for audiovisual products in a quantitative sense, which has sustained the demand for imports. The consumption in theaters, however, is still disproportionately concentrated on local products as one can see by comparing the number of domestic productions and their market shares.

The decrease in the number of domestic productions implies that film production and investments have been concentrated on fewer and fewer projects that are potentially high in commercial value. Whether this trend would decrease the diversity offered by the local film industry, which might eventually decrease the competitive strength in the long run, is currently under debate.[8]

The revival of local cultural production is not something only to be found in film industry. Starting from the late 1990s, popular songs, television programs, and films made in Korea have been drastically increasing their market presence in the neighboring Asian countries, especially in China and Southeast Asian countries. The emergence of Korea as a regional media capital (the Korean wave) can only be explained by complex social, commercial, and cultural factors that reside in Korea and countries at the receiving end. However, such a phenomenon shows the po-

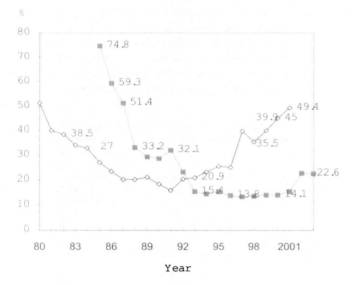

Figure 2. Market share of local films from 1980 through 2003.

Square dot denotes the ratio of local movie titles out of total number of titles exhibited. Diamond dots denote the ratio of audiences of local titles. From Korean Film Council (1981–2003). *Annual Review of Korean Films*, Seoul, Korea: Jib-moon-dong.

Table 2. The Number of Domestic Productions and Imports

Year	Domestic	Import	Direct Distribution	Domestic (%)
1985	80	27	0	74.8
1986	73	50	0	59.3
1987	89	84	0	51.4
1988	87	175	1	33.2
1989	110	264	15	29.4
1990	111	276	47	28.7
1991	121	256	45	32.1
1992	96	319	57	23.1
1993	63	347	64	15.4
1994	65	382	68	14.5
1995	64	358	65	15.4
1996	65	205	53	13.8
1997	59	380	58	13.4
1998	43	290	67	13.7
1999	49	297	74	14.2
2000	59	359	79	14.1
2001	65	355	60	15.5
2002	78	266	79	22.7
2003	79	271	68	22.6

Note. From Korean Film Council (2000, 2003). *Annual Review of Korean Films*, Seoul, Korea: Jib-moon-dong.

tential of Korean cultural industries in the age of global competition. The number of Korean movie prints[9] exported increased from 21 (in 1991) to 90 (in 2000) over the last decade (Korean Film Council, 2004b).

Just as Hollywood producers have benefited from the global market expansion due to the privatization of cultural sectors and communication technology advances over the world, Korean producers, as they were achieving the status of a regional media capital, must have benefited from the same phenomenon that took place in the adjacent regions that are culturally similar in relative terms. Such potential market expansion might have increased the investment on the quality of films, which in turn increased the popular appeal of them.

As the previous description of the Korean market case indicated, the competition between Hollywood and local films is much more complex than tracking the market share changes within a market. During the period when foreign market growth has increased feedback of commercial resources to support Hollywood film production to increase the market power of Hollywood in the global market (Waterman & Jayakar, 2000), the market share of local films in Korea increased at the expense of that of foreign, mostly Hollywood, films. However, at the same time, the number of films imported to Korea did not decrease because the market as a whole was expanding mainly due to the growth of the new communication channels such as cable, satellite, and VCRs. As Waterman & Jayakar (2000) predicted, the increases in film spending by local audiences helped local producers proportionately more than they helped Hollywood. The market growth in adjacent Asian countries also helped Korean producers vis-à-vis Hollywood, which makes it a somewhat unique case.

Competition Along the Intertemporal Dimension

To test the relation between the performances of film over the two windows, theaters and VCR, and the influence of budget on such performance, Pearson correlation coefficients were computed.

Table 3 presents the results for the variables related to the performance of Hollywood films in the Korean market. The variables in the table are performance measures in each sequential window a Hollywood film would go though along with its production budget. They are budget, USBO, KRBO (when the film is exported and exhibited in Korean theaters), USVR, and KRVR.

Table 3 basically shows how the performance in each window is closely interrelated to one another. It shows that the Pearson correlation coefficients among the intertemporal windows over the two countries (USBO, USVR, KRBO when a Hollywood films is exported, and KRVR when a Hollywood movie is released as a home video in Korea) were all positive and very strong (significant at .01 level). A success in the early window, geographical or intertemporal, seems to have been more or less reproduced in later windows, even when a film was exported to another country.

Contrary to the theoretical expectation, production budget has no relation with the film's performance either in theater or home video in the Korean market.

Local Audience Preference

Table 4 presents the regression results on the performance of theatrical films in the home video window (video revenue as dependent variable). To test the difference between local and Hollywood films, a dummy variable denoting the Hollywood production is included. Other variables included, for control purposes, are box office performance in Korean market and film genre dummy variables.[10]

Adjusted R^2 of the model is .31 ($N = 1,787$). As seen in the correlation analysis, box office success is perpetuated in the video sales. Holding the film genre and box office figures constant, Hollywood films perform significantly worse in home video market in Korea compared to the domestic productions. This shows the cultural discount effect in distributing theatrical films in the video window. The addition of the home video window helps local producers proportionately more than it does their Hollywood counterparts.

Table 3. The Relationship Among the Film Performances in Multiple Windows Over the Two Countries (Pearson Correlation)

Variable	Budget	p	N	USBO	p	N	USVR	p	N	KRBO	p	N
USBO	.04	.70	123									
USVR	.10	.28	123	.62*	.00	48						
KRBO	.06	.56	106	.61*	.00	181	.37*	.00	181			
KRVR	.07	.41	123	.55*	.00	218	.52*	.00	218	.65*	.00	1,631

Note. USBO = U.S. box-office figure; USVR = U.S. video revenue; KRBO = Korean box-office figure; KRVR = video revenue in Korea.
*p = .01.

Table 4. Regression on Video
Revenue of Theatrical Films

Variable	B	β	T	p
KRBO	1.62E−03	.48	24.36	.00
Comedy	87.69	.06	2.91	.00
Animation	24.15	.01	0.54	.59
Action/thriller	137.52	.15	6.63	.00
Hollywood	−340.12	−.21	−10.20	.00
Constant	542.05		16.43	.00

Note. The dependent variable is Korean video revenue. KRBO = Korean box-office figure.

Discussion

There seems to be more profound changes going on in the local cultural industries than is often framed under the umbrella term globalization. Globalization does not mean the local culture is being dominated or that local cultural industry withers away under the influence of a global power such as Hollywood. In this article, I have provided empirical evidence of the growth of local media in spite of Hollywood infiltration.

The competition between what is global and what is local is not a zero-sum game that the local and global cultural industries are engaged in. According to Giddens (as cited in Tomlinson, 1996, p. 86), the local and the global are opposing tendencies that engage in dialectical push and pull disembedding and reembedding.

The preceding analysis shows that the technological and industrial changes in the media environment often accompanying the market expansion of audiovisual products over the world produce competitive advantages for both the local industry and Hollywood. The expanded motion picture market in Korea can be attributed to the diffusion of multichannel television and VCRs, increased direct competition from foreign distributors, increasing leisure time, increasing screens and multiplexes, and so on. The increases in film spending by local audiences helped local producers proportionately more than they helped Hollywood in the case of Korea. However, it should be noted that the number of import titles still increased.

Hollywood producers are expanding their market not only in foreign theaters but also in home video. This study provides an empirical evidence of hit orientation. Those films successful in the U.S. market have higher chances to garner more revenues from an export market too. Increased media channels are disproportionately benefiting box office hit films in both the U.S. and export markets. Considering the "ever-openness" of the video window, the disproportionate benefits of the video window to box office hits found in this cross-sectional analysis may well be potentially enlarging in the long run. Although there is a tendency of hit orientation, the influence of budget on film performance seems to be decreasing.

At the same time, the much strengthened local film production industry is benefitting from the increasing market through the advantage offered by the cultural discount. Cultural products produced domestically with domestic stars enjoy an added value by their local audiences. Note also that such proximate cultural values can be formulated into successful cultural products only when a certain level of production quality is met. Cultural products are made with certain cultural values combined with industrial endeavors to make the product commercially viable. Indigenous products with lower production quality would only be rejected by local audiences, and the desire to pursue higher production qualities to consume should not be ignored. It should also be pointed out that in this article, I only showed the difference in preference level for local and foreign content. Future research should address how to measure the cultural discount in a way that it can be compared over time or between products.

According to Wang et al. (2000), the dramatic surge in television program supply capacity in Asia and Europe did not turn audiences' attention from local programs. Top programs in terms of ratings were mostly local despite the fact that the volume of foreign, mostly Hollywood, imports has increased. The percentage of supply in the expanded marketplace for audiovisual products does not mean the level of actual consumption is matched to the comparable level (Wang et al., 2000). In this article, I showed that the market dominance of globally marketed film and television programs had been somewhat overstated.

The Korean cultural industry is eager to globalize its reach, and such endeavors bear fruit in terms of increasing export of its products and stars to many parts of Asia. At the same time, global media firms try to increase their market power in the markets around the world. Therefore, what is local and what is global might not be opposing forces whereby the gain of one side is directly related to the decay of the other.

Newcomb (1996) noted that culture is an adaptive process. However, Newcomb added, the adaptive process is always conducted in the context of unequal distribution of power. Newcomb emphasized that future research should focus on the ways in which culture and cultural industries interact. Hybridization of cultures will go on as long as it produces bigger markets in which blockbusters with heavy investments on production qualities are preferred. However, it is not the only type that is likely to dominate the global audiovisual markets. Jeff Berg, head of the international talent agency ICM, once mentioned that Hollywood was now less a specific place than a metaphor. What Hollywood now evokes, according to Berg, is a set of expectations, high production quality and global appeal, not necessarily a specific country or a mother tongue

(Foroohar, 2002). Hollywood's international influence provides an inspiration, which strengthens local film industries. Some successful Korean movie producers have exactly followed the path.

The new media environment, as this research attempts to point to, brings about a complex web of multilevel influences that should be given due consideration on both global and local levels. Markets cannot be a cause for cultural dominance, or culture becomes succumbed to the industry. What is happening is that markets influence culture, and what goes on at the cultural level influences market competition.

Eun-mee Kim

(eunmee@yonsei.ac.kr)

is an Assistant Professor for the Department of Communication at Yonsei University in Seoul, Korea. Her research focuses on the mass media industry and economics, audience analysis, and computer-mediated communication.

Acknowledgments

An earlier version of this paper was presented at the annual convention of National Communication Association, November 2002, New Orleans, LA.

Endnotes

1. By law, theaters in Korea are obliged to exhibit local films over 146 days per year.
2. As of May 2004, the market share of local motion pictures in Korea reached as high as 68.3%, which is one of the highest local film market share in countries other than the United States.
3. The popularity of Korean cultural products in Asian countries has been drastically increasing over the last decade. Such a phenomenon is referred as "Korean Wave."
4. An anonymous reviewer has noticed that this illustrates the difficulty of getting the theater exhibition opportunity due to a protectionist policy such as screen quota.
5. It costs even less if a rental video is shared by more than one viewer.
6. This data set was obtained from Audiovisual Business Division of Samsung, which belonged to Korea's number one conglomerate. The division shut down its business in 1999. The data set was constructed for their internal use. Although it is not public information for which we can trust the validity of the data, there is no alternative source for such information in Korea.
7. However, only a part of the movie titles had all the necessary information on all variables.
8. This cannot be shown by cross-sectional analysis.
9. Please note that these are prints, not individual films. A film may have multiple prints exported on different contracts.
10. Genres are categorized as drama, animation, action/thriller, and comedy. Production budget was excluded from the model because such information is not available for Korean films. Reliable budget data are not reported in Korea.

References

Cho, E. (1999). An economic analysis of TV program imports from Japan to Korea. *Journalism and Society, 22,* 72–101.

Dupagne, M., & Waterman, D. (1998). Determinants of US television fiction imports in western Europe. *Journal of Broadcasting & Electronic Media, 42,* 208–220.

European Audiovisual Observatory. (2004). Retrieved July 5, 2004, from http://www.obs.coe.int

Foroohar, R. (2002, May 27). Hurray for globowood; As motion picture funding, talent and audiences go global, Hollywood is no longer a place, but a state of mind. *Newsweek,* p. 51.

Fu, W. (1999). *The theory of windowing of motion pictures and empirical evidences : From theaters to home video.* Unpublished manuscript, Northwestern University, Evanston, IL.

Guback, T. H.(1969). *The international film industry.* Bloomington: Indiana University Press.

Hoskins, C., Finn, A., & McFadyen, S. (1996). Television and film in a freer international trade environment: US dominance and Canadian responses. In E. McAnany & K. Wilkinson (Eds.), *Mass media and free trade* (pp. 63–91). Austin: University of Texas Press.

Korean Film Council. (1981–2003). *Annual Review of Korean Films.* Seoul, Korea: Jib-moon-dang.

Korean Film Council. (2004a). Retrieved on July 5, 2004, from http://www.kofic.or.kr/data/kofic_data_detail.asp?page=4&p_part=&p_item=&pds_seq=89

Korean Film Council. (2004b). *Statistical data for the annual review of Korean film 2004.* Retrieved on July 5, 2004, from http://www.kofic.or.kr/attach/II-2,3,4,5.hwp

Moragas Spa, M., & Lopez, B. (2000). Decentralization processes and proximate television in Europe. In G. Wang, J. Servaes, & A. Goonasekera (Eds.), *The new communications landscape: Demystifying media globalization* (pp. 33–51). London: Routledge.

Newcomb, H. (1996). Other people's fictions: Cultural appropriation, cultural integrity, and international media strategies. In E. McAnany & K. Wilkinson (Eds.), *Mass media and free trade: NAFTA and the cltural industries* (pp. 92–109). Austin: University of Texas Press.

Noble, G. (1988). The social significance of VCR technology: TV or not TV? *The Information Society, 5,* 133–146.

Ogan, C. (1989). The worldwide cultural and economic impact of video. In M. R. Levy (Ed.), *The VCR age* (pp. 230–251). Newbury park, CA: Sage.

Schiller, H. I. (1969). *Mass communication and American empire.* New York: Kelley.

Tomlinson, J. (1996). Global experience as a consequence of modernity. In S. Braman & A. Sreberny-Mohammadi (Eds.), *Globalization, communication, and transnational civil society* (pp. 63–88). Creskill, NJ: Hampton.

Wang, G., Ku, L., & Liu, C. (2000). Local and national cultural industries: Is there life after globalization? In G. Wang, J. Servaes,

& A. Goonasekera (Eds.), *The new communications landscape: De-mystifying media globalization* (pp. 52–73). London: Routledge.

Wasko, J. (1994). *Hollywood in the information age.* Austin: University of Texas Press.

Waterman, D. (1985). Pre-recorded home video and the distribution of theatrical feature films. In E. Noam (Ed.), *Video media competition* (pp. 221–243). New York: Columbia University Press.

Waterman, D. (1988, June). World television trade: The economic effect of privatization and new technology. *Telecommunications Policy, 12*(2), 106–202.

Waterman, D. (1996, April). *World motion picture trade.* Paper presented at Northwestern University, Department of Communication Studies, Evanston, IL.

Waterman, D., & Jayakar, K. P. (2000). The competitive balance of the Italian and American film industries. *European Journal of Communication, 15,* 501–528.

Wildman, S. S. (1994). One-way flows and the economics of audience making. In J. Ettema, & D. C. Whitney (Eds.), *Audience making* (pp. 115–141). Thousand Oaks, CA: Sage.

Wildman, S. S. (1995). Trade liberalization and policy for media industries: A theoretical examination of media flows. *European Journal of Communication, 20,* 367–388.

Wildman, S. S., & Siwek, S. E. (1988). *International trade in films and television programs.* New York: Addison-Wesley.

Selling the Niche: A Qualitative Content Analysis of Cable Network Business-to-Business Advertising

■

Walter S. McDowell
University of Miami, USA

Aside from battling for the hearts and minds of audiences, cable networks also must compete for the attention of cable system operators and national advertisers. The purpose of this study was to ascertain how cable networks attempt to achieve these objectives using various niche branding strategies revealed through their business-to-business (B2B) advertising. Adopting a merged conceptual framework of niche theory and brand differentiation, a 10-month qualitative content analysis of over 200 B2B advertisements representing 62 national cable networks revealed several recurring strategies for selling the niche.

In a crowded marketplace where consumer products and services often are more similar than they are different, the need for a highly differentiated and popular brand niche is essential for financial survival. This is no truer than in the tumultuous business climate of cable program networks. In addition to battling for the hearts and minds of audiences, these networks also must compete for the attention of cable system operators and national advertisers. The purpose of this study was to ascertain how cable networks attempt to achieve these objectives using various niche branding strategies revealed through their business-to-business (B2B) advertising. To that end, I conducted a qualitative content analysis of over 200 advertisements representing 62 networks. Although there has been a considerable body of academic work on the goals, approaches, and effectiveness of consumer advertising, there has been far less research addressing B2B advertising and essentially no significant research directed at such endeavors involving the cable industry.

The focus of this study was not concerned with the persuasiveness of advertising so much as with the capacity of advertising to reveal underlying issues facing an industry at a crucial point in its history. Researchers have used advertising as a window or mirror that enables a better understanding of an external culture. By the same token, in this study, I maintained that there exists a business culture that can be understood in part by analyzing the explicit and implicit messages embedded within advertisements aimed at business professionals. For decades, researchers have focused on the revealed attitudes, beliefs, and values of advertising intended for retail consumers, but scant attention has been paid to these factors when the message has been aimed at business people. A basic assumption of this study is that the inherent message of a business advertisement will offer insight into not only the company that created the advertisement but more important, a broader insight into the industry in which the company competes.

On a longitudinal scale, this type of analysis can provide historical benchmarks for seeing changes and developments over time. One would hope that a systematic analysis of B2B advertising would reveal worthwhile information for both scholar and professional. More specific, in this work, I concentrate on niche branding strategies used by American cable networks. The master plan is to conduct an analysis approximately every 6 months. This first study included 62 national cable networks that placed advertising in one of three industry trade magazines–*Broadcasting and Cable, Advertising Age,* and *Media Week* and the Cable Advertising Bureau (CAB; 2004) Web site.

Because of the nature of the previously mentioned goals and the fact that so little prior research exists on this narrow topic, in this study, I took an exploratory posture using a qualitative content analysis methodology. Although openness is key to this type of approach, a basic conceptual framework or guiding principle was employed in collecting appropriate data. This amounted to combining salient elements of media niche theory fostered by Dimmick (2003) and brand equity theory and, more precisely, brand differentiation espoused by Keller (1993, 2003).

Address correspondence to Walter S. McDowell, School of Communication, University of Miami, Coral Gables, FL 33189. E-mail: wmcdowell@miami.edu

Background and Literature Review

Cable networks are programming services that deliver information and entertainment content by satellite to local cable television systems. The cable systems then redistribute the network programs through wires to individual residences in their local franchise areas. The number of cable networks carried by any particular cable system varies and is based on the channel capacity of the system. Newer or upgraded systems may have more than 200 channels. Cable system managers decide which cable networks will be carried. Their decisions are based on analyses of the requirements of their franchise agreement with the local community they serve, on their own economic needs and abilities, and on local audience needs and wishes.

From an economic perspective, cable program networks compete for (a) distribution (usually referred to as *carriage*) on cable systems, (b) subscriber fees paid by the system operators, and (c) commercial revenue from national advertisers. These factors work in concert whereby more distribution translates ideally into bigger audiences (i.e., higher ratings), which in turn translate into higher subscriber fees and higher commercial rates (Carroll & Howard, 1998; National Cable and Telecommunications Association, 2004).

The decade of the 1990s witnessed a stunning increase in the number of cable program networks. The 1992 Cable Consumer Protection and Competition Act stimulated the growth of new multichannel delivery systems, most notably direct to home satellite services (Carlin, 2002). With these new policies in place, the cable industry, for the first time, experienced the threat of competition. The result has been a dramatic increase in the number of national and regional cable program networks. Additionally, the deregulation elements of the 1996 Telecommunications Act stimulated expansion from analog to digital tiers to accommodate more program diversity. According to the Federal Communications Commission (2004), in 1994, most cable operators offered 30 to 53 analog video channels. Today, after investing billions of dollars to rebuild and upgrade systems, operators offer on average 70 analog channels and 120 digital video channels. Coinciding with this onslaught of new program competition has been a steady deterioration in prime time audiences watching the conventional broadcast networks. Since the early 1990s, these networks have lost over half of their prime audiences to alternative media including cable and satellite multichannel offerings. This audience defection spurred the growth of advertising on cable networks and local systems (Bianco, 2004; CAB, 2004). However, in terms of commercial rates, cable still struggles to achieve comparable cost-per-thousand (CPM) pricing with conventional television. This "CPM gap" has frustrated cable networks for years and reflects the pervasive notion among media buyers that cable remains the struggling stepchild of the established broadcast networks. Season after season, despite dramatic and continued losses in audience ratings, broadcast television is able to raise CPMs almost effortlessly. Cable, on the other hand, struggles to play catch-up (Grimes, 2004; Higgins, 2004).

Although this unprecedented increase in the number and diversity of cable programming options has been welcome news for American audiences, it has caused some sleepless nights for both broadcast and cable network executives. The core problem is that audience viewing has not kept pace with the increase in available channels. That is, during the past decade, whereas the number of available channels has nearly tripled, the increase in the number of channels actually viewed has been modest at best. According to Nielsen Media Research (2003), for homes with access to at least 100 channels, the average number of channels actually viewed was only 14.8. Furthermore, in homes capable of receiving 200 or more channels, actual viewership climbed to a paltry 18.9 channels. Looking back a full decade to 1994, which provided less than half the number of channels available today, the average number of channels viewed per household was 10. This is a classic example of the law of diminishing returns wherein more choice has not translated proportionately into more channels viewed. The bottom line consequence is a zero-sum market, meaning that while the number of brands within a product category increases, the number of potential customers for that product category remains unchanged. Therefore, the only way for a brand to attract more customers is to take market share away from direct competitors (Keller, 1993; Porter, 1996). Against this backdrop of a zero-sum market, cable and broadcast networks compete.

The objectives of B2B advertising initiated by the cable networks for the past few years are fairly obvious:

1. Persuade cable system operators to pay higher per-subscriber fees for existing programming. This will result in a direct increase in revenue for the network. Note that the networks typically offer opportunities to insert local commercials (called *adjacencies*) to offset the burden on system operators of increased fees.
2. Persuade cable system operators to accept carriage of a new network or move the network to a more attractive tier (such as basic or enhanced basic). Presumably, this will result in more potential viewers for a network and more satisfied subscribers for the system operator.
3. Persuade national advertisers to purchase commercial time on the networks. This will result in a direct increase in revenue for the network.

Given these three intertwined objectives, the real challenge for the networks and the topic of this study is to create distinctive selling strategies. Schultz and Barnes (1999) maintained that "strategies flow from objectives and are views of how the objectives might be achieved or the alternatives the organization might follow" (p. 106). Once a network has adopted a niche in terms of the program content and intended audience, it must communicate this information to potential viewers and the business community.

B2B Marketing and Advertising

Understanding the historical background of B2B marketing and advertising can be confusing due to changes in terminology and jargon over the years. For several decades, the term *industrial marketing* was the preferred label for this type of activity. An example would be Bellizzi and Lehrer (1983) who advocated "better industrial advertising" (p. 19). Over time, however, the nomenclature of *B2B* has taken precedence in most published research and commentary. Furthermore, within media circles, the term *sales promotion* (as opposed to *audience promotion*) is a common synonym. Along these lines, Adams (2002) reminded media observers and researchers that although the most visible forms of marketing and promotion are aimed at the general public to attract audiences, there are other target groups within the business community that are equally important to most media companies. In addition to launching major marketing efforts to attract and hold audiences, broadcast and cable networks use similar marketing tools to persuade potential advertisers and program distributors to do business with them. Within the context of the cable industry, consumer advertising would be typified by messages aimed at subscribers, whereas B2B advertising would include primarily messages aimed at advertisers and cable system operators.

B2B advertising is different from consumer advertising in terms of objectives. Consequently, different persuasion strategies are employed (Hartley & Patti, 1988). For example, a cable network such as CNN might place an advertisement in *TV Guide* with the goal of persuading audiences to tune in during an upcoming presidential election campaign. The same network might also place an advertisement in *Advertising Age* with the goal of persuading national advertisers and media buyers to purchase commercials during coverage of the campaign.

Substantive and stylistic differences between consumer and B2B advertising can be understood better by paying attention to the target audiences involved. For mass media, consumer advertising is aimed primarily at the general public segmented often into narrower demographic or lifestyle groupings. B2B advertising, however, concentrates typically on a much smaller audience of business decision makers possessing esoteric knowledge.

The idea that the intended receivers of a message are assumed to have unique competencies falls in line with what Lindlof (1995) and other communication scholars have called an *interpretive community*, meaning that the members share a common understanding of what is read, viewed, or heard. In many respects, these audience groups can be perceived as small cultures existing within or overlapping with a larger culture. Indeed, when examining the jargon of cable network advertising, one cannot help but sense that this communication can only be understood adequately within the subculture of the media business community.

To some extent, every group has a unique culture that is shaped by its members' shared history and experiences. Schein (1992) maintained that even businesses have a "corporate culture" in that

> At the heart of every organization there is a paradigm of interrelated and unconscious shared assumptions which directs how members think, feel and act. ... They govern, amongst other things, what the organization feels its fundamental mission to be, how it perceives its environment, and the strategies it judges as appropriate. (p. 5)

Additionally, this corporate culture includes not only the paradigms of a specific company but also the paradigms of the larger industry in which the company operates. Consequently, the following content analysis took on an ethnographic orientation wherein I needed to be familiar with attitudes and behaviors of the business culture under examination. Furthermore, I needed to recognize the media context in which these B2B messages are placed. There is considerable empirical evidence that supports the idea that media context (i.e., the advertising medium in which the advertisement is placed such as a trade magazine) can be an important situational factor influencing how messages are comprehended by readers. Hence, B2B advertisements appear generally in what De Pelsmacker, Geuens, and Anckaert (2002), called "context-congruent" media. That is, advertisements are placed in an editorial environment that addresses similar business interests.

Content Analysis of Print Advertising

For decades, content analysis has been used as a methodological tool for understanding all types of mass media. Most content analyses are quantitative in nature, involving the counting of instances of certain types of messages or techniques used to convey messages. However, there is also justification for qualitative analysis emphasizing the meanings associated with the messages rather than with the number of times message variables occur. Furthermore, qualitative research encourages an inductive approach to understanding wherein theory is derived from observations rather imposed onto observations. The goals of this grounded theory approach are to propose patterns, themes, or shared categories.

Content analysis in advertising has taken several forms, ranging from examinations of compositional form and mechanics focusing primarily on the effectiveness of advertisements on readers to more abstract interpretations focusing on underlying social and cultural themes. One can divide these studies further into consumer and B2B groupings. On the business side, most studies have dwelled on the notion of advertisement effectiveness on targeted readers. In many cases, content analyses have been integrated with surveys to assess the persuasiveness of print advertising. Variables such as layout style, headline composition, color, length of copy, and vocabulary have been utilized (Chamblee & Sandler, 1992; Korgaonkar, Bellenger, & Smith, 1986; Leigh, 1994; Lohtia, Johnson, & Aab, 1995; Naccarato & Neuendorf, 1998). Persuasion approaches also can vary along lines of emotion and reason. For instance, Turley, Kelley, and Scott (1997) found significant differences in message appeals wherein advertising directed toward consumers (or audiences) takes advantage of emotional approaches, but B2B advertising tends to focus on the use of information presented in a logical and rational format.

Moving to a more interpretative or cultural approach, essentially all published content analysis work has been confined to consumer magazine advertising. For example, Busby and Leichy (1993) conducted a longitudinal study of feminism and advertising in women's magazines over a 30-year period. Another example would be Humphrey and Schuman (1984) who looked at the changing portrayal of Blacks in general interest magazines. Regrettably, researchers using this more qualitative technique have ignored B2B advertising. Specifically in the area of electronic media, Eastman's (2000) book-length appraisal of all scholarly work dealing with media promotion found no B2B (or sales promotion) advertising research of any merit. Literature searches of studies that may have surfaced since the book's publication yielded a similar void. Therefore, in terms of conceptual approach and methodology, this qualitative study of cable network B2B advertising breaks new ground.

Within the sphere of qualitative research, there has been a growing trend in media studies to adopt a "hybrid" approach of capitalizing on the advantages of both qualitative and quantitative paradigms. Gunter (2000) asserted that increasingly, researchers are attempting to develop complex thematic analysis of transcripts that combine interpretive sensitivity with systematic coding. In this study, I attempted to take this route using a content analysis technique commonly called *constant comparative*, which I elaborate in the Methodology section.

Theoretical and Conceptual Underpinnings

No content analysis can begin without some type of conceptual framing. Depending on the objectives and prior research on the topic, the degree of framing will vary. Recognizing the aforementioned highly competitive environment for cable networks, in this study, I incorporated salient aspects of niche theory and brand equity as framing tools. Dimmick (2003) offered his theory of the niche as a means of explaining modern media competition and coexistence whereby to survive and prosper, a media business must adapt and evolve through its marketing environment. According to Dimmick, a niche is fundamentally a relation between an individual element and its surrounding "population." Although this population can be biological, sociocultural, or economic, the shared dynamic is the competition for scarce resources. In the case of cable networks, the competition is for channel carriage, subscriber fees, and advertising dollars. The ultimate goal is to cultivate a niche that prospers without exhausting its energies fighting too many similar competitors for the same limited resources.

Within this context, Dimmick (2003) emphasized the notion of coexistence. Rather than competing head to head with all brands in a generic product category, niches are created that in some ways overlap with competitors but in other ways do not. The degree of overlap is called *niche breadth*. Dimmick (2003) asserted that "in short, these populations have evolved differences in niche that limit the inter-population competition for resources and allows them to coexist" (p. 38). In summary, similarity in niches leads to strong competition, whereas niche differentiation leads to coexistence. For a cable network wanting to obtain greater distribution and capture more national advertising dollars, it first must recognize the competitive environment and then make shrewd marketing maneuvers that place it in the most advantageous position or niche. The ideal niche maximizes revenue while at the same time minimizes the costs of battling competitors over system distribution and advertiser budgets.

A second framing device I utilized for this study is brand equity theory with its similar emphasis on differentiation. According to Keller (1993), brand names communicate attributes and meaning that are designed to enhance the value of a branded product beyond its functional value. Brand equity is essentially the power of a brand to be recognized as uniquely superior in customer value. Knowledge of a brand can be divided into two domains, namely, brand awareness and brand image. Awareness deals with basic familiarity with the brand name, whereas image addresses the various meanings associated with that name.

In addition to evoking brand images that are seen as valuable to the customer, a successful brand also must be perceived as truly different. This characteristic has been called brand differentiation. Strong, positive associations are of little consequence if the same associations can be attributed to several competing brands. Porter (1996) of the Harvard Business School in his seminal commentary on business strategy echoed the same thought when he asserted that "Competitive strategy is about being different. It means deliberately choosing a different set of activities to deliver a unique mix of value" (p. 64).

In the same vein, researchers in marketing have long been aware of the inherent problems of measuring simple consumer "satisfaction" in that consumers are satisfied with the performance of most brands, and therefore, one brand becomes an equivalent substitute for several others. Going back to terminology coined by Dimmick (2003), one can say that this substitution phenomenon can be defined as the niche breadth of one brand overlapping too much the perimeters of one or more brands competing for the same limited resources.

When looking at brand differentiation, Keller (2003) recommended an analysis of what he called "points of parity" and "points if difference." As the names imply, *points of parity* would consist of a list of derived associations that are common to several competing brands, whereas *points of difference* would include a list of associations that are unique to a particular brand. Often, these brand differences are based on intangible rather than tangible characteristics. In fact, Keller (2003) insisted that "in many situations intangible image associations may be the only way to distinguish different brands in a product category" (p. 5). For winning audiences, this emphasis on intangibles can be quite effective, but, as will be revealed in this study, national advertisers and media buyers rely heavily on hard data to substantiate abstract selling propositions. As a consequence, media B2B advertising, in general, lacks the more emotional puffery found in consumer advertising.

For a cable network wanting to reach potential national advertisers, brand differentiation comes into play when media buyers assess the value of placing commercials in various media brands. If a brand cannot differentiate itself from a group of other equivalent substitutes, then pricing becomes the predominant negotiating weapon. In this situation, the buyer has the upper hand. However, if a brand is perceived as uniquely valuable, pricing becomes an advantage to the seller. In other words, the highly differentiated brand has found a niche whereby it can coexist with competitors operating in the same media arena. Furthermore, in the battle for system carriage, a highly differentiated network brand will increase the odds of being chosen over rival networks.

Synthesizing the previously mentioned constructs of niche theory and brand differentiation, I can form the conceptual backdrop for this study. Dispensing with theoretical jargon, the basic research question can be stated as follows: What strategies do cable networks use in their B2B advertising to communicate unique brand value?

Methodology

Approach and Design

Because the objective of this study was not enumeration but rather explication, the most appropriate methodology for achieving the goals of this study was a qualitative content analysis. According to Lindlof (1995), constant comparative is a well-recognized qualitative content analysis technique designed to organize and consolidate data into parsimonious groupings. Execution involves four basic stages:

1. Comparative assignment of incidents to categories.
2. Elaboration and reinforcement of categories.
3. Searching for relations and themes among categories.
4. Simplifying and integrating data into a coherent structure.

Procedures

From May 2003 through February 2004, a census was conducted of all advertising supported, cable network display advertisements appearing in *Broadcasting and Cable, Advertising Age,* and *MediaWeek.* For the sake of continuity, I wanted to analyze networks that held a similar advertising based business model. Therefore, advertisements for commercial free or subscription-based networks such Turner Movie Classics and HBO were not included in the study. Within this time frame, in addition to conventional display advertising, *Advertising Age* produced a special cable supplement ("Cable 2003," 2003) featuring scores of cable networks. The publication provided a standardized full-page advertisement layout that included space modules for text (approximately 1,000 words), photographs, a program schedule, and a target audience descriptor. Although giving the initial appearance of an item created by the magazine staff, in fact, each page was a purchased advertisement with all copy and graphics supplied by the sponsoring networks. The only creative restriction was the strict page layout. Also, the CAB (2004) provides a Web site offering information about all its member program networks. As with the special supplement in *Advertising Age,* the CAB provides interested media buyers with a "Cable Network Information" section featuring a modular presentation page format consisting of categories titled "Introduction," "Value to advertisers," "Network Viewer

Profile," and "Advertising Contacts." The individual networks provide copy and graphics. For tabulation purposes, each dedicated computer page was considered an advertisement along with the more conventional hard copy trade magazine display advertisements.

Tabulation was based on unique advertisements for each network. That is, repeated advertisements with the identical copy and graphics were not included. In total, 233 unique advertisements representing 62 cable networks were analyzed (see the Appendix).

A graduate assistant and I began assessing each advertisement for explicit or implicit evidence of niche branding strategies that attempted to portray the network as possessing valuable and unique characteristics. Aside from these ground rules, a constant comparative technique of sifting through the advertisement copy several times was employed.

Results

Approaching the advertisement copy using the niche/brand differentiation mind-set, one overriding framework or grid emerged rather quickly as a means of organizing the data. The first meaningful way to organize the network data was to recognize the fact that all 233 advertisements addressed two primary topics: audiences and program content. Furthermore, these two dimensions seemed to vary considerably in terms of their intended reach.

Two Dimensions of Niche Breadth

Dimmick's (2003) niche-breadth concept was the incentive for generating Table 1. Here the 62 participating networks were broken down according to (a) the demographic breadth of the network's targeted audience and (b) the breadth or diversity of program content. The matrix reveals, in a very rudimentary way, a variety of approaches, thus dispelling the notion that all cable networks strive for essentially the same size niche. For example, the target audience for the USA network (lower right quadrant) appears to be extremely broad, offering a variety of program genres

aimed at different content preferences. On the other hand, the Soap Net (upper left quadrant) channel offers media buyers a highly targeted female audience and a narrow program format consisting mainly of repurposed soap episodes from the broadcast networks. A middle ground would be networks that exhibit a moderate breadth on both dimensions or opposing breadth characteristics in which one appears narrow and the other appears wide. An example here would be the Weather Channel (lower left quadrant), which offers a narrowly defined program format but aims at a wide heterogeneous audience.

Differentiation Strategies

In the second round of analysis, I looked at differentiation strategies. The following list presents the most commonly revealed strategies and a brief definition. With the goal of creating reasonably exhaustive and mutually exclusive categories, eight salient areas emerged from the raw data. Table 2 provides tabulation by specific network. In most cases, a network used a combination of strategies:

1. *Affluence:* Emphasis on the statistical information concerning income and buying power of an audience ("upscale," "professional," and "sophisticated"). This has become am important selling point for cable in differentiating itself from the "poorer" broadcast networks.

2. *Targeted sex/age demographics (underserved ethnic/racial):* Emphasis on statistical information ("The first network for men," "Dedicated to young American Hispanics"). Conceding that in terms of overall household delivery, individual cable outlets rarely break a 2 rating, the best strategy is to concentrate on narrow attractive demographics. Additionally, when even these numbers appear modest, many networks stress ratings growth potential ("fastest growing," "ratings on the rise," and "building on the momentum").

3. *Targeted personality or lifestyle:* Emphasis on some statistical data but also general circumstantial evidence ("Our viewers are a different breed ... Savvy. Curious. Active"; "Passionate in their Pursuits"). Here there is an attempt to take a closer look at the intangibles of an audience.

Table I. Network Matrix Organized by Breadth of Target Audience and Breadth of Program Content

Narrow Audience/Narrow Content	Narrow Audience/Broad Content
Soap Net, Golf, CNBC, Bloomberg, Cartoon, Fuse, MTV, VH1, Speed, Toon, XY.TV, CMT, Great American Country, Sci Fi	BET, Fine Living, Galavision, Nickelodeon, Mun2, Lifetime, We, Oxygen, Spike, Style, Fine Living, Trio

Broad Audience/Narrow Content	Broad Audience/Broad Content
Weather, CNN Headline, CNN, MSNBC, Bloomberg, Fox News, Animal Planet, Comedy Central, Court TV, Fox Sports, ESPN, History, Travel, Food, Game Show, Biography, HGTV, Do-It-Yourself, Outdoors, Outdoor Life	USA, ABC Family, AMC, A&E, Discovery, FX, National Geographic, E!, Hallmark, Nick-at-Night, TLC, WGN, TV Land, TNT, Bravo

Table 2. Network Differentiation Strategies Derived From Advertisement Messages

Strategy	Cable Network
Affluence	Weather, MSNBC, Bloomberg, CNN, CNN Headline CNBC, Style, Fine Living, E!, Speed, Bravo, Biography, Hallmark, Fox Sports, Comedy, TNT, USA, ESPN, Nick-at-Nite, MTV, National Geographic, Oxygen, HGTV
Targeted sex/age demographics (or underserved ethnic/racial)	FX, Weather, Bloomberg, CNN, Fox, A&E, AMC, Style, Spike, Court TV, Food, Fine Living, DIY, CMT, Cartoon, Speed, CNN Headline, BET, Galavision, Sci Fi, Bravo, ABC Family, Hallmark, Great American Country, Game Show, Fuse, Fox Sports, Discovery, Comedy, TNT, TBS, USA, ESPN, TV Land, Nick-at-Nite, Toon/Disney, TLC, VH1, We, WGN, History, Lifetime, MTV, National Geographic, Oxygen, Nickelodeon, Trio, XY.TV, Outdoors, HGTV
Targeted personality/lifestyle	Weather, Bloomberg, Fox News, CNBC, AMC, Style, Fine Living, CMT, Speed, CNN Headline, Biography, Golf, Fuse, VH1, MTV, We. Travel, Lifetime, Oxygen, Nickelodeon, Trio, Outdoor Life, Outdoors, XY.TV
Unique audience behavior	Weather, MSNBC, CNN, Fox News, CNBC, AMC, Spike, Court TV, Food, DIY, Cartoon, Soap Net, Sci Fi , Animal Planet, Biography, Hallmark, Golf, Game Show, Fox Sports, Discovery, Nick-at-Night, Toon/Disney, Travel, History, Lifetime, National Geographic, Nickelodeon, Trio, XY.TV, HGTV
Best off-network hits	Hallmark, TBS, WGN, Nick-at-Nite, USA, TNT
Original/first-run programming	FX, A&E, AMC, Spike, Court TV, Food, E!, CMT, Cartoon, Speed, BET, Galavision, Sci Fi, Bravo, ABC Family, Hallmark, Great American Country, Golf, Game Show, Discovery, Comedy, TBS, USA, TLC, VH1, We, History, Lifetime, National Geographic, Oxygen, Trio
Reputation	FX, MSNBC, CNN, Fox News, CNBC, A&E, CMT, Bravo, ABC Family, Hallmark, Comedy, TNT, TBS, ESPN, Nick-at-Nite, Toon/Disney, WGN, Oxygen, Trio

4. *Unique audience behavior:* Emphasis on audience behavior or attitudinal research beyond basic ratings and demographics such as length of tune-in, Internet usage, loyalty, and satisfaction ("Attracts early adopters—first on the block," " ... among the highest in commercial recall"). Here the network tries to appreciate the practical needs of advertisers placing commercials buys.

5. *The Best off-network hits:* Emphasis on program inventories of broadcast network hits ("Prime Time in the daytime"). Some networks remain highly successful as merely "rerun" vehicles, but this reinforces a long-standing bias that the cable industry is attempting to overcome.

6. *Original/first-run programming:* In opposition to the preceding rerun imagery, this category emphasizes the investment made in programming that cannot be found elsewhere (" ... a great passion and investment behind our vision," "Critically acclaimed"). It is interesting to note that the broadcast networks always air original programming but rarely brag about it.

7. *Reputation* ("risk taking," "Bold," "cutting-edge," "most trusted"): Mostly well-established networks use this strategy that focuses more on intangibles rather than quantitative ratings data.

Discussion

The strategies revealed in this B2B content analysis provide a mosaic of the industry experiencing an ever-increasing number of competitors fighting over the lim-ited zero-sum resources of audiences, system channels, and advertising dollars. As a means for uncovering the typical niche-brand strategies of cable networks, this qualitative content analysis was a good first step in adding new knowledge and, more important, refining a methodology. By adopting the procedures and categories developed in this work, future studies have the option of taking a more quantitative approach, incorporating multiple coders to enhance efficiency and reliability.

When conducting a content analysis, it is difficult sometimes to decide where the Results section should end and the discussion section should begin. In this case, there are items deserving comment for the very reason that they were not found. First, despite allegations of ruthless competition among cable networks for advertising budgets and system carriage, their external B2B advertising was rather polite. There was little mention of direct competitors by name. As alluded to earlier, this could be construed as a deliberate niche approach in that it nurtures coexistence rather than competition. The one major exception was the genre of 24-hr news channels (CNN. FOX, and MSNBC) that went at each other with a vengeance.

A second related consideration is that the cable industry, as a whole, is still attempting to overcome the CPM gap with the broadcast networks. Returning to Keller's (2003) diagnostic tools of points of parity versus points of difference, most of the revealed differentiation strategies presented in Table 2 share a common theme of implicit comparisons with their over-the-air network competitors.

Some depicted cable as similar to the broadcast networks—such as bragging about expensive, first run, star-powered content—whereas other strategies depicted cable as dissimilar to the broadcast networks, such as emphasizing highly targeted audience segments and daring, innovative program content. Although seldom disclosing the rival broadcast networks by name, there was a discernable undercurrent in the advertisement copy that reflected a fixation with the supposed undeserved success of the broadcast networks. Of course, several major cable networks such as TBS, WGN, TNT, and Nick-at-night continue to be in the off-network business. Also, the current broadcast network practice of repurposing programs onto cable (such as recent episodes of NBC's, *Law and Order* series airing on several cable networks) runs counter to this brand-niche strategy and over the long term may hurt the cable industry's crusade to make advertisers believe that cable deserves to charge premium rates. Perhaps the most telling nonobservation from this study was that during the same time span, there was essentially no B2B advertising addressing similar marketing issues placed by the broadcast networks. In terms of advertisement count, the score was 233 to 0.

As mentioned earlier, the one obvious exception to the previously mentioned polite marketing environment was 24-hr cable news. Instead of making inferences about the shortcomings of broadcast news, these three cable combatants attacked each other by name and with a certain zest.

Perhaps the problem for cable is more about arithmetic than anything else. How can 62 cable networks capture 62 highly differentiated brand niches? Overlap and redundancy seem inevitable. This marketing shortfall has serious implications for the cable industry in that media buyers will continue to see only a small handful of networks as indispensable buys. The rest can be substituted readily among an array of undifferentiated brand competitors. Furthermore, cable networks must deal with the often irrational preference among advertisers to choose broadcast television over cable.

Limitations

All qualitative research suffers from the potential problems of subjectivity and reliability. By design, this study was intended to take an inductive approach and allow observations to emerge unencumbered by a predetermined set of analytic categories. Calculations of intercoder reliability in a quantitative sense were not appropriate, but this does not have to be the case in future studies. Now that the much of the groundwork has been accomplished, subsequent rounds of advertisement analysis might be more structured, using multiple coders and stricter protocols for examining data.

Another limitation is that B2B trade publication advertising is not the only means networks use to communicate with cable systems and advertisers. Selling still involves personal contact via letters, phone calls, e-mails, and meetings. I do not claim this study to be the one definitive examination of cable marketing strategies.

Future Research

In addition to continuing this project, there are several related areas ripe for nonproprietary research. In particular, a comprehensive audience analysis of shared viewing among networks would help define network niches by audience behavior rather than program content or gross audience ratings. In the same vein, an analysis of channel repertoires among cable audiences would further help researchers to conceptualize a brand niche. For many years, Arbitron has provided this type of shared audience analysis for its radio clients (e.g., cume duplication), but television and cable professionals are only just beginning to recognize the value of such information. For a cable network, such information probably would find its way into its B2B advertising as means of further selling the niche.

Walter McDowell

(wmcdowell@miami.edu)

is an Assistant Professor at the University Of Miami School of Communication. His research interests include media brand management and audience research methodologies. Before entering academia, McDowell worked in commercial broadcasting for over 20 years.

References

Adams, W. J. (2002). Marketing to affiliates, buyers, and advertisers. In S. T. Eastman; D. A Ferguson, & R. Klein (Ed.), *Promotion and marketing for broadcasting, cable and the web* (pp. 195–210). Boston: Focal Press.

Bellizzi, J. A., & Lehrer, J. (1983). Developing better industrial advertising. *Industrial Marketing Management, 12,* 19–23.

Bianco, A. (2004, July 12). The vanishing mass market. *Business Week,* p. 60.

Busby, L. J., & Leichy, G. (1993). Feminism and advertising in traditional and non-traditional women's magazines 1950s–1980s. *Journalism Quarterly, 70,* 247–264.

Cable 2003 [Special Supplement]. (2003, May 19). *Advertising Age, 74,* pp. C1–C98.

Cable Advertising Bureau. (2004). *Cable network profiles.* Retrieved from http://www.onetvworld.org/?module=displaystory&story_id=704&format=html

Carlin, T. (2002). Direct broadcast satellites. In A. Grant & J. Meadows (Eds.), *Communication technology update* (8th ed., pp. 83–104). Oxford, England: Focal Press.

Carroll, S. L., & Howard, H. (1998). The economics of the cable industry. In A. Alexander, J. Owens, & R. Carveth, *Media economics theory and practice* (pp. 152–174). Mahwah, NJ: Lawrence Erlbaum Associates, Inc.

Chamblee, R., & Sandler, D. M. (1992). Business to business advertising: Which layout style works best? *Journal of Advertising Research, 32,* 39–47.

De Pelsmacker, P., Geuens, M., & Anckaert, P. (2002). Media context and advertising effectiveness: The role of context appreciation and context/ad similarity. *Journal of Advertising, 31,* 49–63.

Dimmick, J. W. (2003). Media competition and coexistence. In *The theory of the niche.* Mahwah, NJ: Lawrence Erlbaum Associates, Inc.

Eastman, S. T. (2000). *Research in media promotion.* Mahwah, NJ: Lawrence Erlbaum Associates, Inc.

Federal Communications Commission. (2004). *Annual assessment of the status of competition in the market for the delivery of video programming* (MB Docket No. 03–172). Washington, DC: Author.

Grimes, J. W. (2004). Cable television. In C. Warner & J. Buchman (Eds.), *Media selling. Broadcast, cable, print, and interactive* (3rd ed.). Ames: Iowa State University Press.

Gunter, B. (2000). *Media research methods.* London: Sage.

Hartley, S. W., & Patti, C. H. (1988). Evaluating business-to-business advertising: A comparison of objectives and results. *Journal of Advertising Research, 28*(2), 21–27.

Higgins, J. M. (2004, March 29). The great divide. Why is the CPM gap widening if cable keeps grabbing viewers from broadcast? *Broadcasting and Cable, 134,* p. 1.

Humphrey, R., & Schuman, H. (1984). The portrayal of Blacks in magazine advertisements: 1950–1982. *Public Opinion Quarterly, 48,* 551–563.

Keller, K. L. (1993). Conceptualizing, measuring, and managing customer-based brand equity. *Journal of Marketing, 57,* 1–22.

Keller, K. L. (2003). *Strategic brand management: Building, measuring and managing brand equity.* Upper Saddle River, NJ: Prentice Hall.

Korgaonkar, P. K., Bellenger, D., & Smith, A. E. (1986). Successful industrial advertising campaigns. *Industrial Marketing Management, 15,* 123–128.

Leigh, J. H. (1994). The use of figures of speech in print ad headlines. *Journal of Advertising, 23,* 17–33.

Lindlof, T. R. (1995). *Qualitative communication research methods.* Thousand Oaks, CA: Sage.

Lohtia, R., Johnston, W. J., & Aab, L. (1995). Business-to-business advertising. What are the dimensions of an effective print ad? *Industrial Marketing Management, 24,* 369–378.

Naccarato, J. L., & Neuendorf, K. A. (1998). Content analysis as a predictive methodology: Recall, readership, and evaluations of business to business print advertising. *Journal of Advertising Research, 38,* 19–34.

National Cable and Telecommunications Association. (2004). *Industry overview.* Retrieved from the National Cable and Telecommunications Association Web site: http://wwwncta.com.

Nielsen Media Research. (2003). *Annual report on television.* New York: Author.

Porter, M. (1996, November–December). What is strategy? *Harvard Business Review, 74*(6), 61–78.

Schein, E. H. (1992). *Organizational culture and leadership.* San Francisco: Jossey-Bass.

Schultz, D. E., & Barnes, B. E. (1999). *Strategic brand communication campaigns.* Lincolnwood, IL: NTC Business Books.

Telecommunications Act of 1996, Pub. LA. No. 104-104, 110 Stat. 56 (1996).

Turley, L. W., Kelly, S. W., & Scott, W. (1997). A comparison of advertising content: Business to business versus consumer services. *Journal of Advertising, 26,* 39–49.

Appendix Participating Cable Networks and Number of Unique Advertisements

Network	No. Advertisements	Network	No. Advertisements	Network	No. Advertisements
ABC Family	5	ESPN	3	Nickelodeon	2
Animal Planet	1	Fox News	3	Outdoor Channel	2
AMC	7	Fox Sports	7	Outdoor Life	4
A&E	7	Fine Living	2	Oxygen	4
Bravo	5	Food	5	Sci Fi	6
Biography	3	Fuse	4	Soap Net	1
BET	4	FX	3	Speed	3
Bloomberg	2	Galavision	2	Spike	1
CNN	8	Game Show Network	4	Style	1
CNBC	2	Golf Channel	3	TLC	2
Comedy Central	4	Great American Country	1	Toon/Disney	2
CMT	3	Hallmark	7	Travel	1
Court TV	5	History	4	VH1	5
Cartoon	4	HGTV	5	Weather	5
Discovery	7	Lifetime	10	We	8
ESPN	3	MTV	4	WGN	4
Do-It-Yourself	3	Mun2	2	XY.TV	1
E!	3	National Geographic	3		

Radio Station Innovation and Risk Taking: A Survey of Programmers and General Managers

■

John W. Owens
University of Cincinnati, USA

Francesca Dillman Carpentier
Arizona State University, USA

We conducted a survey of radio station program directors and general managers to explore the perception and role of innovation within radio programming and the key factors that influence this perception. In the study, we found that, in general, programmers and general managers perceive little innovation in programming except at their own stations. Results also indicate perceptions that more risk taking is needed in radio programming, that risk taking is essential for the financial health of a station, that increased artist diversity and an innovative music rotation influence the perception of innovation at the station level, and that too many commercials are being placed within an average hour of programming.

We are getting to the point where many radio companies are beginning to create a company template for each format. The big loser is the listener, who more and more these days receives generic programming with little innovation. (Guy Zapoleon, Houston-based media consultant [McCoy, 2002, p. E-1])

In 1996, the radio industry began a period of incredible change. The passage of the Telecommunications Act of 1996 (Leeper, 2000), which eliminated national ownership caps and allowed a single company to own up to eight radio stations in a market, led to a flurry of station buying. In 1996 alone, 2,066 radio station transactions were completed, and by the end of 1998, the number of radio station owners had dropped by 11.7% (McConnell, 1998).

The effects of this legislation have been far reaching. From an economic perspective, the industry has flourished. In 1990, the largest radio group (CapCities/ABC) billed about $190 million, but in 2000, the largest group (Clear Channel) brought in over $3.7 billion in advertising revenue (Duncan's American Radio, 2001). In addition, U.S. advertising spending on radio increased from $13.5 billion in 1997 to $19.2 billion in 2000, a 43% increase in just 4 years (Coen, 2001). A poor performing U.S. economy

contributed to a weak advertising market in 2001, as total radio sales dropped 7.4% to $17.9 billion (Coen, 2002). However, radio appears to have weathered this economic storm nicely. Advertising sales have grown each month through September of 2002, placing the industry year-to-date growth rate at 4% (McClellan, 2002). In addition, analysts have predicted that radio will see a 10% growth in advertising sales over the next 4 years ("U.S. Advertising Market Predicted," 2002).

Similar to other consolidated industries, radio groups have benefited from their economies of scale to become more efficient in their organizational structure. Stations under the same corporate banner often share music libraries, consolidate sales efforts for local "clusters," link contesting between markets, and even share general management to positively impact the bottom line (Petrozzello, 1996a, 1996b).

However, radio listenership has not followed this same upward trend. According to industry analyst Duncan (1999), total radio listening has declined by 12% since 1990. Arbitron's Summer 2002 measure of weekly time spent listening for persons 12 and over was just over 20 hr (Arbitron, 2002a; Bachman, 2002). This represents a 13% decrease since 1994 when the average person spent about 23 hr per week with radio (Bachman, 2002). Although the proliferation of media choices for the consumer has certainly contributed to this decline, some have argued that

Address correspondence to John W. Owens, Electronic Media Division–CCM, University of Cincinnati, P.O. Box 210003, Cincinnati, OH 45221–0003. E-mail: owensjw@uc.edu

the audience may be reacting to an industry that lacks an incentive to innovate in its most public area: on-air programming.

Concerns about the impact of consolidation on radio programming quality and diversity have been around since 1996, but a few signs seem to point to an increase in the intensity of such complaints. Open criticism of radio programming from analysts and radio professionals floods today's popular and trade press (Bednarski, 2001; Block, 2002; Browning, 2002; Graybow, 2002). In addition, U.S. lawmakers continue to cast a critical eye on the radio industry, its programming, and the legislation that paved the way for the present state of consolidation (Pfister, 2004).

However, very little primary data is available from the people that design and shape radio formats on a daily basis. In this study, we sought to expand the work of a previous pilot project to more fully understand the opinions of radio station programmers and managers about the state of station programming in this era of consolidation.

The Concern Over "Sameness"

As Croteau and Hoynes (2001) stated in their assessment of the present day media business, "homogenization can be the unintentional outcome of companies minimizing risk and maximizing profits. ... [T]he frequent result is very little innovation and a great deal of imitation" (p. 153). Former Federal Communications Commission commissioner Tristani (1998) was concerned about consolidation's impact on radio programming "sameness" when she said, "Eventually, the danger is that with national play lists, nationally syndicated programming, and outsourced news, everything ends up sounding the same" (p. 3). Moreover, Graybow (2002) cited radio professionals who believe potential audience members are choosing to download their music rather than listen to radio because they are bored by the lack of new music on the airwaves.

There is certainly anecdotal evidence that listeners perceive a lack of diversity in radio programming. In 1998, Capitol Cities/ABC bought KREV in Minneapolis from Cargill Communications. After Capitol Cities/ABC changed the format of the station from progressive rock to heavy metal, a group of local fans of "REV" organized and formed the nonprofit Americans for Radio Diversity (ARD). According to Jerry Wilker (Reece, 1998), ARD's president, "the mega-media corporations coming in and buying up stations have destroyed radio localism ... not to mention that it has really made radio bland" (p. 70). A similar protest group formed in Hawaii when an alternative rock station was removed from the air (Fisher, 1998).

Huntemann (1999) argued that large conglomerates that are driven to maximize profit and stock value do not serve the public properly. Indeed, Huntemann (1999) argued that trends such as regional program directors, sat-

ellite-delivered shows/formats, and the growth of syndicated programming have resulted in "a marked decrease in airplay for local talent and community tastes" (p. 400). However, not all evaluations of radio station consolidation paint such a gloomy portrait of its impact.

Product Variety

According to Stoney Richards, Program Director of Pittsburgh's WDSY–FM, radio stations today do not add much new music to their playlists. "We play hits. We're looking for the broadest audience we can get, so we're not sticking our necks out and taking many chances on unfamiliar artists and songs that aren't getting played"(McCoy, 2002, p. E–1). However, researchers have not often studied product variety in radio stations at the station level. Most examinations of product variety have investigated changes in formats at the market level.

Berry and Waldfogel (2001) used the implementation of the Telecommunications Act of 1996 as a "natural" independent variable in an experiment examining changes in the number of stations and formats within local radio markets. Using Hotelling-style models of competition as their theoretical foundation, Berry and Waldfogel proposed three hypotheses (H) concerning the effect of consolidation on product variety:

H1: Mergers will increase variety because group owners want to avoid competing with their own properties.

H2: Mergers will decrease variety because group owners may shut down stations to reduce costs.

H3: Mergers will increase variety because group owners will differentiate their properties just enough to close "holes" for new entrants to exploit.

Berry and Waldfogel's (1999) regression analysis of market data from 1993 to 1997 showed that whereas the number of owners per market declined, the number of stations per market increased, and the number of formats available in the market increased as well. Berry and Waldfogel argued that the results indicate support for H1 and H3 and a rejection of H2. More specifically, Berry and Waldfogel suggested that overall product variety has increased as a result of group owners wanting to position their "brands" in a complementary fashion and forcing new entrants in the marketplace to directly compete with their established stations.

These results appear to correlate with the messages from the leadership of radio conglomerates. In a recent *Journal of Radio Studies* forum (Keith, 1998), Mark Mays, President and Chief Operations Officer of Clear Channel Communication, said

Owning more signals in a market, we can take a risk with less popular and more diverse formats. ... [T]his trend will continue because the economics of scale at the local level allow operators to make a reasonable return on investment even though one station of the local group may have a relatively small audience share. (p. 5)

Although there is evidence of improved variety as measured by an increase in the number of formats per market, there is still a need to address the amount of diversity within these formats. For example, Huntemann (1999) argued that "canned" formats provided by syndicators and many "hits" formats have very restrictive playlists, and so station choice should not be equated with programming diversity.

However, where are the incentives for stations to provide original or innovative programming? If a loss of audience has not hurt the profit margin since 1996, then why take the risk of providing content that is unique? Are programmers and general managers willing, as Mark Mays stated, "to take a risk with less popular and more diverse formats" (Keith, 1998, p. 4)?

The Case for Innovation

Without question, these media conglomerates will take advantage of their newfound size and progressively learn better ways of capitalizing on their economies of scale. In addition, one could argue that major radio group owners should continue to present the "safe," "tried-and-true" programming formats that have made them so much money over the last 5 years. After all, where is their incentive to change?

Still, there are some real threats and obstacles on radio's horizon. First, as mentioned earlier, there appears to be a drop in size of the listening audience since 1990. Second, satellite radio, with its promised delivery of nearly 100 crystal clear, virtually commercial-free formats, is now a reality. According to Clear Channel's Mark Mays ("Mays Makes Himself Clear," 2002), "No question, satellite is a threat long term that radio has to take seriously. We're going to have to provide compelling product to get consumers to turn on radio and listen to programs" (p. 24). With the launch of XM and Sirius Satellite Radio, terrestrial broadcasters will now have a competitor in an important venue that they have dominated for so long: in-car listening (Wyllie, 2001). According to XM's CEO Hugh Panero (Bachman, 2002)

Radio has become homogenized. You look at radio today and 70 percent of all the stations carry one of five formats: Adult Contemporary, Country, Oldies, Top-40 and Talk. ... We want to do for radio what cable did for TV and what DirectTV did for cable: bring more choice to the medium. (p. 23)

Finally, broadband Internet access continues to grow in popularity. The Internet offers nearly unlimited streaming audio selections including talk, sports, and highly specialized music programming. A joint study by Arbitron (2000a) and Coleman Research indicated that individuals with this service are much more likely to listen/view streaming media. However, respondents did not see it as a complete replacement for radio at this time.

Although new entrants in the audio entertainment business category build the strongest case for a revival in original radio programming, some business scholars would argue that innovation is a prerequisite for business success today. Wolfe (1994) explained that although there is widespread agreement that innovation is a crucial component to organizational effectiveness, the research literature on the subject, "provides little guidance to those who want to influence organizational innovation" (p. 405). However, Tuval (1999) stated that

If you want to survive in the twenty-first century, you have no choice; you've got to learn to create discontinuity, to go against the flow or someone else will and you'll find yourself being swept along in the wrong direction. (p. 27)

In addition, Tuval (1999) argued that as a company grows it becomes more difficult for its leadership to maintain a strong relationship with its customers. Could it be that as radio groups have increased in size, and its management has become less localized, that they have missed signals from the audience that it is dissatisfied with current programming?

Thomke (2001) supported a concept called enlightened experimentation as a means for companies to face competition. Two of its key principles call for "rapid experimentation" and for groups within organizations to "fail often and early" (Thomke, 2001, p. 180). Thomke stated that this experimentation does not equate to random change, but rather it emphasizes carefully crafted, educated advancement that leads to the rapid and consistent development of knowledge.

In fact, innovation may be linked to increased revenues. One study ("Innovation Has Become the New Theology," 1999) that examined 17 successful American innovations of the 1970s found that they averaged a 56% return on investment. In comparison, the average return on investment for all American business over the last 30 years is 16%.

How do radio station program directors and general managers judge the effects of consolidation on programming? By surveying radio station program directors and general managers, we attempted in this study to provide some preliminary insight into this general question while specifically addressing the following research questions (RQs):

RQ1: How do radio programmers and general managers perceive the scope and importance of innovation in programming?

RQ2: What key factors contribute to a programmer or manager's perception of programming innovation?

Methodology

Arbitron (2004b) market sizes 1 through 100 were selected as the base population for this survey. Those markets were then divided into four size categories: 1 through 25, 26 through 50, 51 through 75 and 76 through 100. A random sample of 8 markets per category was identified for a total of 32 markets to be surveyed. Once a specific market was identified, a list was compiled of all viable stations within that market. "Viable stations" is a term used by Duncan's American Radio (2001) that signifies a station's ability to be economically stable within a given market based on audience ratings and revenue data. The viable stations were found within *Duncan's Radio Market Guide* (Duncan, 2001). This selection process resulted in a total sample of 539 radio stations.

Using M-Street Enterprise's STAR (Station Tracking and Ratings) database, station contact information and the names of program directors and general managers were identified. Because radio programming was the key unit of analysis for this study, program directors were identified as the primary contact for each station. However, general managers were tabbed for contact when either no program director was listed for the station or when a program director was listed for multiple stations.

A three-pronged survey method (mail, online, and phone) was implemented to increase the response rate of this hard-to-reach target group. The process began with the mailing of questionnaires to programmers and general managers. At that point, the respondents were asked to either return the completed hard copy questionnaire or go to the survey Web site to complete the instrument online. After about 3 weeks, those individuals that did not respond through mail or Web were contacted by phone. If programmers or general managers were contacted directly, they were asked complete the survey over the phone or via the Web. If the radio professionals were unavailable, research assistants asked for an e-mail address so that the survey Web link could be imbedded into an e-mail message to them. If the research assistant could not obtain an e-mail address, and repeated calls did not result in a direct contact, voice mail messages were left for the professionals directing them to the Web survey.

The survey consisted of 20 questions: 3 regarding station and individual background information and 17 examining the professional's perception of programming innovation or factors related to programming innovation.

The background questions asked for the individual's title, their career experience in their position, and station format. The innovation questions prompted respondents to evaluate their radio station(s) as well as stations in their market and nationwide on a number of aspects. Among these aspects were perceived innovation, music testing, content diversity, market competition, the economic importance of risk, involvement of ownership in programming decisions, advertising clutter, and the impact of satellite radio.

A total of 147 radio professionals completed the survey. Almost three fourths of the respondents (73%) were program directors (N = 107). Another 13% of the respondents were general managers (N = 19), and 21 respondents (14%) listed their position as "other." Most of the respondents were seasoned at their current position, with 54% having been in their position for over 11 years (N = 80). Other respondents had been in their position for 7 to 11 years (N = 28 or 19%), 3 to 6 years (N = 26 or 18%), or for less than 2 years (N = 13 or 9%).

The majority of stations represented were primarily music oriented (N = 116 or 79%). Only 21% (N = 31) of the represented stations were not music oriented. Adult contemporary (N = 28 or 19%) and rock (N = 28 or 19%) formats dominated the sample, followed by news/talk (N = 22 or 15%), oldies (N = 12 or 8%), country (N = 11 or 8%), contemporary hit radio (N = 10 or 7%), sports (N = 8 or 5%), urban (N = 8 or 5%), and religious (N = 5 or 3%). Fifteen respondents (10%) categorized their radio station format as "other."

Results

Preliminary Analyses

Position title was used as a categorical factor in analyses of variance (ANOVAs). Station music orientation was dummy coded as 1 for an affirmed music orientation and 0 for a station that was not primarily music oriented. This would be used both as a correlate with other variables and as a factor in ANOVAs. Responses to years of experience were coded appropriately (1 = less than 2 years; 2 = 3–6 years; 3 = 7–10 years; 4 = 11+ years) to reflect increasing numbers of years in the position.

The item asking for a description of the competitive environment between radio stations within the market was coded on a 5-point scale ranging from 1 (*Extremely contentious*) to 5 (*Extremely good-natured*). Descriptions of the current state of the station's programming and the station's current music rotation as well as local programming nationwide and in the market were coded on scales ranging from 1 (*Extremely unoriginal*) to 5 (*Extremely innovative*). Descriptions of the variety of artists within music rotations also used a 5-point scale ranging from 1 (*Extremely repeti-*

tive) to 5 (*Extremely diverse*). Descriptions of the importance of music testing for the selection of songs for the station's format were measured on a scale ranging from 1 (*Extremely unimportant*) to 5 (*Extremely important*). Descriptions of ownership's acceptance of risk taking in the station's programming were measured on a scale ranging from 1 (*Extremely unsupportive*) to 5 (*Extremely supportive*). Descriptions of ownership's involvement in programming decisions were measured on a scale ranging from 1 (*Extremely uninvolved*) to 5 (*Extremely involved*).

Likert-type, 5-point scales ranging from 1 (*Strongly disagree*) to 5 (*Strongly agree*) were used to code the following assessments of risk: "Radio stations should take more risks within their programming"; "Radio stations provide ample opportunity for the inclusion of music from new artists"; "Radio stations, on average, place too many commercials within an hour of programming"; "Voice-tracking has improved the quality of radio station programming"; "Listeners are not satisfied with the programming that radio stations are providing"; "Risk-taking is essential for the financial well-being of a radio station"; and "Traditional radio stations will have to change their programming in response to satellite radio." The items regarding the existence of too many commercials and dissatisfaction of listeners were not reverse-coded.

Items regarding perceptions of innovation, willingness to take risks, and perceptions of risks were used as single-item measures after internal consistency analyses on various combinations yielded questionable reliability coefficients ($\alpha s < .80$).

Perceptions of Programming Innovativeness and Risk Taking

Descriptive statistics were used to examine the first RQ about perceptions of the scope and importance of programming innovation. Respondents were not overly impressed with innovation nationwide ($M = 2.9$, $SD = 1.0$). Regarding programming within their market, respondents were slightly more complimentary, with half of the respondents judging the content as innovative ($M = 3.3$, $SD = 1.0$). Still more complimentary, respondents placed their own station in a very positive light; over two thirds of the respondents rated their station's output as innovative ($M = 4.0$, $SD = 0.78$). Interestingly, respondents generally felt that the air of competition in their own market was slightly aggressive ($M = 1.9$, $SD = 0.87$), with only 13 respondents rating their market as good natured.

Consistent with their positive station outlooks, respondents from music-oriented stations largely agreed that their current music rotation was innovative ($M = 3.79$, $SD = 0.86$) and that the variety of artists presented within their rotation was diverse ($M = 3.6$, $SD = 1.0$). Also positive, a little over half of the respondents agreed that radio stations in general provide ample opportunity for the inclusion of music from new artists ($M = 3.3$, $SD = 1.9$). However, just over half of the respondents felt that stations air too many commercials per hour ($M = 3.5$, $SD = 1.1$), which may be related to their assessment that market competition is somewhat aggressive ($M = 1.9$, $SD = 0.87$). Finally, respondents exhibited an even spread of opinions regarding listener dissatisfaction ($M = 2.9$, $SD = 1.0$).

Specific to risk taking, most respondents agreed that risk taking is essential to the financial well-being of a station ($M = 3.4$, $SD = 1.1$). In fact, many felt that radio stations should take more risks with their programming ($M = 3.7$, $SD = 0.87$). This is interesting when coupled with the opinion among music oriented station managers that music testing is very important ($M = 4.4$, $SD = 1.0$). When asked whether traditional radio will have to change its programming in response to satellite radio, however, over half of the respondents disagreed that stations will need to make any programming changes ($M = 2.6$, $SD = 1.1$). This may indicate that respondents felt that risk is much more necessary for basic economic viability than as a mere defense against new technologies.

With regard to the respondents' perceptions of their station owners, most respondents felt that their ownership was fairly supportive of risk taking ($M = 3.6$, $SD = 1.2$) and in addition, that their ownership was somewhat involved in station decision making ($M = 3.2$, $SD = 1.3$).

Influences on Perceptions of Risk and Innovation

Backward regression analyses were used to explore the second RQ regarding key factors that may contribute to perceptions of innovativeness at the national, market, and station levels. For each analysis, the regression model that exhibited the largest F change from the previous model, which also happened to be the most conservative model, was selected for study. Five main predictors emerged from the analysis of perceived innovation at the respondent's station (see Table 1). Innovation in the current music rotation and innovation of programming at the market level were the top two predictors in this model. For perceived innovativeness at the market level, five key factors were found to be most influential (see Table 2). Not surprisingly, the strongest predictors here were perceptions of innovation nationwide and at the station. In looking at contributors to perceptions of innovation at the national level, Table 3 shows the three best contributors to the model. Interestingly, the belief that stations should take more risks had a negative weight in predicting perceived innovation nationwide.

To determine if respondent position (program director, general manager, and other) had any influence on perceptions of innovation and risk, univariate ANOVAs were con-

Table 1. Factors Contributing to Perceived Programming Innovation at the Station Level

Factor	B	SE B	β
Innovativeness of current music rotation	.342	.069	.393**
Programming innovation at the market level	.293	.061	.380**
Years of experience in position	−.112	.058	−.148*
Belief that too many commercials are aired	.082	.052	.123
Nature of station competition in market	−.098	.066	−.116

Note. Model R^2 = .40; $F(5, 104)$ = 13.6, $p < .01$.
*$p < .10$. **$p < .01$.

Table 2. Factors Contributing to Perceived Programming Innovation at the Market Level

Factor	B	SE B	β
Programming innovation nationwide	.485	.072	.518**
Programming innovation at the station level	.353	.094	.271**
Perceived listener dissatisfaction	−.129	.071	−.133*
Nature of station competition in market	.139	.077	.126*
Belief that stations should take more risks	.139	.080	.124*

Note. Model R^2 = .52; $F(5, 104)$ = 22.2, $p < .01$.
*$p < .10$. **$p < .01$.

Table 3. Factors Contributing to Perceived Programming Innovation at the National Level

Factor	B	SE B	β
Programming innovation at the market level	.613	.080	.575**
Belief that voice-tracking improves station quality	.179	.065	.207**
Belief that stations should take more risks	−.169	.086	−.141*

Note. Model R^2 = .482; $F(3, 106)$ = 31.9, $p < .01$.
*$p < .10$. **$p < .01$.

ducted for each relevant item. Position only significantly affected perceptions that too many commercials air in an hour, $F(2, 144)$ = 4.6, $p < .05$, with program directors (M = 3.6) agreeing that too many commercials are aired more so ($p < .05$) than general managers (M = 2.8). Respondents in other positions (M = 3.5) were similar in agreement to program directors, a marginally significant difference from general managers ($p < .10$).

ANOVAs were also run using station orientation (music oriented vs. not music oriented) as an independent factor to see if the type of station influenced perceptions. This item had a main effect only on perceptions of owners' risk-taking acceptance, $F(1, 145)$ = 7.3, $p < .01$, indicating that music stations owners appeared more accepting of risk (M = 3.7) than were owners of talk-dominated stations (M = 3.1). A marginally significant influence of station orientation was found for perceived innovation in the local

market, $F(1, 145)$ = 3.4, $p = .069$; respondents from music stations were slightly more apt to judge programming in the market as more innovative (M = 3.4) than respondents from nonmusic stations (M = 3.0).

Correlates of perceived station, market, and nationwide innovation. Correlations were run to see which items related significantly to perceptions of programming innovativeness in the nation, market, and station, irrespective of other item influences. Table 4 shows the relations to each level of perceived innovation. As evident in the table, the correlation patterns for each level of perceived innovativeness somewhat differed. For example, certain factors, such as music rotation, only related to the respondent's own station, whereas other factors, such as voice tracking, only related to the more global perceptions of innovation in the market and nationwide.

Correlates with station risk acceptance. Correlations were also run for items deemed integral to perceptions that stations should take more risks. The highest correlate with this belief was agreement that risk is good for a station's financial well-being ($r = .55$, $p < .01$). Current music rotation innovativeness was also related to support of station risk ($r = .23$, $p < .05$). The next highest correlate indicated that as station risk-taking acceptance grew, the perceived importance of music testing weakened ($r = −.21$, $p < .05$). Relations with nationwide and station programming innovation (see Table 4) were next in strength, followed by the belief that change was needed in response to satellite radio ($r = .17$, $p < .05$). Last, the perceived good nature of the market's station competition related negatively with station risk ($r = −.16$, $p < .05$).

Correlates with perceptions of ownership. Ownership's risk-taking acceptance and ownership's involvement in decision making also played a role in influencing innovation judgments. As seen in Table 5, the profile of items that corresponded with the roles that ownership was perceived to play in station innovation were markedly different from the profiles seen for perceptions of innovation at the station, market, and nation. In addition, profiles for ownership roles differed from each other, with only the perceptions of innovation in the station's current music rotation that related both to ownership risk-taking acceptance and involvement in decision making.

Discussion

Consistent with the results of the pilot study, programmers appeared to see very little innovation in radio station programming outside of the walls of their own station. Although it was not surprising that managers were self-serving in their responses about their "home" facility,

Table 4. Correlates With Perceived Innovation at the Station, Market, and National Levels

	Perceived Innovation Level		
Factor	Station	Market	Nation
Programming innovation at the station level	—	.442***	.241***
Programming innovation at the market level	.442***	—	.678***
Programming innovation nationwide	.241***	.678***	—
Nature of station competition in market	ns	.224***	.148*
Innovativeness of current music rotation	.488***	.211**	ns
Diversity in the variety of artists	.227**	ns	ns
Belief that music testing is important	ns	.160*	.192**
Belief that stations should take more risks	.167**	ns	-.198**
Belief in ownership's acceptance of risk taking	.198**	.223***	ns
Belief that voice tracking improves station quality	ns	.349***	.383***
Belief that too many commercials are aired	ns	ns	-.203**
Perceived listener dissatisfaction	-.141*	-.380***	-.412***
Belief that change is needed due to satellite radio	-.145*	-.161*	ns

Note. Items not appearing in this table did not correlate with perceived programming innovativeness at the station, market, or national level. Markings of *ns* (nonsignificant) denote that the corresponding item (row) did not correlate with the indicated perceived innovation (column).
*p < .10. **p < .05. ***p < .01.

Table 5. Correlates With Perceptions of Ownership Roles in Station Innovation

	Perceived Ownership Roles Factor	
Factor	Acceptance of Risk Taking	Involvement in Decision Making
Years of experience in position	ns	-.170**
Programming innovation at the station level	.198**	ns
Programming innovation at the market level	.223***	ns
Innovativeness of current music rotation	.288***	-.188**
Diversity in the variety of artists	.164*	ns
Belief that music testing is important	ns	.157*
Opportunity for new artists in rotation	.164**	ns
Belief that too many commercials are aired	.147*	ns
Belief that voice tracking improves station quality	.161*	ns
Belief that change is needed due to satellite radio	ns	.139*

Note. Items not appearing in this table did not correlate with perceived ownership roles in station innovativeness. Markings of *ns* (nonsignificant) denote that the corresponding item (row) did not correlate with either indicated ownership role (column).
*p < .10. **p < .05. *p < .01.

their view of the industry as a whole was consistent with many criticisms expressed in the popular and trade press about radio content. This result was even more interesting when viewed in relation to their view of competition in the local market. These professionals perceived a very competitive and contentious radio marketplace, yet saw very little programming innovation. Shouldn't competition spur program innovation? It is quite possible that innovation is occurring within stations, but just not on the programming front. Further investigation is needed to judge the competitive/innovative atmosphere in such divisions as marketing and sales.

This survey more precisely addressed the issue of program diversity in comparison to other studies. It was obvious that radio professionals perceive their playlists as innovative, diverse, and open to the inclusion of new artists. This was in direct contrast with the opinion of media critics that there is little variety on radio and that musical artists and listeners want change. In addition, the strongest correlations with perception of station-level innovation were innovation in the current music rotation and perception of artist diversity. Moreover, the regression analysis revealed that innovation in the current music rotation was the strongest predictor of perceived innovation at the station level. A content analysis of station playlists would be helpful in determining if this station level assessment of music/artist diversity is valid. However, if their evaluation of their own station was any indication, programmers and general managers appeared to value the inclusion of a wide assortment of artists in their formats.

A very intriguing result of this study was that a strong majority of programmers and general managers believed radio stations should take more risks within their programming. This opinion was strongly and positively correlated with the view that risk taking was essential for the financial well-being of a radio station. This was an important result, as it shows a perceived link between risk taking and the economic bottom line of the organization. This study appears to have found common ground between radio station managers and their critics: Innovation in programming could be a win–win scenario for the audience and the company.

The results clearly indicate that programmers and general managers perceived a great deal of support for risk taking from their ownership. A strong majority (67%) believed that their owners were either somewhat or extremely supportive of taking chances. The perceived acceptance of risk by ownership was also positively correlated with the perception of innovation at the market and station levels. Whereas critics of today's radio programming complain about overly tested playlists and "cookie cutter" formats, these professionals indicated that their directives from ownership leaned more toward taking chances than playing it safe.

Another interesting finding was the negative relation between perception of innovation at the nationwide and market levels and perceived listener dissatisfaction. In other words, as these professionals judged programming as more innovative across the country and in the market, they were more likely to disagree with the statement that, "Overall, I believe listeners are not satisfied with the programming that radio stations are providing." This finding appears to indicate that programmers and general managers believed audience members appreciate innovative fare. However, it should be noted that a lack of dissatisfaction cannot be equated to feelings of satisfaction. Therefore, future research must more precisely assess the measurement of audience fulfillment.

When it comes to nonmusic programming, a strong majority of respondents believed there are too many commercials placed within an hour of radio programming. In addition, the correlation analysis revealed that as these radio professionals perceived innovation on a national scale more positively, they were more likely to agree with the statement that, "I believe radio stations, on average, place too many commercials within an hour of programming." However, when examined by title, general managers tended to indicate that current spot loads were not a problem. This may be an example of the traditional organizational structure at work: the general manager having primary responsibility of maintaining the station's profitability and the program director taking control of the station "sound." Historically, the presence of too many commercials has been viewed as the number one reason listeners tune away from a radio station. Even industry insiders point to increased spot loads over the past 5 years, with increases in the neighborhood of 10% to 20% in a given hour of programming (Weil, 2002). With listening levels dropping over the last decade, general managers and program directors would be well advised to seek new ways to satisfy the needs of their advertisers while dropping the number of minutes per hour devoted to commercial spots.

Finally, the respondents did not perceive satellite radio as a strong competitor at this point and therefore changes in broadcast programming are not likely until these services attract a larger subscriber base. However, these professionals did link the importance of taking risks in station programming with the belief that change will be needed in response to satellite radio, which may indicate that more programming risks will be taken as satellite radio becomes more of a competitive threat.

Future research should focus on the radio listeners to provide an unbiased assessment of their perception of this industry as well as the industry's role in their lives. Also, multiple research methodologies should be implemented to obtain qualitative and quantitative data pertaining to station innovation. For example, focus group research or depth interviews might provide a more detailed analysis of how radio professionals define innovation and where it appears throughout the station. Content analyses of radio programming would provide specific data concerning artist diversity and repetition of music that could be compared to earlier survey results.

John W. Owens

(owensjw@uc.edu)

is interested in media management and sales, programming, and production. He joined the faculty of the Electronic Media Division of the College Conservatory of Music at the University of Cincinnati in 1999. He serves as faculty advisor to BearCast, the Electronic Media Division's student Internet radio station.

Francesca Dillman Carpentier

(Francesca.Carpentier@asu.edu)

is interested in informational and emotional processing of mass media, with specific attention to motivations driving selective exposure to mediated messages. She joined the Psychology faculty at Arizona State University in 2002, where she works in their Program for Prevention Research with hard-to-reach populations.

References

Arbitron. (2000, October 2). *The broadband revolution: How superfast internet access changes media habits in american households.* Retrieved August 1, 2003, from www.arbitron.com/downloads/broadband.pdf

Arbitron. (2002a, Summer). *American radio listening trends: Persons using radio report.* Retrieved August 1, 2003, from http://wargod.arbitron.com/scripts/ndb/ndbradio2.asp

Arbitron. (2002b). *Arbitron radio market rankings: Spring 2002.* Retrieved May 10, 2002, from http://www.arbitron.com/radio_stations/home.htm

Bachman, K. (2002, March 25). Reaching for the stars: Satellite companies want to be the next big thing in radio. *Mediaweek, 12,* 22 –28.

Bednarski, P. J. (2001, January 1). A screed against greed: If bigger is better the issue becomes better for whom? *Broadcasting and Cable, 131,* 32.

Berry, S. T., & Waldfogel, J. (2001, August). Do mergers increase product variety? Evidence from radio broadcasting. *The Quarterly Journal of Economics, 116,* 1009-1025.

Block, V. (2002, April 22). City prides itself on diversity; radio formats do not station conglomerates tune into bottom line. *Crain's New York Business,* p. 4.

Browning, L. (2002, June 19). Making waves on the air: Big radio's bad boy. *The New York Times,* p. C1.

Coen, R. (2001). *Coen's spending totals for 2001.* Retrieved October 14, 2002, from http://www.adage.com/page.cms?pageID=906

Coen, R. (2002). *Coen's spending totals for 2002.* Retrieved August 25, 2003, from http://www.adage.com/page.cms?pageID=1010

Croteau, D., & Hoynes, W. (2001). *The business of media: Corporate media and the public interest.* Thousand Oaks, CA: Pine Forge Press.

Duncan, J. (1999). *A speech to the Paine Webber media conference.* Retrieved March 1, 2003, from http://www.duncanradio.com/Jim%20Duncan%20at%20PaineWebber.htm

Duncan, J. (2001). *Duncan's radio market guide.* Cincinnati, OH: Duncan's American Radio.

Duncan's American Radio. (2001, June 22). *Radio ownership update: America's highest billing groups.* Retrieved March 1, 2003, from http://www.duncanradio.com/PR%20on%20Radio%20Ownership.htm

Fisher, M. (1998, June 2). The great radio rebellion: The turned off fight back. *The Washington Post,* p. D01.

Graybow, S. (2002, April 13). As top 40 and mainstream rock radio further encroaches on the genre's territory, stations rethink programming practices. *Billboard, 114,* p. 71.

Huntemann, N. (1999, October). Corporate interference: The commercialization and concentration of radio post the 1996 Telecommunications Act. *Journal of Communication Inquiry, 23,* 390-407.

Innovation has become the new theology. (1999, February 20). *The Economist,* p. S8.

Keith, M. C. (1998). JRS forum. *Journal of Radio Studies, 5,* 1-8.

Leeper, S. E. (2000). The game of radiopoly: An anti-trust perspective of consolidation in the radio industry. *Federal Communications Law Journal, 52,* 473-496.

Mays makes himself clear: The head of the biggest U.S. radio group responds to the company's critics. (2002, September 2). *Broadcasting & Cable, 132,* 24.

McClellan, S. (2002, December 9). Radio is hot in the fourth quarter. *Broadcasting and Cable, 132,* 20.

McConnell, B. (1998, November 16). FCC moving cautiously, on ownership. *Broadcasting & Cable, 128,* 27.

McCoy, A. (2002, March 10). How radio picks the songs: Successful programming retains an art form that's difficult to master. *Pittsburgh Post-Gazette,* p. E-1.

Petrozzelo, D. (1996a, October 28). Consolidation a boon for programmers. *Broadcasting & Cable, 126,* 73-74.

Petrozello, D. (1996b, October 14,). Sales, personnel new challenges of consolidation: Radio owners suggest different approaches to business. *Broadcasting & Cable, 126,* 46.

Pfister, B. (2004, January 28). FCC boss to get an earful at S.A. hearing today: Meeting focuses on who controls the broadcast airwaves. *San Antonio Express-News,* p. 1A.

Reece, D. (1998, April 4). KREV fans rally for radio diversity. *Billboard, 110,* 70.

Thomke, S. (2001). Enlightened experimentation: The new imperative for innovation. In *Harvard Business Review on innovation* (pp. 179-205). Boston: Harvard Business School Press.

Tristani, G. (1998). *Keeping the local in local radio.* Retrieved March 1, 2003, from http://www.fcc.gov/Speeches/Tristani/spgt811.html

Tuval, Y. (1999). *Against the flow: A new strategic framework for business success in the 21st century.* London: Orion Business Books.

U.S. advertising market predicted to grow 6% in 2003: New Global Insight study forecasts ad revenues for 2002 through 2006. (2002, November 25). Retrieved March 1, 2003, from http://www.globalinsight.com/About/PressRelease/PressRelease209.htm

Weil, D. (2002, February 3). Confusion on the airwaves: Aftermath of area radio consolidation means more ad revenue, but less choice for listeners. *The Palm Beach Post,* p. 1-F.

Wolfe, R. (1994). Organizational innovation: Review, critique and suggested research directions. *The Journal of Management Studies, 31,* 405-431.

Wyllie, D. (2001). *Sirius announces limited February launch.* Retrieved March 1, 2003, from http://www.gavin.com/news/article.php?art_id=899

Optimizing Radio Advertising in North Queensland, Australia: A Mathematical Programming Approach

■

Adee Athiyaman
James Cook University, Australia

Decision making could be described using 2 steps: (a) understanding the effects of a particular course of action and (b) selecting an action given this knowledge of effects. It is my contention that businesses wanting to advertise in radio have only partial information about the marketplace. There are approximately 500 commercial and community radio stations in Australia. However, only commercial radio stations, which make up 47% of the total radio stations in the country, systematically conduct radio surveys. In this article, I profile radio audiences in North Queensland, Australia using the list of values measure (LOV; Kahle & Kennedy, 1989). Also, I present the combinations of commercial and community radio stations that could deliver the maximum possible impact on the pertinent target market.

There are around 37 million radio sets across Australia or an average of 5 radio sets in every household in the country (Neilsen Media Research, 2003a, 2003b). The households have the option to tune into one of the 256 commercial radio stations; or 230 community radio stations; or 5 national radio stations of the Australian Broadcasting Service; or 1,500 low-power, narrow casting, and temporary community stations in the country (Commercial Radio Australia, 2003a). Because radio can be accessed anywhere, anytime, by anybody, advertisers consider the medium to be effective for (a) creating awareness of a new brand, (b) products targeted at younger people (85% of 10- to 17-year-olds listen to radio), and (c) use in an integrated multimedia campaign (Commercial Radio Australia, 2003b).

Media expenditure in Australia is estimated at $8 billion per annum (Neilsen Media Research, 2003b). In 2003, approximately $702 million was spent on radio advertising (Advertising Federation of Australia, 2004). Predictions are that it would increase to $740 million in 2004: a 5.49% increase over the 2003 spending (Commercial Radio Australia, 2003b).

Although most of the commercial and community radio stations are located in regional areas (approximately 80% as of 2003), only metropolitan stations attract "national" advertising. Specifically, 58% of advertising revenue for metro stations comes from national advertising, whereas only 27% of advertising expenditure for regional radio emanates from this source (Australian Broadcasting Authority, 2003). One major reason for this difference is the widespread presence of network stations in metropolitan areas and their ability to produce and broadcast advertising at a lower cost than individual radio stations. Another reason would be the continual availability of audience estimates for commercial, metropolitan radio stations: eight market surveys each year compared to one survey a year for regional commercial radio stations.

Nielsen Media Research (2003b), the firm that holds the contract with Commercial Radio Australia Limited to provide audience rating service to stations, has a software package called Radio Advisor (Version 2.1, 2003) that analyzes radio surveys and provides businesses analyses such as session ranking, reach and frequency, station loyalty, and predictions about changes to listenership from one period to another. What is missing in this approach is information about the community radio audience.

More than three decades ago, Clark and Sexton (1970) highlighted that all marketing decisions have two components: (a) understanding the effects of a particular course of action and (b) selecting an action given this knowledge of effects. It is my contention that businesses wanting to advertise in radio have only partial information about the marketplace. Specifically, little is known about the audiences of community radio and the combination of commercial and community radio that would deliver the maximum possible reach or coverage of the pertinent target market. In this article, I attempt to bridge this gap in knowledge.

Address correspondence to Adee Athiyaman, School of Business, James Cook University, Townsville, QLD 4811, Australia. E-mail: Adee.Athiyaman@jcu.edu.au

This article is organized as follows. In the next section, I highlight a behavioral framework that guides radio-audience measurement. In the subsequent section, I employ the framework to profile radio audience in North Queensland, and finally, I present an optimization model for advertising in radio in the North Queensland region.

Audience Analysis: A Conceptual Framework

The most common approach to audience analysis is the use of geographic and demographic variables to describe the population of interest (Shultz, Block, & Custer, 1977). For example, the Regional Radio Bureau (2003) described the four commercial radio stations in Townsville, Queensland, in terms of audience age (e.g., 35–54), format of the station (for instance, adult contemporary), and the station's desired positioning in the marketplace (e.g., "best songs of all time"). However, as aptly observed by Lipke (2000), geodemographic variables are causally remote to consumer behavior. For example, two households with identical demographics may have different beliefs and outlooks on life. Because of these differences, each household would respond to marketing messages in a different way and more important, each household might purchase and consume different products and brands. What is required is a profiling approach that would help radio stations highlight to media buyers the future consumer behavior of their audience, not their geodemographic details and their past purchase behavior. What variable or set of variables could assist radio stations to construct such a causally relevant classification scheme?

Howard & Seth (1969) posited that values implicit in a culture or subculture, for example, an ethnic group, affect consumption behavior. In other words, values, which are enduring beliefs concerning desired states of existence toward which humans strive, regulate the manner in which this striving takes place (Vinson, Scott, & Lamont 1977). Table 1 lists the conceptual definition of value and differentiates it from other related constructs such as self, lifestyle, and personality. Note that personality is a second-order factor, with value, self, and lifestyle forming the first-order factors (Figure 1). In other words, values shape one's evaluation of oneself: People utilize values to determine the appropriateness of their beliefs, attitudes, and behavior and also directly influence the way in which a person lives his or her life. The sum total of all the preceding concepts is personality: one's generalized patterns of response to stimuli.

Note that in Figure 1, value, self, and lifestyle are hypothesized to be first-order factors with personality being the latent variable that accounts for correlations among the 3 first-order factors. Consider Figure 2. It suggests that

Table 1. Conceptual Definition of Value and Related Constructs

Construct	Definition
Value	Beliefs concerning desired states of existence
Self	Evaluation of oneself as an object; this evaluation is based on beliefs about desired state of existence (personal values); behavior will be directed toward the furtherance and enhancement of self-concept
Lifestyle	A distinctive mode of living of an individual or a group of individuals; for example, individuals who view themselves as "liberals" are more likely to watch foreign movies; lifestyle is a consequence of personal values
Personality	Generalized patterns or response to stimuli

a consumer's value orientation will affect the consumer's product choice but not brand choice. For instance, a consumer's general belief that "one should protect the environment in which one lives in" might affect the type of automobile (large, medium, and small) that the consumer purchases but not the brand purchased. Empirical support for this assertion can be gleaned from Henry (1976), and Sheth, Mital, and Newman (2000). Note that unlike attitudes and opinions, values are stable and slow changing. This suggests an extended "shelf life" for applied research that utilizes consumer values.

To describe radio audience, I employed "personal values" as the profile variable. This is based on the reasoning that products are purchased as a means to satisfy a desired end state (e.g., buying a sports car for

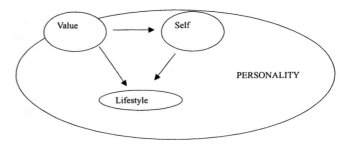

Figure 1. Relations among value, self, lifestyle, and personality.

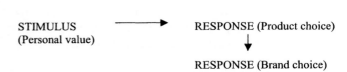

Figure 2. Relation between personal values and consumer behavior. Note that product choice will be the stimulus for brand choice.

self-expression purposes; see the means–end chain conceptualization offered by Gutman, 1988). In summary, my interest in this article was to profile radio audiences using personal values and to suggest an optimal combination of commercial and community radio that would deliver the maximum reach or target audience coverage in North Queensland.

Method

The setting for this research is Townsville, the largest regional center in Australia with a population of 144,000 persons. The city of Townsville is home to two community radio stations and four commercial radio stations (Table 2).

To gather radio listening data, 1,000 households in the Townsville region were contacted. A systematic random sampling procedure was employed to choose the respondents and to ensure the accuracy of the information. The Telstra White Pages directory on CD (2002/2003 edition) was used as the sampling frame.

A self-administered, structured questionnaire was employed to gather the information. Respondents were asked to indicate the specific stations listened to during each 15-min time period for the past 24 hr. From this information, the listening patterns for different time segments were derived. In addition, respondents were also asked to complete the list of values (LOV) profile (Kahle & Kennedy, 1989). LOV, an abbreviated measure of Rokeach's Value Survey (Rokeach, 1968), uses terminal values, that is, ideal states of existence to capture personal values of individuals. Respondents provide importance rankings or ratings for a set of nine terminal values (see Table 5). Conceptually, the rank orderings represent the "value system" of an individual or a group such as a subculture (Rokeach, 1968). The value system helps one to choose among competing interests. For instance, if a situation in life activates more than one value, then the value system is used to choose the means that satisfy the most important value or end state (Kamakura & Novak, 1992).

Measurement of Values

One assumes that the value rankings provided by an individual are error-prone observations of the individual's true value system. Specifically,

$$U^k_i = V^k_i + \varepsilon^k_i,$$

where U^k_i = the observed, error-prone importance of value k to individual i, V^k_i = the true importance of value k to individual i, and ε^k_i = the stochastic error term that is assumed to be independent and identically distributed across all individuals i.

In probability terminology, the preference ranking of LOV items by an individual can be expressed in the form

$$P(U^k_i > U^l_i) \text{ for all } l \, \varepsilon \, A, l \neq k,$$

where set A contains all nine LOV items.

Rewriting the preceding function using true score and error score components results in the function

$$P\{(V^k_i + \varepsilon^k_i) > (V^l_i + \varepsilon^l_i)\} \text{ for all } l \, \varepsilon \, A, l \neq k,$$

or by rearranging terms, one has

$$P\{(V^k_i - V^l_i) > (\varepsilon^l_i - \varepsilon^k_i)\} \text{ for all } l \, \varepsilon \, A, l \neq k.$$

As mentioned earlier, if one assumes the ε_i to be independent and identically distributed (iid) normals over the population, then $E(U^k_i) = E(V^k_i)$. This formulation was used in this article to capture the importance ratings of LOV items assigned by radio listeners. Because I used type of radio station as the segmentation variable—that is, the six commercial and community radio stations in Townsville—I computed personal values for each of the radio stations and combined them into a value system using behavioral motivations related to the values (Table 6).

Determining Optimal Radio Advertising

To prescribe the optimal mix of radio stations, the following objective function was maximized:

$$Z = \text{effective reach} = \Sigma c_{jk}x_j,$$

where c_{jk} = number of listeners during the kth hour (k = 1, 6 a.m. to 7 a.m. to 18, 11 p.m. to 12 a.m.) with the jth (j = 1 to 5) value system (for instance, "security"; see Table 6); x_j = radio station j (j = 1 to 6; $x1$ = 4TO, $x2$ = HOT FM, $x3$ = MIX FM, $x4$ = SEA FM, $x5$ = 4TTT, and $x6$ = 4KIG) subject to the constraint

$$\Sigma a_{jk}x_j \leq b_k,$$

Table 2. Radio Stations Broadcasting From Townsville

Type of Radio Station	Station Identification	Format
Community	4k1G	Indigenous
	4TTT	General format
Commercial	4TO	Adult contemporary
	Hot FM 103.1	Hot adult contemporary
	Mix FM 106.3	Hot adult contemporary
	Sea FM 100.7	Classic and modern rock

where a_{jk} = technical or production coefficient j such as the cost of placing a 30-sec commercial during the hour k (Table 3), and b_k = available productive resources such as advertising time constraint, that is, the maximum number of advertising insertions possible in an hour k (Table 3).

Note that the problem requires an integer solution. In other words, the optimal solution should be whole numbers. Although it may sound reasonable to round off the fractional solutions obtained by implementing a linear program, research has demonstrated that the practice of

Table 3. Constraints of the Model

Constraint No.	Model	Description
1	$110x1 + 99x2 +$ $45x3 + 49x4 +$ $50x5 + 40x6 \leq 2,500$	Average cost of placing a 30-sec commercial in the stations with $2,500 being the maximum budgeted expenditure for an hour[a]
2	$x1 \geq 2$	Minimum exposure requirement for 4TO[b]
3	$x2 \geq 2$	Minimum exposure requirement for HOT FM[b]
4	$x3 \geq 2$	Minimum exposure requirement in MIX FM[b]
5	$x4 \geq 2$	Minimum exposure requirement in SEA FM[b]
6	$x5 \geq 2$	Minimum exposure requirement in 4TTT[b]
7	$x6 \geq 2$	Minimum exposure requirement in 4KIG[b]
9	$x1 \leq 20$	Maximum number of advertisements in 4TO in any 1 hr[c]
10	$x2 \leq 20$	Maximum number of advertisements in HOT FM in any 1 hr[c]
11	$x3 \leq 20$	Maximum number of advertisements in MIX FM in any 1 hr[c]
12	$x4 \leq 20$	Maximum number of advertisements in SEA FM in any 1 hr[c]
13	$x5 \leq 10$	Maximum number of advertisements in 4TTT in any 1 hr[d]
14	$x6 \leq 10$	Maximum number of advertisements in 4KIG in any 1 hr[d]

[a]Advertising rates for commercial radio can be gleaned from Regional Radio Bureau (http://www.rrb.com.au). For community radio, see http://www.4ttt.com.au, and http://www.4kig.com.au. The $2,500 budget is a hypothetical figure. [b]The two-exposure hypothesis is based on Krugman's (1972) assertion that advertising message processing requires two exposures to cause communication effects. [c]This is based on the assumption that commercial radio stations can sell up to 10 min of airtime for every hour of broadcast, and the length of advertisement is 30 sec. [d]Community radio can sell up to 5 minutes of sponsorship/advertising time for every hour of broadcast (see Clause 2(2)(b)(ii) of Schedule 2 of Broadcasting Services Act 1992). This translates to 10 thirty-sec commercials per hour.

rounding off the solution will not result in an optimal solution (Best & Ritter, 1985). To ensure that the problem solution results in whole numbers, I employed an integer-programming algorithm. Specifically, because the variables have lower and upper bounds, I utilized the "branch and bound" method to solve the problem (see Table 3; Hu, 1970).

Results and Discussion

Of the 528 persons who responded to the survey, 507 (96%) had listened to at least one radio station during the past 24 hr. Because there are 128,865 persons in the target population, that is, persons aged 15 and above in the Townsville region, the number of radio listeners for a 24-hr period works out to 123,708 persons (factor weight = 244).

Market Share of Community and Commercial Radio Stations

Table 4 identifies the percent of radio audience that was listening to each identified station during each hour. Appendix A provides estimates of listenership for the population. The percentage for each hour is an average of the respective 4 quarter hours. The quarter-hour share was computed by taking all stations listened to for at least 8 min and summing them for all respondents, then dividing the total into the number of times each station was mentioned for the respective time period.

In words, radio station share equals number of each station mentions divided by total number of station mentions. Note that 4TTT, a community radio station, has the second largest market share or radio listenership in the Townsville region. This shows that any media optimization effort that does not take into account the listeners of community radio will produce suboptimal solutions.

Values of Radio Station Audiences

Table 5 lists the values endorsed by the radio listeners and highlights their association between the five motivational domains discussed by Schwartz and Bilsky (1987, 1990) and Kamakura and Novak (1992). In addition, Table 5 highlights whether the motivational orientations serve individualist, or collectivist, or mixed interests. As the label implies, an individualist orientation is concerned with self-interest, a collectivist orientation refers to furthering the interests of a group—for example, the family—and mixed interests include both self-interest and group interest. Note that the causal direction is from personal values to motivation.

Table 4. Estimated Average Quarter Hour Listening Share for Each Radio Station for Each Hour

	Radio Station					
	4TO	Hot FM 103.1	Mix FM 106.3	Sea FM 100.7	4TTT	4KIG
6–7 a.m.	22	1	6	6	9	6
7–8 a.m.	24	2	7	7	10	4
8–9 a.m.	23	4	7	6	13	2
9–10 a.m.	19	6	3	7	17	2
10–11 a.m.	17	3	3	8	18	1
11–12 p.m.	16	4	4	7	18	0
12–1 p.m.	21	2	3	6	17	1
1–2 p.m.	23	2	2	8	18	2
2–3 p.m.	19	2	2	8	18	2
3–4 p.m.	18	2	3	9	17	3
4–5 p.m.	15	2	3	8	15	0
5–6 p.m.	16	3	6	11	13	0
6–7 p.m.	19	2	4	2	9	3
7–8 p.m.	21	3	4	3	14	1
8–9 p.m.	23	2	6	3	23	0
9–10 p.m.	26	2	4	4	15	1
10–11 p.m.	21	3	4	3	13	1
11–12 a.m.	16	7	4	2	12	5
Daily share[a]	20	3	4	6	15	2
Number of listeners[b]	24,741	3,711	4,948	7,422	18,556	2,474

[a]Entries are weighted average of hourly listening shares. [b]Market projection of market share. For example, a daily share of 2% would translate into # of listeners to radio × 2% = 123,708 × .02 = 2,474 listeners. See Appendix A for hourly projections.

Table 5. LOV Items Endorsed by Respondents and LOV's Relation With Motivational Domains

Value	M Score[a]	Rank	Motivational Domain	Interest Served
Self-respect	2.86	1	Self-direction	Individual
Warm relationships	2.78	2	Maturity	Mixed
Security	2.76	3	Security	Mixed
Accomplishment	2.73	4	Self-direction	Individual
Fun and enjoyment	2.68	5	Enjoyment	Individual
Self-fulfillment	2.67	6	Self-direction	Individual
Well respected	2.65	7	Achievement	Individual
Belonging	2.64	8	Maturity	Mixed
Excitement	2.29	9	Enjoyment	Individual

Note. LOV = list of values.

[a]Computed using a 3-point scale ranging from 1 (*low importance*) to 3 (*high importance*). The three-step scale is a reduced form of the original nine-step measure. The rescaling was performed to enable readers to compare the results of this study with that of other studies that have used three-step scales to measure value systems of individuals (see, e.g., Kamakura & Novak, 1992). Note that there is no loss of information about relation among variables because of rescaling. The rescaling is in fact a scalar multiplication of the determinant of the original, nine-step, variance–covariance matrix.

Self-respect was rated the most important value. This value operates through the self-direction motivational domain. According to Schwartz and Bilsky (1987), self-direction refers to reliance on one's independent capabilities for decision making, creativity, and action. Product-purchase behavior associated with this motivation includes books, personal computers, music instruments, cameras, cars, skis, parachutes, hang gliders, and rollerblades (Durgee, O'Connor, & Veryzer, 1996).

Warm relationships with others, the second most important value of radio listeners in the region, maps into maturity motivation. *Maturity* is defined to include toler-

ance, faith in one's convictions, deep emotional relationships, and appreciation for the beauty of creation (see Kamakura & Novak, 1992). Product purchases associated with this motive include greeting cards, art, flowers, and clothing.

Security includes family security, national security, and world peace. Durgee et al. (1996) identified and listed 33 products associated with security. These range from financial security products such as mutual funds to tangible safety products such as alarm systems and smoke alarms.

Fun and enjoyment and excitement map into socially acceptable enjoyment pursuits such as watching a movie,

Table 6. Frequency of Values–Motives Classification

Value of Respondents	Motivational Domain	Interest Served	Respondents in the Category (%)
Self-respect, accomplishment, and self-fulfillment	Self-direction	Individual	35
Warm relationships and belonging	Maturity	Mixed	23
Fun and enjoyment and excitement	Enjoyment	Individual	19
Security	Security	Mixed	12
Well respected	Achievement	Individual	11
Total			100

vacations, and desserts. Finally, being well respected stimulates product purchases such as a house and brand name clothing (achievement motive).

Table 6 groups respondents according to their shared motivations, Appendix B lists the value-system of each of the six radio stations' audience, and Appendix C highlights some of the product–value associations discussed in the extant literature.

Maximizing Advertising Reach

Using the information given in Appendix A and Appendix B, I derived the following objective function for the value system self-direction for the time period 6 a.m. to 7 a.m.:

$$\text{Maximize } Z = 3{,}982x1 + 174x2 + 1{,}165x3 + 1{,}125x4 + 1{,}472x5 + 933x6$$

Note that the objective function captures the number of listeners with self-direction oriented values for each of the radio stations. For example, station $x5$ (4TTT) attracts a share of 4,601 listeners during the 6 a.m. to 7 a.m. time period (Appendix A). Appendix B highlights that 32% of the 4,601-listener audience expressed self-direction related values. The product of the two figures is the coefficient of $x5$ in the objective function, that is, $x5 = 4{,}601 \times .32 = 1{,}472$.

The optimization problem, which included all of the 13 constraints, was submitted to the H02BBF routine (NAG Fortran Library, 2004). This routine solves integer-programming problems using the branch and bound method. Table 7 shows the result of this exercise.

The results of the optimization run suggest that businesses advertising during the 6 a.m. to 7 a.m. time period, attempting to appeal to the self-direction values of the population, should purchase 7 min of airtime with the commercial radio station 4TO, 5 min of airtime with the

community radio 4TTT, and 1 min from each of the other four commercial/community radio stations. Appendix D highlights the optimal advertising placements for all of the values-motive combinations for the 6 a.m. to 10 a.m. time period. Optimal solutions for all other time periods (e.g., the "drive time" starting at 3 p.m. and concluding at 6 p.m.) can be constructed using data given in Appendixes A, C, and information provided in Table 3.

Summary and Conclusion

The results of this study offer two sets of guidelines to marketing decision makers in the North Queensland region. First, the study identified "triggers" or stimuli for product purchases, and second, the study prescribed optimal mix of commercial and community radio stations that should be used to reach potential purchasers of products. For example, a sports car marketer in the region would identify from Appendix C that the motive (stimulus) relevant for a sports car purchase is achievement. Then, based on the information given in Appendix D, they may decide to place twenty 30-sec commercials in 4TO and six 30-sec commercials in 4TTT during the 8 a.m. to 9 a.m. time period. Note that this combination of commercial and community radio offers the maximum reach or coverage of the target audience (32,396 people with an achievement motive).

It is a marketing truism that no brand can appeal to all consumers. Marketers who understand the value orientation of consumers and through marketing communications appeal to that value would attain competitive advantage. This research has shown that targeting both commercial and community radio audiences would maximize sales response from consumers in the North Queensland region.

Table 7. Results of the Integer Programming Run: Self-Direction Related Values, 6 a.m. to 7 a.m. Time Period

Variable	$x1$	$x2$	$x3$	$x4$	$x5$	$x6$
Station	4TO	HOT FM	MIX FM	SEA FM	4TTT	4KIG
No. with self-direction values	3,982	174	1,165	1,125	1,472	933
Optimal no. of advertisements	14	2	2	2	10	2

Adee Athiyaman

(Adee.Athiyaman@jcu.edu.au)

is Associate Professor and Director of the Centre for Business and Economic Research at James Cook University, Australia. His research focuses on marketing models. His work has appeared in Australasian Journal of Marketing Research, European Journal of Marketing, Journal of Contemporary Business Issues, and Marketing Intelligence & Planning.

References

Advertising Federation of Australia. (2004, March 1). *Advertising Federation of Australia: Industry info.* Retrieved March 3, 2004, from http://www.afa.org.au/

Australian Broadcasting Authority. (2003). Retrieved March 3, 2004, from http://www.aba.gov.au/tv/content/index.htm

Best, M., & Ritter, K. (1985). *Linear programming: Active set analysis and computer program.* Englewood Cliffs, NJ: Prentice Hall.

Clark, W. A., & Sexton, D. E. (1970). *Marketing and management science: A synergism.* Homewood, IL: Irwin.

Commercial Radio Australia. (2003a, May). *All Australian listening report* (Media Release). Retrieved August 1, 2003, from http://www.commercialradio.com.au/news.cfm

Commercial Radio Australia.(2003b, December 1). *Radio campaign hits the mark* (Media Release). Retrieved August 1, 2003, from http://www.commercialradio.com.au/news.cfm

Durgee, J. F., O'Connor, C., & Veryzer, R. (1996). Translating values into product wants. *Journal of Advertising Research, 36,* 90–101.

Gutman, J. (1988). Laddering: Theory, method, analysis and interpretation. *Journal of Advertising Research, 28,* 11–31.

Henry, W. (1976). Cultural values do correlate with consumer behavior. *Journal of Marketing Research, 13,* 121–127.

Howard, J., & Sheth, J. (1969). *The theory of buyer behavior.* New York: Wiley.

Hu, T. C. (1970). *Integer programming and network flows.* Reading, MA: Addison-Wesley.

Kahle, L., & Kennedy, P. (1989). Using the list of values (LOV) to understand consumers. *Journal of Consumer Marketing, 6,* 5–12.

Kamakura, W., & Novak, T. (1992). Value system segmentation: Exploring the meaning of LOV. *Journal of Consumer Research, 19,* 119–132.

Krugman, H. E. (1972). Why three exposures may be enough. *Journal of Advertising Research, 12,* 11–14.

Lipke, D. (2000, October). Head trips: A new way to understand consumer psychology. *American Demographics, 22,* 38–40.

NAG Fortran Library. (2004). *H02BBF.* Retrieved March 3, 2004, from http://www.iec.co.uk/numeric/FL/manual/html/genint/FSnews.asp

Nielsen Media Research. (2003a). *All homes in Australia have at least one radio.* Retrieved March 3, 2003, from http://www.Acneilsen.com.au

Nielsen Media Research. (2003b). *Industries and issues.* Retrieved March 3, 2004, from http//www.Acneilsen.com.au

Radio Advisor (Version 2.1) [Computer Software]. (2003) Sydney, Australia: Nielsen Media Research.

Regional Radio Bureau. (2003). *Queensland.* Retrieved August 1, 2003, from http://www.rrb.com.au/stations/qld/qld.htm

Rokeach, M. (1968). *Belief, attitude and value.* San Francisco: Jossey-Bass.

Schwartz, S., & Blisky, W. (1987). Toward a universal psychological structure of human values. *Journal of Personality and Social Psychology, 53,* 550–562.

Schwartz, S., & Blisky, W. (1990). Toward a theory of the universal content and structure of values: Extensions and cross-cultural replications. *Journal of Personality and Social Psychology, 58,* 878–891.

Sheth, J., Mital, B., & Newman, B. (2000). *Customer behavior: Consumer behavior and beyond.* Fort Worth, TX: Dryden.

Shultz, D., Block, M., & Custer, S. (1977). A comparative study of radio audience measurement methodology. *Journal of Advertising, 7,* 14–22.

Vinson, D., Scott, J., & Lamont, L. (1977, April). The role of personal values in marketing and consumer behavior. *Journal of Marketing, 41,* 44–50.

Appendix A Estimate of the Number of Persons Listening to Each Station During Each 1-Hr Time Period

Time	4TO	Hot FM	Mix106.3	Sea FM	4TTT FM	4KIG
6 a.m. to 7 a.m.	11,714	526	3,148	2,885	4,601	3,011
7 a.m. to 8 a.m.	13,158	973	3,781	3,671	5,405	2,168
8 a.m. to 9 a.m.	12,360	2,358	3,906	3,253	7,121	1,145
9 a.m. to 10 a.m.	9,371	2,783	1,721	3,515	8,369	717
10 a.m. to 11 a.m.	7,448	1,382	1,382	3,418	7,679	238
11 a.m. to 12 p.m.	6,270	1,544	1,544	2,795	7,042	200
12 p.m. to 1 p.m.	7,872	758	1,232	2,355	6,633	203
1 p.m. to 2 p.m.	8,431	730	730	2,816	6,383	665
2 p.m. to 3 p.m.	6,798	705	705	2,725	6,240	705
3 p.m. to 4 p.m.	7,472	967	1,382	3,941	7,147	1,077
4 p.m. to 5 p.m.	5,535	719	1,161	2,853	5,415	705
5 p.m. to 6 p.m.	4,483	680	1,609	3,135	3,643	358
6 p.m. to 7 p.m.	4,240	298	975	513	1,939	538
7 p.m. to 8 p.m.	2,742	363	500	394	1,863	136
8 p.m. to 9 p.m.	2,657	201	666	350	2,635	136
9 p.m. to 10 p.m.	3,100	434	465	494	1,811	182
10 p.m. to 11 p.m.	2,070	271	366	301	1,256	119
11 p.m. to 12 a.m.	1,975	242	353	282	1,361	91

Appendix B   Personal Values of Radio Listeners

4TO

Motive	6 a.m. to 7 a.m.	7 a.m. to 8 a.m.	8 a.m. to 9 a.m.	9 a.m. to 10 a.m.	10 a.m. to 11 a.m.	11 a.m. to 12 Noon	12 p.m. to 1 p.m.
Selfdirection	34	34	34	34	34	28	34
Maturity	21	24	24	24	15	23	24
Enjoyment	20	18	18	16	20	20	17
Security	13	12	12	13	16	15	13
Achievement	12	12	12	13	15	14	12

Motive	1 p.m. to 2 p.m.	2 p.m. to 3 p.m.	3 p.m. to 4 p.m.	4 p.m. to 5 p.m.	5 p.m. to 6 p.m.	6 p.m. to 7 p.m.	7 p.m. to 8 p.m.
Selfdirection	34	31	29	29	32	36	43
Maturity	24	23	23	23	23	24	0
Enjoyment	17	19	20	20	19	17	29
Security	13	13	14	14	13	12	14
Achievement	13	13	14	14	13	12	14

Motive	8 p.m. to 9 p.m.	9 p.m. to 10 p.m.	10 p.m. to 11 p.m.	11 p.m. to 12am
Selfdirection	34	33	33	33
Maturity	14	22	22	22
Enjoyment	26	22	22	22
Security	13	11	11	11
Achievement	13	11	11	11

HOT FM

Motive	6 a.m. to 7 a.m.	7 a.m. to 8 a.m.	8 a.m. to 9 a.m.	9 a.m. to 10 a.m.	10 a.m. to 11 a.m.	11 a.m. to 12 Noon	12 p.m. to 1 p.m.
Selfdirection	33	33	36	33	33	33	33
Maturity	22	22	21	22	22	22	22
Enjoyment	22	22	21	22	22	22	22
Security	11	11	9	11	11	11	11
Achievement	11	11	12	11	11	11	11

Motive	1 p.m. to 2 p.m.	2 p.m. to 3 p.m.	3 p.m. to 4 p.m.	4 p.m. to 5 p.m.	5 p.m. to 6 p.m.	6 p.m. to 7 p.m.	7 p.m. to 8 p.m.
Selfdirection	33	33	33	33	33	33	33
Maturity	22	22	22	22	22	22	22
Enjoyment	22	22	22	22	22	22	22
Security	11	11	11	11	11	11	11
Achievement	11	11	11	11	11	11	11

Motive	8 p.m. to 9 p.m.	9 p.m. to 10 p.m.	10 p.m. to 11 p.m.	11 p.m. to 12am
Selfdirection	33	33	33	33
Maturity	22	22	22	22
Enjoyment	22	22	22	22
Security	11	11	11	11
Achievement	11	11	11	11

MIX FM

Motive	6 a.m. to 7 a.m.	7 a.m. to 8 a.m.	8 a.m. to 9 a.m.	9 a.m. to 10 a.m.	10 a.m. to 11 a.m.	11 a.m. to 12 Noon	12 p.m. to 1 p.m.
Self-direction	37	37	36	36	36	36	33
Maturity	21	22	24	24	24	24	22
Enjoyment	20	19	17	16	16	16	22
Security	13	13	12	12	12	12	11
Achievement	8	9	12	12	12	12	11

Motive	1 p.m. to 2 p.m.	2 p.m. to 3 p.m.	3 p.m. to 4 p.m.	4 p.m. to 5 p.m.	5 p.m. to 6 p.m.	6 p.m. to 7 p.m.	7 p.m. to 8 p.m.
Self-direction	38	38	36	38	29	33	33
Maturity	25	25	24	25	29	22	22
Enjoyment	13	13	16	13	14	22	22
Security	13	13	12	13	14	11	11
Achievement	13	13	12	13	14	11	11

Motive	8 p.m. to 9 p.m.	9 p.m. to 10 p.m.	10 p.m. to 11 p.m.	11 p.m. to 12am
Self-direction	34	33	34	34
Maturity	24	24	23	24
Enjoyment	17	19	20	19
Security	12	12	12	12
Achievement	12	12	12	12

SEA FM

Motive	6 a.m. to 7 a.m.	7 a.m. to 8 a.m.	8 a.m. to 9 a.m.	9 a.m. to 10 a.m.	10 a.m. to 11 a.m.	11 a.m. to 12 Noon	12 p.m. to 1 p.m.
Self-direction	39	39	40	40	39	39	39
Maturity	19	19	21	21	21	21	19
Enjoyment	18	18	16	16	16	16	18
Security	15	15	13	13	14	14	15
Achievement	9	9	11	11	10	10	9

Motive	1 p.m. to 2 p.m.	2 p.m. to 3 p.m.	3 p.m. to 4 p.m.	4 p.m. to 5 p.m.	5 p.m. to 6 p.m.	6 p.m. to 7 p.m.	7 p.m. to 8 p.m.
Self-direction	35	35	38	38	38	38	38
Maturity	23	23	21	20	20	20	20
Enjoyment	17	17	17	19	19	19	19
Security	15	15	14	14	14	14	14
Achievement	11	11	10	9	9	10	9

Motive	8 p.m. to 9 p.m.	9 p.m. to 10 p.m.	10 p.m. to 11 p.m.	11 p.m. to 12am
Self-direction	38	38	38	38
Maturity	20	20	20	20
Enjoyment	19	19	19	19
Security	14	14	14	14
Achievement	10	10	10	10

(continued)

Appendix B (Continued)

4TTT

Motive	6 a.m. to 7 a.m.	7 a.m. to 8 a.m.	8 a.m. to 9 a.m.	9 a.m. to 10 a.m.	10 a.m. to 11 a.m.	11 a.m. to 12 Noon	12 p.m. to 1 p.m.
Self-direction	32	29	28	29	29	29	30
Maturity	25	24	27	26	26	26	24
Enjoyment	23	24	23	23	24	24	24
Security	13	13	13	12	13	13	12
Achievement	8	9	9	9	9	9	10

Motive	1 p.m. to 2 p.m.	2 p.m. to 3 p.m.	3 p.m. to 4 p.m.	4 p.m. to 5 p.m.	5 p.m. to 6 p.m.	6 p.m. to 7 p.m.	7 p.m. to 8 p.m.
Self-direction	30	30	31	31	31	28	32
Maturity	25	25	24	23	23	24	23
Enjoyment	23	23	23	23	23	24	23
Security	13	13	12	11	11	12	11
Achievement	10	10	9	11	11	12	11

Motive	8 p.m. to 9 p.m.	9 p.m. to 10 p.m.	10 p.m. to 11 p.m.	11 p.m. to 12am
Self-direction	32	32	31	33
Maturity	23	23	23	22
Enjoyment	23	23	23	22
Security	11	11	11	11
Achievement	11	11	11	11

4KIG

Motive	6 a.m. to 7 a.m.	7 a.m. to 8 a.m.	8 a.m. to 9 a.m.	9 a.m. to 10 a.m.	10 a.m. to 11 a.m.	11 a.m. to 12 Noon	12 p.m. to 1 p.m.
Self-direction	31	38	38	38	35	35	37
Maturity	25	25	25	25	25	25	25
Enjoyment	19	13	13	13	13	13	13
Security	13	12	12	12	13	13	13
Achievement	13	12	12	12	13	13	13

Motive	1 p.m. to 2 p.m.	2 p.m. to 3 p.m.	3 p.m. to 4 p.m.	4 p.m. to 5 p.m.	5 p.m. to 6 p.m.	6 p.m. to 7 p.m.	7 p.m. to 8 p.m.
Self-direction	36	36	36	36	36	36	36
Maturity	25	25	25	25	25	25	25
Enjoyment	14	14	14	14	14	14	14
Security	13	13	13	13	13	13	13
Achievement	13	13	13	13	13	13	13

Motive	8 p.m. to 9 p.m.	9 p.m. to 10 p.m.	10 p.m. to 11 p.m.	11 p.m. to 12am
Self-direction	36	36	36	36
Maturity	25	25	25	25
Enjoyment	14	14	14	14
Security	13	13	13	13
Achievement	13	13	13	13

Note. Value system shows percent of listeners with motive.

A. Athiyaman

Appendix C Products (Means) and Their Values (End)

Values (Desired End States)	Motive Triggered by the End State or Terminal Values	Product Purchases Associated With the End State (Means)
Accomplishment, self-fulfillment, and self-respect	Self-direction	Skis Hair coloring Running shoes Tennis racquet Television Books Musical instrument Bicycle Golf Exercise machine Personal computer Camera Hang glider Boat Vacuum cleaner Rollerblades
Warm relationships and belonging	Maturity	Greeting cards Art Crafts Furs Flowers Wedding ring Clothing
Fun and enjoyment and excitement	Enjoyment	Bowling Musical instrument Movie Vacation Hot tub Swimming pool Desserts Cookies Jewelry Cosmetics
Security	Security	Mutual fund Alarm system Smoke alarm Telephone Blanket Drugs Raincoat Toothbrush Dishwasher Cleansers Bottled water Frozen food
Well respected	Achievement	Sports car Air travel House

Note. Adapted from Durgee, O'Connor, and Veryzer (1996).

Self-Direction

Time Period	Objective Function	Optimal No. of Advertisements		Obj Fn
		4TO	4TTT	
6 a.m. to 7 a.m.	$3,982x1 + 174x2 + 1,165x3 + 1,125x4 + 1,472x5 + 933x6$	20	6	88,472
7 a.m. to 8 a.m.	$4,501x1 + 324x2 + 1,414x3 + 1,441x4 + 1,558x5 + 813x6$	20	6	99,368
8 a.m. to 9 a.m.	$4,237x1 + 857x2 + 1,388x3 + 1,287x4 + 2,008x5 + 429x6$	20	6	96,778
9 a.m. to 10 a.m.	$3,197x1 + 928x2 + 623x3 + 1,391x4 + 2,445x5 + 269x6$	18	10	82,577

Maturity

Time Period	Objective Function	Optimal No. of Advertisements		Obj Fn
		4TO	4TTT	
6 a.m. to 7 a.m.	$2,347x1 + 117x2 + 677x3 + 548x4 + 1,134x5 + 753x6$	18	10	54,013
7 a.m. to 8 a.m.	$3,166x1 + 216x2 + 822x3 + 697x4 + 1,317x5 + 542x6$	20	6	71,222
8 a.m. to 9 a.m.	$2,954x1 + 500x2 + 925x3 + 679x4 + 1,932x5 + 286x6$	18	10	73,029
9 a.m. to 10 a.m.	$2,277x1 + 618x2 + 415x3 + 733x4 + 2,163x5 + 179x6$	18	10	63,029

Enjoyment

Time Period	Objective Function	Optimal No. of Advertisements			Obj Fn
		4TO	4TTT	4KIG	
6 a.m. to 7 a.m.	$1,511x1 + 117x2 + 618x3 + 511x4 + 1,069x5 + 565x6$	15	10	10	38,318
7 a.m. to 8 a.m.	$2,890x1 + 216x2 + 723x3 + 651x4 + 1,317x5 + 271x6$	18	10		65,715
8 a.m. to 9 a.m.	$4,760x1 + 500x2 + 668x3 + 515x4 + 1,667x5 + 143x6$	20	6		105,202
9 a.m. to 10 a.m.	$2,803x1 + 618x2 + 267x3 + 556x4 + 1,943x5 + 90x6$	18	10		70,394

Security

Time Period	Objective Function	Optimal No. of Advertisements		Obj Fn
		4TO	4TTT	
6 a.m. to 7 a.m.	$1,480x1 + 58x2 + 412x3 + 438x4 + 583x5 + 376x6$	20	6	33,098
7 a.m. to 8 a.m.	$1,632x1 + 108x2 + 493x3 + 558x4 + 676x5 + 271x6$	20	6	36,696
8 a.m. to 9 a.m.	$1,516x1 + 214x2 + 463x3 + 421x4 + 909x5 + 143x6$	18	10	36,654
9 a.m. to 10 a.m.	$1,182x1 + 309x2 + 208x3 + 455x4 + 1034x5 + 90x6$	18	10	31,831

Achievement

Time Period	Objective Function	Optimal No. of Advertisements				Obj Fn
		4TO	MIXFM	SEAFM	4TTT	
6 a.m. to 7 a.m.	$1,378x1 + 58x2 + 265x3 + 256x4 + 356x5 + 376x6$	20				30,380
7 a.m. to 8 a.m.	$1,533x1 + 108x2 + 329x3 + 325x4 + 507x5 + 271x6$		20	14	6	19,003
8 a.m. to 9 a.m.	$1,438x1 + 286x2 + 463x3 + 351x4 + 606x5 + 143x6$	20			6	32,396
9 a.m. to 10 a.m.	$1,182x1 + 309x2 + 208x3 + 379x4 + 784x5 + 90x6$	18			10	29,331

Note.   The two-exposure requirement for each station was relaxed in computing the optimal insertions. This is to maximize the number of audiences reached in any 1 hr. The Obj Fn (Objective Function) provides estimates of reach for the chosen mix of radio stations.

The Wired Homestead, An MIT Press Sourcebook on the Internet and the Family

edited by Joseph Turow and Andrea L. Kavanaugh

☐

reviewed by Navneet Anand

Theoretical Approach/ Methodology

Has the book a theoretical approach? Is the applied methodology useful for the author's objectives? Is the context of the information clear? Is the publication positioned within existing literature? Are the terms clearly defined? Is the information consistent?

Structure

How does the chosen structure help the reader to understand the information?

Depth of the Analysis

Is the content sufficient to explain the described phenomenon?

Contribution to New Knowledge

How does it contribute to existing knowledge? Does it use up-to-date data?

Applicability

Is the content useful? Does it help in solving practical problems?

Clarity and Style of Writing

Are the ideas presented in a clear and comprehensible way? Are specific and illustrative examples given? Is the information concise?

The Setting: A Networked Society

The 21st century has heralded a whole set of new developments. Global power equations have been altered, many nations have emerged out of the shadows of economic and military mismanagement, trade barriers between nations have diminished, internationalization has led to intermingling of cultures and communities like none in the past, and communication systems have metamorphosed.

A new revolution has been simultaneously sweeping human existence. A new thread of human bonding has been stretching along the global landscape. The Internet or World Wide Web (WWW) has been pervading us all like nothing did in the past. A system of networking, the Internet has redefined the way humans communicate, do business, transact, trade, negotiate, persuade, and establish relationships.

McLuhan and Fiore (1967) said decades ago, "Time has ceased, space has vanished. We all live in times of allatonceness" (p. 67). They were talking in the context of traditional forms of media. In the modern era, when the new media has made a grand entry, the prophecy seems truer than ever before.

Leyden (1995) wrote in the *Star Tribune*

> We are living through an extraordinary moment in human history. Historians will look back on our times, the 40-year span between 1980 and 2020, and classify it among the handful of historical moments when humans reorganized the entire civilization around a new tool, a new idea. These decades mark the transition from the Industrial Age, an era organized around the motor, to the Digital Age, an era defined by microprocessor. (p. 5)

Cairncross (1997), a journalist of *The Economist,* wrote a celebrated book in 1997, *The Death of Distance,* in which she discussed how the arrival of modern communication technologies has given a new dimension to our personal and professional landscapes. Their impact is felt both at the microlevel (e.g., individual communication) and macrolevel (e.g., global business). The growth of home PCs, multimedia tools ,and technologies, which enabled faster speed of access to the Internet especially, brought microhuman relationships under microscopic scrutiny. The spotlight has often been on children, women, family relationships, crime, and violence.

The Work: Wired Homestead

A rigorous academic treatise exploring various dimensions of the Internet and family in the form of *The Wired Homestead: An MIT Press Sourcebook On Internet and the Family*, edited by Joseph Turow and Andrea L. Kavanaugh, is critically timed and highly desirable. This book by MIT Press under their "sourcebooks" series fills in a gap in academic discourse on a subject of good importance. It is comprehensive in its scope, rigorous in research, and meticulous in bringing together a diverse range of ideas and perspectives.

What makes the book inspiring is the ideal collection of communication theorists, scientists, and social scientists with deep insights into the Internet and the family. The editors are also an ideal duo, specializing in communication and computing. Although Joseph Turow is the Robert Lewis Shayon Professor of Communication at the Annenberg School for Communication, University of Pennsylvania, Andrea L. Kavanaugh is Senior Research Scientist and Assistant Director at the Human Computer Interaction Center, Department of Computer Science, Virginia Polytechnic Institute and State University. Their training and backgrounds are reflected in the choice of subjects, chapters, and their arrangements. The advances in technology often brings with it simultaneous changes in social structures and processes. It has wide ramifications for the society. Social scientists since time immemorial have been exploring the subject, looking at the way social institutions such as the family, marriage, religion, education, and social processes like socialization are impacted with the advent of new technologies.

In the whole of the 1960s and 1970s, one found many studies around television. The interest was understood given the emergence of this medium, which promised to redefine entertainment and dissemination of information. For instance, Trenaman and McQuail (1961) worked on *Television and the Political Image*, Seymour-Ure (1973) wrote on *The Political Impact of Mass Media*, and De Fleur (1964) wrote an article on "Occupational Roles as Portrayed on Television." A series of academic works have also emerged around the great industrial revolution, where technology was the key again. In fact, Marx (Marx & Engels, 1998) put a great deal of emphasis on the industrial system and did a prognosis of a society, which would have problems such as alienation. Durkhiem (1951) too talked of division of labor and processes such as suicide and crime in an industrial setup. Bell's (1873) *The Coming of Post Industrial Society* is also a celebrated book in this area. All these works have given a distinct academic perspective to these new eras.

The Internet is a decade-old phenomenon, especially in the context of the West. It has many unique features—the Web's digital nature means that users can send, retrieve, transform, and store the material that moves across it—

that makes it particularly relevant for the social and public spheres. However, still no serious academic work has come to light that analyzes the implications of the Internet on the family unit and its members interrelated social lives. The many stand-alone exercises are at best scattered. In this context, this work assumes great significance. Going beyond the conventional models of analyzing relations between new technology and family, the book attempts to look at the interrelation of Web, family, and home in creative ways. The use of the Internet in homes rivals the advent of the telephone, radio, or television in social significance. Daily use of the WWW and e-mail is taken for granted in many families, and the computer-linked Internet is quickly becoming an integral part of the audiovisual and physical environment of parents and children in American society. The Internet era beings with it crucial features of interactivity, personlization, and information abundance that raise profound new issues for parents and children.

The Discussions: Virtuality, Connectivity, and Family

This book has been divided into four parts: "The New World in Context," "On Parents and Kids," "The Wired Homesteads and Online Life," and "The Wired Homestead and Civic Life."

There is a logical progression from the first to the fourth section. Although academic-type readers may find it convenient to move from first to the last chapter in order, general readers may pick a chapter of their choice. She or he may not find it comfortable browsing through chapters with a quantitative orientation.

Each section comprises rich essays, some of which are based on extensive surveys mapping peoples' minds on some crucial issues. The five essays in the first section are devoted to explore conceptual frameworks and comparative historical perspectives on the Internet and the family and what we should study about it.

Ellen Wartella and Byron Reeves look at the historical trends in research on children and media between 1900 and 1960 in the third chapter. Recognizing the need for media effect studies around children, Wartella and Reeves point out that there has not been any tradition of research on children and media under the broader framework of mass communication research in America. "The study of media effects on youth has developed independently of the broader media effects tradition" (p. 55), Wartella and Reeves say, underlining the significance of this stream. In the chapter, they also rightly note that the origin of research about children lies in concern expressed by each medium as it was introduced. The 1933 Payne Fund studies (Blumer & Hauser, 1933), for instance, represents a detailed look at the effect of films on such diverse topics as knowledge about foreign cultures, attitudes about violence, and delinquent behavior. Some other important studies of this period are Blumer's (1933) *Movies and Conduct*, Frank's *Comics, Radio and Movies and Children* (New York, Public Affairs Office, 1949) and *Television in the Lives of Our Children* by Schramm, Lyle, and Parker (1960). In the tradition of media scholarship, the authors in the essays extensively borrow from disciplines such as sociology, family studies, psychology, cognitive development, and social history to develop their arguments.

In the first chapter, Joseph Turow provides an "information-boundaries" perspective that provides a model for viewing family in relation to the Web. According to Turow's model, there are two notions about the role played by the Web for the family. The first one suggests that rapid commercialization of the Internet is helping to reinforce divisive tensions that researchers say are typical of U.S. families today. The other hails e-mails and related activities as countering the dysfunctional development by strengthening family relationships and reducing stress. The conceptual framework puts subsequent discussions in perspective.

Turow also notes that home-based Internet connectivity allows commercial interests to contact various family members directly, thereby bypassing a spouse or a parent. Elihu Katz borrows the concept of "disintermediation" and explains in chapter 2 that this is not the first time that parents have been bypassed or disintermediated by the media. Parents have traditionally tried to act as intermediaries or gatekeepers with regard to most aspects of their children's lives, seeking to deflect them from media exposure, which they consider a negative one. What makes the Internet different from books or TV selections is the fact that the range and diversity of content is vastly greater, easier to access, and more difficult to monitor. In chapter 4, Daniel R Anderson and Marie K. Evans focus on TV's effects on children as they relate to cognitive and emotional processes such as attention, comprehension, memory, emotion, and social attribution. Anderson and Evans show the utility of using cognitive psychological research on the impact of TV as a measuring stick to assess the Internet's implications for children. Ellen Seiter brings in element of critical sociology in chapter 5 to bear on the similarities that she finds between the family dynamics that surround television and those that seem to be evolving around the internet. Seiter observes, "as personal computers proliferate in middle class homes, the boundaries between leisure and work time, public and private space, promise to become increasingly blurred" (p. 95).

The second part of the book shifts to discuss more specific Web issues that concern parents and kids. The section rightly begins by a scanning of the data available on family and the Internet by Maria Papadakis. It highlights the fact that we know very little when it comes to the correlation between family and the Web. The next essay by

Amy B. Jordan of the University of Pennsylvania notes that the family use of media not only reflects but also shapes the overall norms and beliefs of the home environment. Joseph Turow and Lilach Nir present results of a national survey in 2000 of parents and youngsters and paint a complex and potentially controversial picture of the attitudes parents and youngsters hold toward the various aspects of the Web. Then there is a global collation of views on the Web and the family's attitudes toward it as well as the consequences of Web and family interface in the rest of the three chapters in this section.

The third section is an exhaustive evaluation of the implication of the Web for the family members' lives. There are pertinent issues discussed and questions raised about the shape of things to come. Thus, Steven Izenour wonders how the Web will alter the home architecture. David Frohlich, Susan Dray, and Amy Silverman ask whether in the future, family life will center on internet-linked PCs or on so-called Internet appliances that spread different aspects of the Web experience around the house. Much like Izenour, Robert Kraut, Sara Kiesler, Bonka Boneva, Jonathon Cummings, Vicki Helgeson, and Anne Crawford explore whether the Internet reduces social involvement and psychological well being. Sherry Turkle looks at the way in which some people use the Internet in search of interpersonal connections outside the home—in virtual worlds that she describes as "neighborhoods in cyberspace." Using sound metaphors to capture the essence of "Virtuality and Its Discontents," as her chapter is called, Turkle borrows from anthropologist Ray Oldenberg who considered local bars and coffee shops to be the heart of social integration and community vitality. Turkle observes

> Today we see a resurgence of coffee bars and bistros, but most of them do not serve, much less recreate, coherent communities and, as a result, the odor of nostalgia often seems as strong as the espresso. Some people are trying to fill the gap with neighborhoods in cyberspace. (p. 385)

Turkle notes that people reach out to cyberspace from the home to find personal satisfaction, but do they also do it with an awareness of the relationship of their home and family to the world around them? The four essays in the last section of the book, with "The Wired Homestead and Civic Life," are devoted to addressing this question. It begins with an essay by Jorge Reina Schement on the relationship between "households and media in the creation of 21st century communities." Next, it presents three case studies to illustrate the interaction between the Web, the homestead, and its surroundings. Andrea L. Kavanaugh explores the extent to which a "networked" community can encourage people to reach out to one another in various ways. Lodis Rhodes then presents a "literary festival" in a Black and

Hispanic neighborhood to illustrate how the interplay of families and community-based organizations led to the incorporation of Internet technologies into a neighborhood's daily activities. In the final chapter, Keith Hampton and Barry Wellman find evidence that no-cost, high-speed Internet connection in a suburban Toronto development can encourage neighborhood socialization, awareness of local issues, and political mobilization.

The Direction: Mediated

The book uses both qualitative and quantitative approaches and addresses a host of key issues on the role of the Internet in family life. It answers many of the lingering debates, gives rise to new ones, and provides a certain sense of direction to the otherwise nascent research tradition in this area. Although the context that it deals in—families in the United States—is quite pertinent and will certainly enable policymakers and parents to look afresh at the Internet, a reference to nations where the Internet is still in its evolutionary stages is missing. Such countries with lower literacy rates and traditional social structures are more likely to face the negative consequences of a medium such as the Internet, which has the potential of pervading privacy and straining family relations given its anonymity and speed of establishing "virtual relationships." However, the book certainly provides the contours of research and perspective for social scientists of such countries.

In brief, the book has a global relevance. It conveys sound intellectual overtone. The production, including typesetting and layout, is neat and meticulous.

References

Bell, D. (1973). *The coming of post industrial society.* New York: Basic Books.

Blumer, H. (1933). *Movies and conduct.* New York: Macmillan.

Blumer, H. & Hauser, P. M. (1933). *Movies, delinquency, and crime.* New York: Macmillan.

Cairncross, F. (1997). *The death of distance: How the communications revolution is changing our lives.* Cambridge, MA: Harvard Business School Book.

De Fleur, M. (1964). Occupational roles as portrayed on television. *Public Opinion Quarterly, 28,* 57–74.

Durkheim, E. (1951). *Suicide.* New York: Free Press.

Frank, J. (1949). *Comics, radio and movies and children.* New York: Public Affairs Office.

Leyden, P. (1995). The historic moment in on the edge of digital age. *Star Tribune,* p. 5.

Marx, K., & Engels, F. (1998). *Economic and philosophic manuscripts of 1844 and the Communist Manifesto* (M. Milliagan, Trans.). New York: Prometheus Books.

McLuhan, M., & Fiore, Q. (1967). *The medium is the massage: An inventory of effects.* New York: Bantam.

Schramm, W., Lyle, J., & Parker, E. B. (1960). *Television in the lives of our children.* Stanford, CA: Stanford University Press.

Seymour-Ure, C. (1973). *The political impact of mass media.* New York: Constable.

Trenaman, J. S. M., & McQuail, D. (1961). *Television and the political image.* London, UK: Methuen.

Rating

Rating Criteria	Rating
Theoretical Approach/Methodology	++++
Structure	+++
Depth of the Analysis	+++
Contribution of New Knowledge	+++
Applicability	++
Clarity and Style of Writing	+++

Rating Points: excellent: +++++   poor: +

MIT Press, 2003

502 pages

ISBN 0–262–70094–8

www.mitpress.mit.edu

Review Author

Navneet Anand
The Times of India, India
anandnavneet@hotmail.com

Media and Economics,
Volume 1/1: Foundations of Media Economics:
Communication and Media Science, Economics;
Volume 1/2: Foundations of Media Economics:
Sociology, Culture, Politics, Philosophy, International, History,
Technology, Journalism

edited by Klaus-Dieter Altmeppen and Matthias Karmasin

☐

reviewed by Gürhan Kurucu

The fast evolving activities in the media economics research and teaching landscape are undoubtedly indicating the accruing establishment of this field. Surprisingly, introductory teaching books on media economics still seem not only to be rare but often too narrow in focus. Furthermore, publications terminologically and perspectively often reflect the adjacencies to a superior mother discipline, typically economics or communication/media science, making it especially difficult for beginners and laymen to get involved in the field.

These mentioned shortcomings seem even more obvious when looking at available native publications for the German speaking and teaching language area. Identifying this lack, Klaus-Dieter Altmeppen (Technical University of Ilmenau, Germany) and Matthias Karmasin (University of Klagenfurt, Austria) took on the challenge of editing an ambitious and comprehensive book project still in progress.

Media and Economics (original title: *Medien und Ökonomie*) is conceptualized in four volumes. The first two volumes (1/1 and 1/2) form a unit by focusing on the fundamentals and basic questions of media economics analysis. Volumes 3 and 4 concentrate on problems and application fields of media economics. Based on information from October 2004, the last volume still has not been published.

The first volume (1/1) is split up into three major parts. The first part contains a single article on media economics from the very general perspective of the philosophy of science. Parts 2 and 3 take a close look at media economics from the views of the media science discipline and the economics discipline, respectively. The part of the book that focuses on economics consists of six articles and is twice as long as the media science outlook, which in comparison contains three articles.

The second volume (1/2) is structured accordingly, but now introduces the perspectives from eight additional fields on the study of media economics. These single parts mostly cover only a single chapter of approximately same length and go about things from the standpoints of sociology, cultural science, political science, media philosophy, international perspective, history, technology, and journalism in detail.

By presenting the various perspectives, the editors claim not only to give an overview of the diversity of the approaches, but also to provide access to the different and typical terminology in each case, their theories, models, and even their focal research interests. Despite the disparities, Altmeppen and Karmasin emphasize four guidelines in which all contributions of all volumes can be assigned. The first one corresponds to the level of analysis. Media economic analysis is usually located on the classical levels of analysis from individual (microlevel), organizational (mesolevel), to the societal level (macrolevel). The contributions underline a strong actual orientation on the mesolevel of media organizations regardless of their background as a rather communications/media science or economic investigation. This is even truer for pieces in business management, whereas classical economic attempts are still dominated from a microperspective or macroperspective. The second guideline is seen in the double entendre of functions, structures, actors, and activities of and in media. All contributions are embedded between the monetary and societal functions of media, economic, and communication structures (rules and resources) and how they are created, interpreted, changed, and (ab)used by actors such as media managers and journalists and their corresponding activities. The third guideline refers to "system and environment." Particular elements of the environment of the media are, for example, legal regulations, political interests, technological developments, cultural patterns of interpretation, or recipients. With all their inherent mechanisms and structures, these elements are factors affecting the media system and vice versa. The last guideline relates to "creation, production, and distribution" as phases of a simultaneously economic and communications circuit wherein media originates. The editors point out that there exists a recursive relation between the economic and communications side of the phases in which economic changes also affect changes in the way of journalistic work. This illustrates the dependency of various media communication forms in the society on media economic variations.

Volume 1/1 starts out with an article by the editors themselves from the mentioned general perspective of science (Part 1). Altmeppen and Karmasin introduce areas, methods, and methodologies of media economics. They reconstruct its status quo and developments. Their discussion of the different methodological and general theoretical approaches makes them argue for a transdisciplinary concept of media economics, considering both the character of media as a cultural as well as an economic good. This concept pleads for media goods to not be reduced to their communicative, economic, social, political, or cultural functions. The article concludes with a consideration of contingent problems and the overall potential of such a conception.

Part 2 takes the view of the media science discipline. Martin Löffelholz criticizes that developments in media and communication are often described in catchphrases without proper theoretical underpinnings (e.g., "New Media," "Multimedia," and "Information Highway"). These metaphors often can not be classified theoretically and therefore can not be harnessed academically. To deepen understanding of current transformations and to overcome this semantic vagueness, the author analyzes central metaphors from four different levels of reference, namely, media, societal change, computer networks, and dynamics of systems.

"Everyday public communication" takes center stage in Manfred Rühl's article. Rühl argues that economic problems of public communication are far easier to deal with if addressed with terms, methods, and theories of communication science. For further insights, Rühl takes a closer look at the economic character of everyday public communication goods from the standpoint of the theories of political economy.

Thomas A. Bauer considers media pedagogy as a reasonable and useful mediator bridging the gaps between media economics and media culture. Bauer's implementations bring the relations of the normative outlooks of media culture and those of media economics closer together for a better media usage of the individual.

The economics section (Part 3) begins with a formal analysis of the markets for media, advertising, and consumer goods and their interplay. Rüdiger Pethig sees the triangle relations between media businesses, media consumers/consumers, and advertising markets as the key for understanding the media economy. Pethig applies theoretical models of industrial economics to illustrate the relations under different market constellations and to derive ex-post explanations (positive analysis). Under the assumptions of welfare economics, Pethig even extends explanations to a normative level by illustrating inefficiencies of the media sector.

Johannes Ludwig focuses on the microeconomics aspects of media. In more detail, Ludwig examines the effects of high first-copy costs on the way of financing media production by cross-subsidization with revenues from advertising markets. Integrating specific consumer needs and media recipient behavior, Ludwig describes the microeconomic problems of pricing and costing with concrete examples of media products.

Werner A. Meier argues that communication is subjected to power and engages himself with the Anglo-American political economy of communication and media. Sketching the development of political economy as a discipline itself, Meier makes its strengths and weaknesses transparent and points out its contributions to media economics. In highlighting the impact of capitalistic production on societal communication via mass media, Meier provides the argumentative munition for discourses in power and control on issues such as deregulation, globalization, or commercialization of media and culture.

New institutional economics has been one of the most promising paradigms in economic analysis over the past two decades. Jürgen Heinrich and Frank Lobigs begin to make this approach utilizable for media analysis. After introducing the reader to its cornerstones, Heinrich and Lobigs follow a positive comparative institutions analysis by demonstrating how journalistic competition as a market institution allows for efficient control of media by recipients. Hereon, in a normative, comparative institutions analysis, they examine what characteristics institutions of a democratic media supply should fulfill.

An additional innovative approach is conducted by Karl-Heinz Wigand, who transfers theoretical approaches from the supply of services and its management to the production and distribution of media supply. Wigand interprets media supply as services from media for recipients and analyzes this on the basis of according theories from services management. Wigand finds that services production in the media is highly dependent on the participation of recipients as external production factors.

Last but not least, Marco Czygan and Hermann H. Kallfaß present the main features of competition theory and apply them to the media. These include functions of competition, normative guiding principles, and instruments of competition policy followed by an introduction to the structure-conduct-performance paradigm of industrial economics as a tool for competition analysis. Furthermore, they provide studies on analysis in the media concerning market structure, market performance, or market boundary definitions. These studies enable the reader to understand the impact of political parameters and frameworks on media market structures, behavior, and performances and therefore also empower one to formulate alternative political advice.

The sociological perspective is the first article of the second volume (1/2) of *Media and Economics*. Michael Jäckel asks if it is justifiable that communication science assumes the recipient of media goods to be a "rational man." For sociologists, this concept has to be examined under the task to sort out the difference of perceived needs between social strata.

The cultural studies perspective is taken by articles from authors Udo Göttlich and Ulrich Saxer. Göttlich investigates the relation of cultural studies and media economics. Economic activities in the media are seen as cultural phenomena with societal and institutional consequences. Saxer, on the other hand, deals with media economics and media culture in specific. Saxer pleads for strengthened intermediation of media competence in educational systems reinforcing the low demand for sophisticated offerings in the media because elite-cultural offerings can not simply be transferred into popular-cultural offerings without endangering their identity.

Gerhard Vowe looks at the regulation of public communication from a political point of view. To assess the influence of politics in the media sector, Vowe develops a multidimensional model of media policy on the basis of public-choice theory and describes driving factors that influence regulation of public communication.

The philosophical perspective is addressed by Matthias Ruth. Ruth asks whether ethics dominate the media economy or vice versa and if both might fit together comfortably at all. After all, Ruth points out that ethical questions concerning the media economy are ethical questions of general economic actions.

The contribution of C. Ann Hollifield, Alison Alexander, and James Owers reflects the international perspective and by the way, is the only article of both volumes to be composed in English. Hollifield et al. start out with the combined effects of economic, political, technological, and sociological forces on the structure and behavior of media industries in the United States since the 1980s. Hollifield et al. not only show how these developments have intersected and transformed the U.S. media economy but also examine how those changes and U.S. media companies' strategies may affect media industries in other countries at both the local and global levels.

Scientific works on the history of the academics of media economics are almost nonexistent. Hans Bohrmann takes the journey to follow the traits of media and economics from a historical perspective. Bohrmann finds that the late professional establishment of the field is due to the fact that the academic debates in already established communication/media science would most often focus on issues of journalistic production only. Underlying economic issues were widely and systematically ignored. Surprisingly, there is also no evidence for a systematic and continuous dealing with mass communication on the side of economics and business science until recently.

The continuous change of information and communication technologies and their effect on the media system motivate Maria L. Kiefer to take a closer look at media economics and media technology. Giving a survey on economic theories in the field of technological change and innovation, Kiefer tries to employ those theories to evaluate their potential for application on technologically induced changes in the area of the media.

Susanne Fengler and Stephan Ruß-Mohl finally take the journalistic perspective and pursue an economic analysis of journalistic decision making on the basis of the example of media reporting on media itself. Fengler and Ruß-Mohl plead for a change of paradigm in employing rational choice theory rather than usual attempts based on system theory. They reveal that the assumption of a journalist as a "homo oeconomicus" can be quite fruitful, especially because recent research in the field allows considering altruism as part of self-serving decision making.

The first two volumes of *Media and Economics* are an outline of media economics in its broadest sense. The status quo of media economics currently defines it as a heterogeneous field tangent to many academic disciplines. Therefore, an introductory text on media and economics quite naturally faces issues of classification and evaluation as well as terminological diversity and ambiguity despite a common theme of analysis interest. Often the same is meant, but the perspectives taken are different.

The two volumes at hand represent this status quo, the viewpoint of different perspectives, their evolved linguistic rules, and terminologies. In a rather loosely organized fashion, contributions are bundled into 11 perspectives pointing toward a still opaque center. Attentive readers will be able to distinguish between diverse normative differences and levels of valuation that are always based on corresponding research interests. Therefore, it allows assessing the same media economic phenomenon differently depending on the perspective taken. Media economics seems more approximated and circumscribed than defined.

Up-to-date data on media and economics is rarely given in both books. This point is, however, excusable due to the fact that the authors' intention was to create an introductory book with fairly basic subject matter. Nevertheless, some commendable characteristics of both books need still to be highlighted. Each article is equipped with commented references at the end, helpful for readers who need to further deepen their reading. Furthermore, definitions and key statements are visually accentuated in the text. The usefulness of the index seems restricted: terms such as *media*, abundant throughout the texts, are listed only once or do not appear at all. The last section of the volumes is dedicated to the authors' academic backgrounds. A closer look reveals that the majority of authors have a communications or media science background reasoning some of the linguistic idiosyncrasies and the impression that the way of argumentation is often closer to these disciplines than to economic thinking.

All in all, the volumes' usefulness lies in providing a grid of orientation within this upcoming field. Although there are parts that would be quite advanced for newcomers, there still remains helpful information from which any reader could benefit.

Rating

Rating Criteria	Rating
Theoretical Approach/Methodology	+++
Structure	++++
Depth of the Analysis	+++
Contribution of new Knowledge	++
Applicability	++
Clarity and Style of Writing	++

Rating Points: excellent: +++++ poor: +

Westdeutscher Verlag, 2003

Volume 1/1: 340 pages

ISBN 3-531-13631-3

Volume 1/2: 266 pages

ISBN 3-531-13632-1

www.westdeutscher-verlag.de

Review Author

Gürhan Kurucu
Witten/Herdecke University, Germany
Kurucu@aol.com

A Handbook of Cultural Economics

by Ruth Towse

□

reviewed by Josh Heuman

Every day, with heroic pluck and determination, media managers and scholars face all kinds of difficult challenges. None of these challenges, however, begins to approach the herculean labors of the handbook editor and contributors. Ruth Towse's *A Handbook of Cultural Economics* demonstrates many of the advantages of the handbook form: It offers a panoramic view of the field, it accrues the considerable authority of its many voices, and it can claim a natural resting place on the library reference shelves. However, more pointedly, it also reveals the limitations of that form: Without a strong principle of organization, its panoramic perspective sometimes drifts toward fragmentation and even incoherence, many of its voices lose some of their authority in trying to compress a very large corner of the field into a very brief summary, and its good fit on the reference shelves does not guarantee its usefulness for readers. All together, it succeeds only partially as a survey of the field and presents something less than an essential resource for media managers and scholars.

Along with a brief editorial introduction, *A Handbook of Cultural Economics* comprises 61 entries, arranged alphabetically from "Anthropology of Art" to "Welfare Economics." Most entries are written by European academics, although others come from the field of policy and the art worlds themselves and some from outside of Europe. The entries spread more or less evenly over topics in the fine and performing arts, in the heritage industries, and in the media and cultural industries. Some entries address specific forms and media ("Ballet," "Opera," "Television"), others broader problems or players in the field ("Awards," "Nonprofit organizations," "Tax concessions"), and others more theoretical questions ("Baumol's cost disease," "Contingent valuation," "Value of culture"). Several longer entries run more than a dozen pages; several shorter ones run less than a few pages. Most essays lean toward abstraction and theorization of their topic, although many remain more closely tied to a practical context.

Already in its form and orientation, there are difficulties here. First, the *Handbook*'s 61 alphabetical entries tend to leave the reader feeling as if the forest has been lost for the trees. Apart from Towse's all too brief introduction, there is very little concern to define and situate the field of cultural economics. If a handbook should work as a kind of guidebook, the visitor (or resident) of that field might like a more substantial sense of the lay of the land—rather than only a discontinuous procession of landmarks with no connections between them except for cross-references at the end. Cultural economics develops through a particular history, it finds a home in particular institutions, it defines itself with reference to particular problems and problematizations, and it orients itself with and against particular scholarship in other disciplines. These questions receive insufficient attention in the *Handbook*, which would be much stronger with an introductory section of essays to contextualize the field.

Furthermore, if there is not much attention to the big picture, the little pictures of the 61 entries might be arranged more harmoniously. Why allot separate entries for "Cinema" and "Motion Pictures"? Why separate "Digitalization" and "Internet culture"? Why not allow for much closer connections (and even conversations) among those entries, ones on "Broadcasting," "Television," and so on? In contrast, like its sibling volumes in a series from BFI, Hilmes's (2003) *The Television History Book* comprises six themed sections (each with its own scene-setting introduction), each in turn comprising a half dozen or so short essays, most with short sidebars to pursue some questions further. The difference between the two volumes is more than cosmetic; forms of discourse structure knowledge in important ways. In *The Television History Book,* trees of knowledge grow higher in growing together, building on shared foundations (for only the most banal example, in saying more in fewer words); in many ways, the *Handbook* seems to frustrate rather than flatter knowledge of cultural economics, sometimes falling into redundancy and often losing opportunities for more depth of analysis across entries.

In their sometimes extreme compression, individual entries do not allow for very much depth of analysis. Entries such as "Digitalization" offer pleasant surprises in going as far as they do—in that case, moving in only a few pages from a broad and airy conceptual background to an informed and intelligent discussion of arguments over technologies for digital rights management. However, even such a strong entry lacks the depth and currency of a developed newspaper article. What is even more troubling is how constraints of space tend to push practical application and concrete context off the table in favor of more theoretical and abstract economic analysis. Sometimes this perspective helps clarify the topic at hand; "Digitalization" helpfully depoliticizes some of the more overwrought discussion of digital rights management. More often, however, although it is perhaps more of an indictment of the field of economics than this handbook, such lack of careful attention to context carries unfortunate consequences.

In "Music business," for example, we learn that "apart from exceptional instances when the Majors overlook the consumer appeal of a new creative artist, by and large new and smaller record companies are only able to compete for artists rejected by dominant record companies" (323). It is an understatement to say that this generalization might be complicated by further empirical analysis—such narrowly economic understanding of the business almost wholly neglects the very complicated relations between independents and majors (as in major-label flexibilizing practices of enlisting independents as boutique partners in pressing and distribution deals, explored much more fully in the geographic literature on postfordist production).

Similarly, "Anthropology of Art" mentions in passing how anthropology can "dignify the lives of people by illustrating the artistry in daily life" (p. 18). Within the terms of anthropological arguments about relations between subjects and objects of knowledge, this is a very contentiously phrased claim—does the folk artist have no dignity until the arrival of the anthropologist? In a few more pages, this difficulty might have been explored or at least acknowledged; instead, important questions of context fall off the table.

In one last example, "Globalization" dismisses almost cavalierly cultural nationalist arguments against free-trade liberalism. Whatever the merits of cultural protectionism, it is a credible enough position to be taken more seriously. Adding insult to injury, perhaps, the author's full length study of cultural trade disputes gives a much more careful and nuanced account of the issues in play; again, compression becomes the enemy of depth in the handbook, and often what is lost first are those perspectives that would draw attention to what is beyond the narrow bounds of economic theory.

There are of course happy exceptions to this rule. The entry on "Dealers in art" recalls the close reading of concrete cultural forms that characterizes the best sociology of culture—although it only whets the appetite for the author's more extended work on the topic. Similarly, "Cultural tourism" convincingly seasons narrowly economic analysis with historical and critical approaches. Sadly, entries such as these remain the exception, and in the end, it is questionable whether a handbook such as this is the best way to approach and explore the field of cultural economics. What's more, it is also questionable whether cultural economics as presented here is the best way to explore the economics of culture and especially, the economics of the mass media. This is a book that is useful on the library reference shelf; unlike Vogel's (2004) *Entertainment Industry Economics* and Albarran's (2002) *Media Economics: Understanding Markets, Industries, and Concepts*. How-

ever, it is less useful in the media manager's office, unlike Cowen's (1997) *In Praise of Commercial Culture* or Caves's (2000) *Creative Industries: Contracts Between Art and Commerce*; it is no good on the beach; and unlike Becker's (1982) *Art Worlds* or Bourdieu's (1994) *The Field of Cultural Production*, it is no good behind the barricades. Although perhaps it is unfair to expect it to be something different than it is, it is not wrong to hope for something more.

References

Albarran, A. (2002). *Media economics: Understanding markets, industries, and concepts* (2nd ed.). Ames: Iowa State University Press.

Becker, H. (1982). *Art worlds.* Berkeley: University of California Press.

Bourdieu, P. (1994). *The field of cultural production* (R. Nice, Trans.). New York: Columbia University Press.

Caves, R.(2000). *Creative industries: Contracts between art and commerce.* Cambridge, MA: Harvard University Press.

Cowen, T. (1997). *In praise of commercial culture.* Cambridge, MA: Harvard University Press.

Hilmes, M. (2004). *The Televison History Book.* London: BFI.

Vogel, H. (2004). *Entertainment industry economics: A guide for financial analysis* (6th ed.). Cambridge, England: Cambridge University Press.

Ratings

Rating Criteria	Rating
Theoretical Approach/Methodology	+++
Structure	+
Depth of the Analysis	++
Contribution of New Knowledge	++
Applicability	++
Clarity and Style of Writing	++++

Rating Points: excellent: +++++   poor: +

Edward Elgar, 2003

494 pages

ISBN 1-84064-338-2

www.e-elgar.co.uk

Review Author

Josh Heuman
University of Calgary, Canada
jheuman@ucalgary.ca

Calendar of Events

2005

February

■ 02/24/2005 to 02/25/2005

World Newspaper Advertising Conference
Rome, Italy
http://www.wan-press.org/rome2005/

■ 02/24/2005 to 02/26/2005

Women in the Media: Power and Influence
Chicago, USA
http://www.mediamanagementcenter.org/center/web/
seminars/WIM/wim.htm

March

■ 03/04/2005 to 03/06/2005

Over the Waves: Music in/and Broadcasting
Hamilton, Ontario, Canada
baadec@mcmaster.ca

■ 03/22/2005 to 03/23/2005

German Society for Online Research (GOR) Conference
Zurich, Switzerland
http://www.gor.de/index_e.htm

April

■ 04/02/2005 to 04/03/2005

**National Cable & Telecommunications Association
Annual Convention**
San Francisco, USA
http://www.cablecenter.org/education/academic_
seminar/index.cfm

■ 04/06/2005 to 04/09/2005

Cinema and Technology Conference
Lancaster, United Kingdom
http://www.lancs.ac.uk/fss/cultres/events/cinematech/
cinematech.php

May

■ 05/20/2005 to 05/21/2005

Digital Utopia in the Media: From Discourses to Facts
Barcelona, Spain
http://cicr.blanquerna.edu

■ 05/23/2005 to 05/25/2005

Communication and Mass Media
Athens, Greece
http://www.atiner.gr/index.php?section=3&subsection=
31

June

■ 06/16/2005 to 06/20/2005

Digital Games Research Association Conference
Vancouver, Canada
http://www3.educ.sfu.ca/conferences/digra2004/ocs/

July

■ 07/11/2005 to 07/14/2005

The Radio Conference
Melbourne, Australia
http://www.rmit.edu.au/adc/appliedcommunication/
radio2005

(continued)

■ 07/12/2005 to 07/16/2005

Commercial Integration or Cultural Dialogue in the Context of the Information Society
Buenos Aires, Argentina
http://www.comunicacion.fsoc.uba.ar/engl.htm

■ 07/25/2005 to 07/30/2005

International Association for Media and Communication Research Conference
Porto Alegre, Brasil
http://www.pucrs.br/famecos/iamcr/textos/iamcr.htm

August

■ 08/10/2005 to 08/13/2005

AEJMC Convention—Media Management and Economics Division
San Antonio, USA
http://www.aejmc.org/convention/

September

■ 09/30/2005 to 10/01/2005

Challenges at the Top: Leadership in Media Organizations
Jönkoping, Sweden
cinzia.dalzotto@ihh.hj.se

October

■ 10/05/2005 to 10/09/2005

Internet Generations—Conference of Association of Internet Researchers
Chicago, USA
http://www.aoir.org/resources.html